P9-AOF-124

Peru

LATIN AMERICAN HISTORIES

JAMES R. SCOBIE, EDITOR

James R. Scobie: *Argentina: A City and a Nation,* SECOND EDITION

Charles C. Cumberland: *Mexico: The Struggle for Modernity*

Henry F. Dobyns and Paul L. Doughty: *Peru: A Cultural History*

Ralph Lee Woodward, Jr.: *Central America: A Nation Divided*

Rollie E. Poppino: *Brazil: The Land and People,* SECOND EDITION

Peru

A CULTURAL HISTORY

HENRY F. DOBYNS

and

PAUL L. DOUGHTY

New York · Oxford University Press · 1976

Copyright © 1976 by Oxford University Press, Inc.
Library of Congress Catalogue Card Number: 76-9224

Printed in the United States of America

Preface

We did not accept lightly the challenge of writing a book about a nation as old and complex as Peru. In the New World where Peru and Mexico stand historically as the greatest examples of Native American achievement, Peru is the least known. Moreover, Peru's natural environment is one of the most varied and striking in the world.

Because our editors inevitably allowed us fewer pages than we wished in which to review, document, and theorize about one of the most intriguing countries on earth, we treat the major themes of Peruvian life with broad strokes. Climate, land, and water are powerful influences on human life and what Peruvians have done with these resources is important. Yet what people have done with and to each other in this geographic context provides unending and ever more complex subjects for study.

Peruvians already possessed an ancient culture when the Incas rose to power in the fifteenth century. As a remote, yet vital, source of great riches for the rulers of Spain and Europe during almost three centuries of colonial domination, Peru developed as a unique amalgam of Europe and America. The modern nation still responds to these earlier forces while seeking a contemporary identity to parallel the Inca past.

Here we recount and analyze the interwoven processes by which this culture matures, changes, and distinguishes itself. We write not only about those individuals and institutions at the center of power in their times, but also about the "little traditions" and the "common people" who made the pottery, sowed the fields, and cut the stones. The lives of provincial folk are not easily documented, but it is essential to make the attempt. Peru cannot otherwise be understood either in the past or at present.

The cultural and historical path we journey is strewn with obstacles, like stones fallen on an Andean trail. Some of these we have handled, removed, or rearranged, but some "intellectual" stones we necessarily left in the path. We hope that students who follow will accept the weight of their challenge. If by reading our work they find themselves better prepared than we were, we shall be pleased and rewarded.

Our preparation for writing this book began many years ago when both of us worked with the Cornell University Peru Project under the direction of the late Allan R. Holmberg. Under his inspiration we became "Peruvianists," and we are greatly indebted to him and his many insights about Peru and the cultural process. Since 1960, we have collectively (but independently) spent about eight years in Peru at various times engaged in anthropological research on agrarian reform and socioeconomic development, migration and urbanization, community life and ethnohistory. Consequently, we owe many intellectual debts to friends and colleagues in Peru and the United States for sharing their research and ideas with us, as well as several U.S. government civilian agencies, universities, and private foundations which supported our research financially.

With respect to this book, the University of Florida library greatly aided us, and its Center for Latin American Studies, through Tinker Foundation funds, allowed Kirk Webster and Charles Palmer to convert our sketches into maps. Christine Krueger helped us to track down much obscure data in compiling tables. A final but major note of thanks must also go to Mary Faith Dobyns and Mary F. Doughty for their steadfast help at all critical moments and to Carol F. Doughty, Luz Graciela Joly, and Sally Lawson for their invaluable assistance with the index.

We wish to express our sincerest appreciation to the many Peruvians who have given us their steadfast friendship and help for many years. To them we acknowledge our debt with the hope that this book will stand as testimony of our interest as serious scholars and our goodwill toward Peru.

Gainesville, Florida
December 10, 1975

Henry F. Dobyns
Paul L. Doughty

Contents

Maps

Tables

Peru

Introduction

Peru is a land of dramatic extremes.

The startling contrasts of water, desert, mountain fastness, snow-capped peaks, and tropical jungle always awed observers. Yet, only when astronauts orbiting the southern hemisphere in the 1960s shot unique photographs of western South America could everyone truly appreciate the fantastic juxtaposition of major physiographic divisions.

Seen from space, the deep green carpet of the western Amazon basin rain forest in eastern Peru seems to stretch endlessly, filling the horizon. In fact, the emerald jungle halts only 250 kilometers from the Pacific coast, where the forbidding brown ramparts of the Andean mountain chain sharply delimit the western edge of the forest.

To the viewer from space, the enormously eroded canyons of the eastern Andes constitute one of the outstanding features of the impressive landscape. The ever-widening chasms that split the seemingly impregnable bastion of the Andean highlands testify to the erosive power of glacially fed streams, invisible from space, that rise in the snowcapped peaks and glacial lakes of the high plateaus of the Andes. These streams form the headwaters of one of the world's greatest river systems, the Amazon.

The great snowcapped peaks, high plateaus, and intermontane valleys of the Andes Mountains can themselves be barely distinguished from space, so prominent is the corrugated effect of the mountains that run north and south. Except in southern Peru and Bolivia, where they widen greatly, the Andean heights are a scant 200 kilometers wide. The view from space also fails to reveal the marvelous ecological complexity of the highland regions and, indeed, it is almost impossible to distinguish those places that support human life, although human habitation and modification of natural vegetation began there over twenty millennia ago.

Beyond the Andes to the west, the thin beige line of the coastal littoral outlines the continent's ocean perimeter. Seldom more than 50 kilometers wide, the coastal desert does not impress the space traveler. So minute are the irrigated agricultural valleys that interrupt the sand and rock desert that the observer is hard put to locate even the largest of them. West of the desert edge, the Pacific Ocean floor drops rapidly to great depths. Seen from space, the Peruvian sea is a solid deep blue, failing to show the course of the Humboldt Current with its cold, fish-laden waters that constitute the world's richest fishing zone.

The contemporary Peruvian nation lives and prospers to a significant extent from its maritime resources. One of Peru's startling historical contrasts, however, is that in the past it was not a predominantly maritime country. For hundreds of years, some eighty peasant fishing villages scattered along the Pacific coast caught only enough food fish for the needs of their inhabitants and for a small sale of fresh and dried fish to urban dwellers. Then in midtwentieth century, commercial fishermen began to use industrial techniques intensively to exploit the anchovy resources of the Humboldt Current. Peru zoomed from nowhere in world fisheries statistics to first place, surpassing for several years even the U.S.S.R. and Japan not only in total catch but also in export volume.

In 1946, because of geopolitical concerns, Argentina declared sovereignty over 200 miles of continental shelf and waters off its coast, although the declaration provided for "freedom of navigation" within this area. Peru and Chile followed suit in 1947. International claims upon this ocean area, which we consider one of Peru's four major regions, were at that time negligible. Neither the United States nor any other national interest was active in the area. Even Peruvian exploitation of these maritime resources was then technologically primitive and limited.

The Peruvian-Chilean-Argentine maritime sovereignty declarations nevertheless evoked a U.S. challenge to their 200-mile figure. The Latin American nations countered with the argument that they had acted in accord with the thrust of U.S. President Truman's 1945 fisheries and natural resources proclamations. These had stated the right of the United States and other nations to develop control and conservation rights over ocean resources that distance off their shores and on underlying seabeds. Peruvians and other Latin Americans therefore interpreted the U.S. opposition to their assertions of sovereignty over 200 miles of adjacent maritime resources as U.S. arrogance. They concluded that the U.S. reserved to itself alone the power to extend sovereignty beyond the traditional three- and twelve-mile limits, disregarding the rights of South American nations. This conflict in concept and philosophy subsequently led to increasingly agonized relations between Peru and the U.S.

Peru continues to maintain its position among the largest fish producers in the world by heavily exploiting its maritime resources. Since 1968, the Peruvian government has even further expanded the country's food-fish catch and its domestic consumption.

While the fishing industry has provided Peru with its largest source of foreign exchange since midcentury, it has also been subject to unpredictable fluctuations. The miraculous currents offshore are not inexhaustible. Changes in the availability of fish occur because of the buildup of equatorial warm waters from the north pushing the cold Humboldt Current out to sea. When this occurs, as it did in 1972 and 1973, the fish simply disappear until the waters return to their normal courses. Another reason for this acute decline may be over-fishing of the shoals by the very efficient purse-seiners of the 1,450-vessel Peruvian fleet.

Heavy exploitation of the anchovy shoals has created a serious problem for farmers. Cormorants or *guanay* are birds that live off the anchovy in the Humboldt Current and deposit their dung on small offshore islands. As the fish that have sustained *guanay* for centuries are put to other uses, the *guanay* population decreases considerably. That results in a sharp decline in the production of dung, termed *guano,* used as a high-nitrogen-content field fertilizer since pre-Columbian times.

Peru's newly exploited "fourth region," the sea, is subject to this delicate environmental balance despite its apparent wealth and agelessness. The complexity of the maritime region parallels the environmental diversity of the Peruvian land area, which Peruvians long ago learned to utilize.

The coastal littoral, the first of the three major land divisions, forms the northern portion of one of the world's true arid deserts. Ranging from sea level up to 2,000 meters, the littoral differs completely from the rain forest. None of the verdant Amazonic plants grows naturally on the Pacific coastal desert. Seen at ground level, this desert exhibits somber pastel shades of brown, red, green, gray, and even black and white. These are the colors of bedrock, talus slopes, and sandy wastes unmodified by vegetation. Some of the earth's largest sand dunes move massively across the littoral wastes. For hundreds of kilometers certain peculiar climatic conditions allow one plant—a rootless aerophyte that sucks its water supply from seasonal fogs—to live on the coastal desert.

Within the Peruvian portion of this long, narrow coastal desert of South America, some fifty-seven rivers rising high in the Andes long ago carved alluvial valleys reaching the ocean. Twenty-one of those streams are today virtually unusable. The other thirty-six irrigate valley oases. The environmental contrast between an irrigated, fertile oasis and the stark and barren desert on either side could not be more extreme. On one side of the highest irrigation canal at the valley margin lies barren desert. On the other, lower side, green fields of cultivated plants of numerous species stretch between borders of towering shade and fruit trees—lúcuma, pacai, guava, molle, willow—and thickets of pseudobamboo or fields of tall sugar cane.

The fogs produced by the Humboldt Current seasonally cool the atmosphere over many of these valley oases. The cloud cover helps to maintain even temperatures that characterize the oases. Together with irrigation water and fertile soils, these temperatures have made the oases into subtropical paradises in which an amazing array of cultivated plants prospers the year round. Rain falls directly on the coastal desert only a few times each century.

People have exploited the enormous agricultural potential of the river-watered oases since the domestication of South American plants during the third millennium B.C. Native Americans then began to plant cotton, gourds, and beans, but they soon learned that they could not long depend on yields from narrow riverine fields naturally watered by spring floods. Soon they mastered the skills needed to dig irrigation canals to carry water to larger fields above river level. Thus they created oases. Growing populations eventually required the construction of enormous irrigation works.

Notable advances of this type took place in the Chicama and Moche valleys, in which the contemporary city of Trujillo is located. This area was populated from very early times at a place known as Huaca Prieta in the northern Chicama Valley. The irrigated zone expanded to encompass most of the land readily available for irrigation agriculture. A canal system built in Mochica times (A.D. 200-600) carried water from the Andean foothills by an aqueduct over 2 kilometers long and 30 meters high and then through a series of canals. Many of these, such as the Pongo Chongo in the Chicama Valley, still play a major role in distributing water at plantations such as Cartavio, Chiclín, and Chiquitoy, and to village communities such as Santiago de Cao.

The inhabitants of the coastal oases have long been stratified into socioeconomic classes divided by sharp distinctions of power and privilege. Those who controlled the irrigation waters dominated the oasis populations. Such appears to have been the case in prehistoric times, and certainly characterizes historic times. Building upon a pre-Columbian infrastructure, Spaniards developed large-scale commercial agriculture in the colonial period in the coastal oases of a dozen major river valleys such as Zaña, Nepeña, Chancay, Cañete, and Ica. The economic and political history of such areas can be understood only if one is aware of the special economic importance of irrigation water available when needed and the consequent political power of controlling it.

To point to only one sociopolitical consequence of the special conditions that exist in these irrigated oases, the country's most important political movement of this century grew out of a struggle between the sugar workers' labor organizations in the north coast oases and the landed—which is to say the "watered"—ruling groups of the region. Economically speaking, contemporary Peru's key export crops, sugar and cotton, grow in the irrigated oasis fields and diversify the national export economy significantly beyond temporary reliance on any single commodity such as the tremendously profitable fish meal made from Humboldt Current anchovies.

By 1000 B.C., the major coastal oases were heavily populated and increasingly organized into state societies. Substantial urban settlements developed after 500 B.C. at many places in the Rímac, Moche, Chancay, Lurín, and Nazca valleys. Religious leaders motivated peasant masses to erect great ceremonial centers featuring vast sun-dried brick pyramids, buildings, and public squares. Within the area of the contemporary city of Lima alone, there were approximately 100 large temple mounds. During this period at Moche, the popularly named "Pyramid of the Sun" rose from a base 365 meters long and 137 meters wide. The Mochica people employed more than 130,000,000 sun-dried bricks in its construction. Standing over 40 meters high, although in ruins, this pyramid still dominates the oasis landscape.

Prehistoric planners tried to hold residential areas to barren locations adjacent to the irrigable fields to make certain these fields remained in food and fiber production. Thus, they created a third environment—the city or urbanized farm town—between the valley oasis and the barren desert. Historic inhabitants of the oases have all too often preempted the flat irrigated areas for urbanization in accord with Old World cultural patterns, at the cost of part of Peru's irrigable land base.

Today, Peru's greatest urban settlements lie in the coastal valleys, dominated by the national capital of Lima, situated along the Rímac River on the central coast. Ironically, Lima and its port city of Callao have the worst climate for dense human settlement of all the places along the littoral. The peculiar interaction of natural phenomena occurring there—the Humboldt Current, acting on the Andean foothills high in elevation yet still desert terrain—produce a thermal inversion. This results in a cloud ceiling that hangs over the area for about five months each year, May through September. The cloud cap shuts out the sun, creating a cool temperature (18°C.), high humidity (90%), and a misty fog called *garua,* for which Lima is infamous.

Also trapped in the inversion are airborne wastes such as desert dust, automobile exhaust, and factory fumes, all of which ultimately shower on the city over 18 tons of toxic pollutants per square mile each year. This is a problem severe enough to rank Lima eighth worst in world urban pollution statistics. Even though Lima's residents suffer a constant round of bronchial and pulmonary discomforts stemming from this situation, the city continues to grow.

That the coastal region contains a total area of 161,000 square kilometers, or 12 percent of the nation, matters less than its stark extremes between barren desert and irrigated oases. What is significant is the fact that the river valleys contain only 6,500 square kilometers of land that may be considered arable or even habitable. Scattered along the bleak, 2,000-kilometer-long coastal desert, the 6,500 square kilometers of fertile area constitute less than one percent of the national territory. The oases nevertheless hold 45 percent of the population, having in 1972 over 6,000,000 inhabitants with a density of 938 persons per square kilometer. This made the coastal oases one of the most densely settled regions in the world. Despite their minuscule size, the coastal valleys produce most of Peru's export crops as well as a major portion of its domestic urban food supply.

Only mineral desposits and petroleum resources make the true desert areas economically productive. These are so antagonistic to human life that oil and mine camps appear as artificial environments standing on moonlike landscapes. Oil fields at La Brea and Pariñas in the northern department of Piura have long been exploited. Control

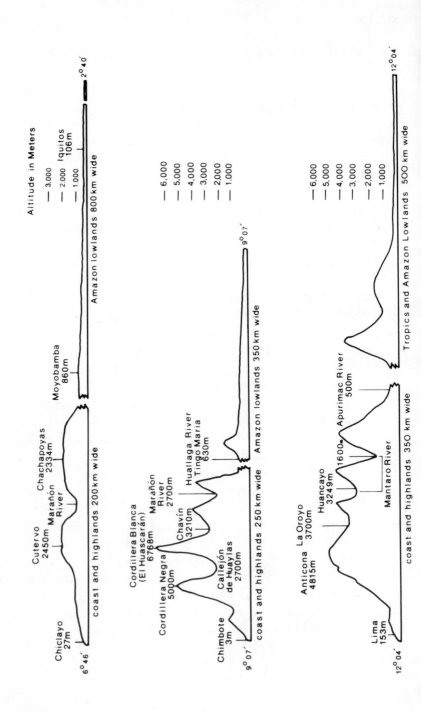

Altitude in Meters

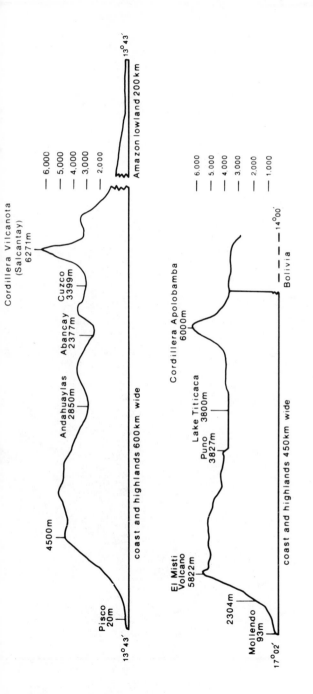

PROFILES OF THE PERUVIAN ANDES AND LOWLANDS

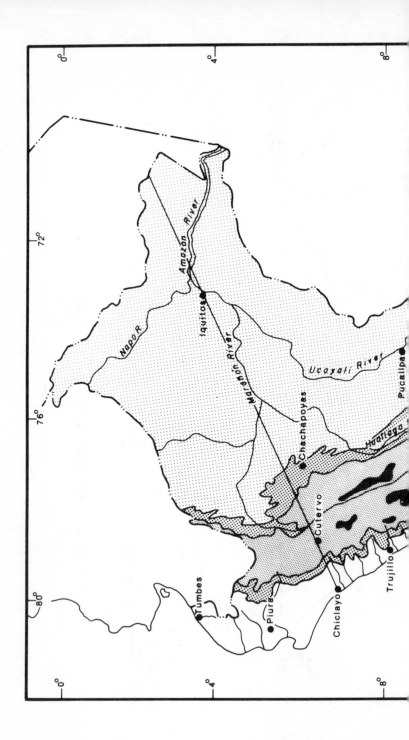

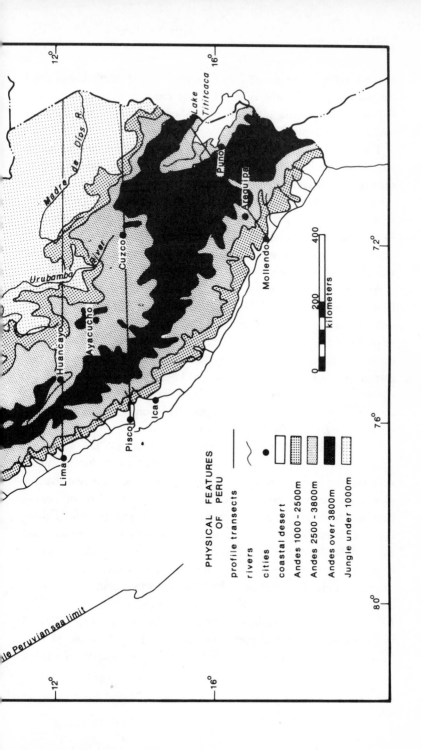

PHYSICAL FEATURES
OF PERU

profile transects

rivers

cities

coastal desert

Andes 1000 - 2500m

Andes 2500 - 3800m

Andes over 3800m

Jungle under 1000m

0   200   400

kilometers

of this wealth has produced enormous conflict and international political turmoil since World War I. On the southern desert, vast copper
deposits at Toquepala and iron ore at Marcona have boosted the economy since midcentury.

The spectacular productivity of the coastal valleys, the enormous
wealth of the Peruvian sea, and the recently discovered mineral resources have accentuated the extreme concentration of people in the
littoral oases. Moreover, administrative centralization in combination
with these factors has brought some 3,341,700 people to reside in
Peru's primate city of Lima. The coastal area thus accounts for vastly
more of the national wealth than either its fertile area or gross size
would initially indicate.

At some points along the coast, the Andean ramparts directly confront the ocean waves. Thus, the mountains divide the littoral into
sections, rising abruptly from the sea to altitudes of over 5,000 meters
at peaks of the western range. Andean elevations drop off into intermontane valleys or high altitude plateaus before rising again farther
east in the central and eastern ranges. Their peaks strain beneath the
weight of the permanent ice of hundreds of mountain glaciers. Only a
small portion of the mountain ice pack melts onto westward draining
slopes to irrigate the Pacific coastal oases.

Peruvians uniformly speak of these elevations as "the Sierra," as
though they were some sort of a homogeneous area. In historic times,
an enduring Indianness of the highland populations has lent the peoples of the Sierra a kind of specious likeness, at least in the eyes of
capital city bureaucrats and members of the ruling elite. During
colonial times, Spanish officials in Lima remained for the most part
far more familiar with the royal court, Peninsular cathedrals, and the
docks of Cadiz or Seville than with the peoples and places of "the
Sierra" of Peru. Republican-era bureaucrats in the capital city likewise
display a similar ignorance of "the Sierra," an area they most probably
have never visited. Members of the upper class are often multilingual
in European tongues and perfectly at home in Paris, London, Madrid,
Washington, New York, and Miami Beach, yet understand neither

major Indian language spoken daily by millions of highlanders and have not visited even one provincial capital in their own nation located in the varied natural environments of the Andes.

Extreme environmental variation characterizes "the Sierra" even more than any other of Peru's four major regions. The high altitude glaciers in the Andes form no connected icesheet, even though the permanent snow line uniformly begins at 5,000 meters above sea level. The mountain glaciers are islands of frozen precipitation glittering like multifaceted diamonds as the bright sun burns away the clouds that frequently shade and cool them. Below the glaciers sparkle hundreds of small crystalline lakes impounded by the huge moraines of earlier and larger ice flows.

Tallest of the glaciated mountains, *El Huascarán,* reaches 6,768 meters. Only the Himalayan mountain peaks jut farther into the atmosphere than those in the Andes. Half a dozen summits on the Chile-Argentina border reach higher than *El Huascarán,* but its 22,205-foot summit is much higher than North America's Mt. Mc-Kinley at 20,320 feet, or Europe's El'brus at 18,510 in the Caucasus, or Mont Blanc at 15,771 in the Alps. Surrounded by dozens of slightly lesser glaciated peaks, *Huascarán* dominates the brilliant 200-kilometer-long range known as the *Cordillera Blanca.* Its eastern slopes drain into the Marañon, a major tributary of the Amazon. The western slope forms one side of the hilly, intermontane valley called the *Callejón de Huaylas,* drained by the Santa River, largest of the streams emptying into the Pacific.

The 300 glacial lakes in the *Cordillera Blanca* store irrigation and hydroelectric power generating waters, as do hundreds more in the Andes. In these invaluable waters lurks, however, an ever-present threat to the inhabitants of the lower valley. When heavy rains raise a lake over its impounding moraine, valley settlements are flooded, often with severe consequences. In 1941, for instance, 5,000 people drowned in the flood at Huaráz. In addition, when an iceberg-size piece breaks off from a glacier, it can precipitate an avalanche of incredible speed and destructive power. In 1962 and 1970, ice from *El*

Huascarán destroyed the towns of Ranrahirca and Yungay, killing over 10,000 persons.

The Callejón de Huaylas is representative of intermontane Andean valleys. Its "penetration" roads from the coast wind tortuously up the western canyons to traverse passes at 4,200 meters before entering the Callejón. The Santa River, its major waterway, rises in the glacial lakes at Conococha, near one pass. Dropping, it flows through several environmental zones before cutting abruptly through the spectacular Cañon del Pato toward the Pacific. At its headwaters at 4,000 meters, the river is surrounded by verdant grasslands that serve as pasture for peasant pastoralists who live dispersed over their range. Known as *puna,* these grasslands are distinguished by their cold, clear atmosphere the year round, and their water-catchment function, acting like a huge natural sponge that collects precipitation to sustain streams to irrigate the oases that feed the people. Here air temperatures frequently drop to freezing and seldom rise above 65°F.

As the terrain drops to 3,000 meters, the climate turns more benign, and highly specialized agricultural villages appear along the road. River waters wash ores at the Ticapampa lead mine. Recuay and Catac are centers for extensive cattle and sheep grazing and potato growing. As the altitude lessens, the population grows and villages appear every five kilometers.

In the middle altitudes of Sierra valleys such as the Callejón de Huaylas, a wide array of temperate and subtropical crops prosper under an Andean sun that warms the air to a comfortable 75°F. in the day. Evening temperatures seldom fall below 40°F. Just as in the coastal valleys, irrigation plays a fundamental role, particularly during the dry season lasting from April to October. During the other five months, the Sierra is subject to torrential rains that play havoc with the narrow dirt roads and irrigation canals, cause numerous landslides, and speed the erosion of the steep cultivated hillsides.

The sun-dried brick and tile-roofed homes of the native peasantry are surrounded by hand- or oxen-plowed fields—wheat, barley, quinoa, and rye at higher elevations and maize, alfalfa, and vegetable crops lower down. Called *chacras,* such fields are often bounded by century plants or tall rows of eucalyptus trees.

By the time the Santa River has dropped 2,000 meters in a distance of 60 kilometers, its waters flow through canal networks to irrigate low-altitude, warm-climate fields such as the orange groves in the neighborhood of Caráz. The oasis character of the irrigated intermontane valley stands clearly revealed at this elevation where precipitation supports only an occasional hardy cactus or deep-rooted thorny shrub.

In southern Peru, the high-altitude *puna* widens into an extensive plateau, the *altiplano.* These natural pastures produce most of Peru's cattle and other animals, including all its cameloid llamas and alpacas. Grazing animals and shepherds on the *puna* inhabit a more-or-less uniform environment, but it is extremely harsh, oxygen-short, and cold. The *altiplano* stretches hundreds of kilometers south of Cuzco into Bolivia. The world's twentieth largest fresh-water lake, Titicaca, moderates the harsh climate on the international border, and cattle browse on its giant lush bulrushes. In adjacent fields, however, drought kills one crop in five, on the average, while frosts or hailstorms destroy another.

The intermontane valleys and gorges opening on both the Pacific Ocean and Amazon Basin have vastly differing microenvironments determined by complex variations in oxygen content in the air, degree of slope relative to sunlight, soil quality, mineral content, water availability, night and day wind patterns, air humidity, and other factors. Because of the extreme diversity of microclimates and microenvironments in the Andes, native flora and fauna have adapted to a very wide range of special environmental niches. Of special significance to mankind, these diverse microenvironments of the Andes prehistorically became one of the world's principal centers for plant domestication. Despite the fact that 68 percent of the Andes thrusts over 3,000 meters, the Native American peoples inhabiting these mountains developed domesticated plants adaptable to each of the habitable Andean microenvironments. Prehistoric cultivators developed the color, taste, texture, and growth characteristics of tuberous crops specialized to high altitudes. Many varieties of potatoes, ollucos, ocas, and other colorful tubers delight the local gourmet because of the fine flavors they signal. They confound, on the other hand, the foreign visitor familiar only with the white-fleshed, bland potato grown the world over. The mislabeled "Irish" potato is one major Andean contribution to the world's diet.

In addition to tubers, Native American cultivators domesticated dozens of other crop plants to serve as the basis for ancient Andean life. These included squashes, beans, cereal-like seeds, fruits in great variety, palms for wood and fruit, cacti, many kinds of plants whose leaves yield teas, salad greens, herbs and condiments, fiber plants, a soap-plant, dye-plants, and gourds, not to mention ornamental "flowers." Such ancient Andean cultigens continue to play a major role in the diet of contemporary highland populations, particularly the peasantry. To this rich Andean agricultural base the Spanish conquest added Old World crops such as wheat and other small grains, numerous common vegetables, and some fruits.

The Europeans also introduced their Neolithic barnyard, which greatly enriched the food production capacity of the Andean populations. Ancient Peruvians domesticated far more animals than did any other Native Americans: llamas, alpacas, guinea pigs, and muscovy ducks. Yet donkeys, cattle, sheep, goats, pigs, and chickens were major additions, even during the long colonial decades when imperial policy kept horses out of the hands of Indians. All these Old World animals adapted quickly to the wide range of altitudes and other environmental factors in the Andes.

The mountains have created special conditions for human life, just as they have for other living things, especially mammals. Anyone who customarily lives near sea level will experience a variety of reactions when visiting high-altitude areas such as Cuzco or Huancayo. In both cities, located over 3,000 meters high, the traveler may experience hypoxia caused by oxygen scarcity. This may cause shortness of breath, dizziness, headache, nausea, nose bleeds, and even a pulmonary edema that can be fatal. The dry, cold air also parches the skin and piercing sunlight can burn an unwary person with ultraviolet radiation. Most individuals fortunately usually have to endure only one or two of the discomforts until the body adjusts to the new conditions.

Since the first humans colonized the Andes at least 20,000 years ago, an evolutionary process of selection has prepared their descendants to cope with the extreme high-altitude environments. To meet the stress caused by decreased oxygen in the air, the lung capacity of native highlanders is increased as much as 40 percent compared with that of sea level natives, with richer capillary beds. The body contains 25 percent more blood, a greater number of red corpuscles per equivalent volume, and is more viscous. The heart enlarges 40 percent to handle its increased load. The body tends toward compactness, with short extremities resulting in low stature.

The Sierra amounts to over 30 percent of the national territory, or 388,000 square kilometers. The 44 percent of the population that lives there is concentrated in mountain valleys and habitable portions of the altiplano, which, as in the case of the coast, amounts to only a fraction of the total, 4.5 percent or 17,460 square kilometers of cultivated land. On about 93,120 square kilometers of Sierra land natural high-altitude pasture thrives and these areas are inappropriate for agriculture.

Despite this, the Sierra contains more than half the nation's arable land. For all the immenseness of the highland region, it has a population density of 343 persons per square kilometer of habitable, arable land. Of the rest, craggy slopes and barren heights are at every hand. Here and there, often at altitudes exceeding 4,500 meters, mineral deposits have been discovered and mining camps established. Lead, zinc, silver, mercury, and numerous other metals are extracted from harsh, inhospitable surroundings by hardy Andean people whose physiques permit them to perform arduous labor at great altitudes.

Seen from space-capsule altitude, Peru's Amazon Basin, the third of the land terrains, spreads like a dark green carpet widely across the earth. Seen from ground level, on the other hand, this region immediately resolves itself into two extremes from a human point of view—the dense jungle and the giant river. The moist, hot rain forest grows so thickly, the shrubs crowding so densely under the upper-story trees, that human beings find overland travel extremely difficult. Even trails cut through the rain forest soon grow up with stout trunks and tough vines. In addition, the humid rain forest microenvironment harbors clouds of voracious stinging insects. Even where roadways are built, the Atlantic weather system dumps so much rain upon the forest that wheeled vehicles tend to mire unless these roadways are carefully constructed and maintained or paved. Giant river channels drain the forest, however, and provide easy transportation routes that have carried watercraft from time immemorial.

The Amazonian forest comprises approximately 57 percent of Peru, 736,000 square kilometers, an area twice the size of Italy. Yet it contained 11 percent of the national population in 1972, which lived on the scant 3,312 square kilometers of arable land. Thus, despite the vastness of the region, population density here is 446 persons to each scarce bit of arable land.

Human occupation of the Ucayali and other important streams draining this basin began early in the course of human expansion in South America. The readily arable land was always to be found largely along the river banks. Renewed each year through flooding as enriched torrents descended from the Andes, these lands supported dense prehistoric populations. Then as now, riverine peoples made a comfortable living from seasonal planting and fishing. The ox-bow lakes formed by the meandering rivers, which often change their courses to leave curved sections behind as independent bodies of water, provided excellent places for permanent settlements. The waters still teem with large, superb fish that have not been properly appreciated outside the region because of its isolation.

The promise of such rain forest "paradises" constantly reinforces legends about the riches to be gained in Amazonia. Such legends began to grow at least as early at 1800 B.C., the period when ceremonial organization clearly emerged in Andean settlements. Both the coastal and highland oasis dwellers traded actively with the jungle peoples. Many plants and animals utilized in the coastal valleys and in the Andes came across the mountain passes. They included manioc, coca,

caygua, peanut, sweet potato, tree tomato, pineapple, papaya, and cotton, and such animals as birds and monkeys. Rain forest denizens such
as the jaguar, harpy eagle, and cayman became features of mountain
and coastal iconography in all major pre-Columbian horizons. Then, as
now, Peruvians depended upon a plethora of medicinal plants from
the Amazonian tropics. Several have proved to be important sources
for modern pharmacology. Tropical herbs and cures have long formed
the basis of the native medical kit, and today such items are widely
sold throughout Peru.

In the high rain forest which reaches 1,600 meters up the eastern
slope, the ground is broken by the Andean ridges, chasms, and rough
terrain. This region, known as "The Eyebrow of the Jungle," has long
produced the major harvest of leaves of the coca plant. Masticated
with lime, coca leaves constituted the favorite "chaw" of ancient Andean and littoral dwellers from the time interregional trading began.

In the lower jungle, the dense rain forest presents a tangle that has
discouraged all but the most dedicated explorers. For this reason, people have throughout history stayed largely by the rivers, and populations followed their courses all over the Amazon. Stronger tribes,
when they entered the region, pushed others upriver into less desirable
areas. Eventually the more timid, less numerous, or defeated groups
found themselves in the headwaters regions of the river networks.
Some perforce eked out a living in the forest away from rivers of note,
but the largest numbers were still riverine peoples. Thus, at the time
of Spanish conquest, the first explorers in the area reported heavy native settlement along each of the principal rivers. By the same token,
the uplands in the Andean foothills comprised refuge areas. In the irony
of historic contact, the more powerful, settled riverine groups became
the first Native Americans to succumb to the impact of European
conquest—at first mostly by Old World diseases, it seems. The tribal
groups that survived with any degree of success survived by virtue of
their isolation in the aboriginally less desirable refuge areas.

Today the Amazonic tribes remaining in Peru number about fifty-
five with a growing estimated combined population of approximately
100,000. The largest ethnic groups are the Aguaruna, Amuesha,

Campa, Shipibo-Conibo, and Cocama-Cocamilla. Virtually all the surviving tribes have lived in contact with the populations outside the Amazon Basin since the first years of European conquest when early explorers traversed the region.

Missionaries began to work relatively early, establishing missions along the edge of the Andes. Others came to the rain forest lured by its legends, but seeking places where they could make a customary kind of living. A gradual colonization took place as highlanders slowly moved into adjacent forest areas, some eventually forming permanent settlements. Large commercial interests promoted an economy based upon rubber, coca, coffee, tea, and cacao—all introduced plantation crops except for coca and rubber.

The rain forest trees constitute a singular resource of the Amazon that has scarcely been utilized. Location, felling, concentration, and especially transportation across the Andes to urban highland or coastal markets pose great difficulties. Peruvian investment in trans-Andean roads has yet to meet the needs of entrepreneurs lured into the rain forest by its legends of riches. Presently, sawmills are increasing and plywood factories are coming into production with external subsidies in such towns as Tingo María and Pucallpa.

Peruvians have proved to be reluctant pioneers despite much rhetoric about the wealth of the rain forest. Few have possessed the kind of adventuresome spirit needed to endure the Amazonic challenge. The process of economic development of the Peruvian part of the basin will take more years than some optimistic planners and policy-makers foresee.

Meanwhile, the environmental extremes of Amazonian life are daily compounded by man's economic pursuits. Modern aircraft fly tropical fish and animals captured by forest tribesmen out of Iquitos airport to Miami for sale to hobbyists in North America. As another Peruvian irony, until such aircraft linked Iquitos to Lima, this rain forest metropolis remained closer to London by sea than to its own national capital.

Today Peru claims a continental area of 1,285,120.7 square kilometers plus 94.9 square kilometers of Pacific islands. This makes Peru the third largest country in South America, after Brazil and Argentina. Peru is a vast and complex country. Its rich human culture and national endowments are endlessly tangled in a web of prehistoric events, colonial tradition, and modern needs.

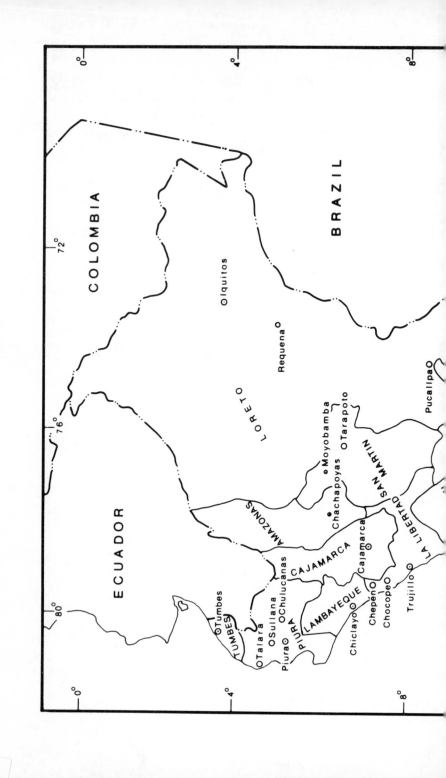

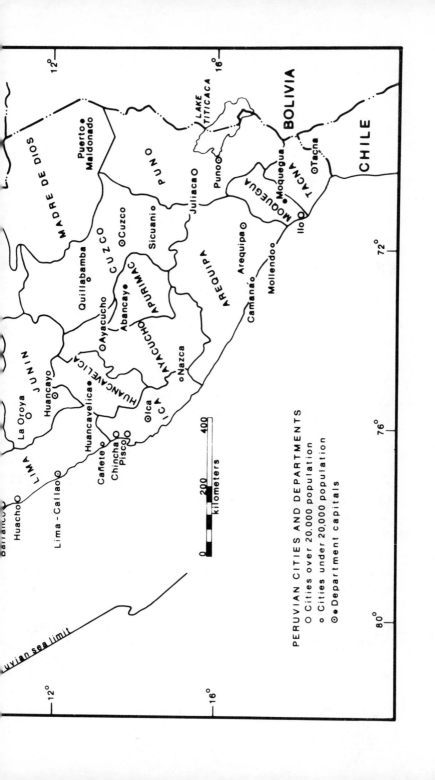

PERUVIAN CITIES AND DEPARTMENTS
O Cities over 20.000 population
o Cities under 20,000 population
⊙● Department capitals

Chapter 1 • The Formation of Andean Culture: The Pre-Incaic Period

By what routes Native Americans first entered Peru's three terrestrial environments and at what point in history remain something of a mystery. Certainly the first groups to arrive came from the north through Central America, but in how direct a movement remains unknown. Did hunters and gatherers wander into South America long after the ancient interglacial period during which their ancestors crossed from Asia to North America, or did some of the original groups that had crossed over race directly to the southern continent in pursuit of late glacial-age big game?

Presently available evidence appears to favor the conclusion that the earliest Native Americans to brave the terrestrial environments of Peru were descended from pioneer migrants from Asia who had entered the New World very much earlier. The best techniques for dating prehistoric remains indicate that hunters inhabited Pikimachay Cave near modern Ayacucho around 17,650 B.C. (±3,000 years). Clearly people had taken some time to settle this central Andean area and adjust to the rigors of its high altitude. The biological adjustment needed to permit successful permanent human settlement at an altitude of nearly three miles above sea level may have already been made.

Archeologists have recently found convincing evidence that Native Americans have exploited the highland Ayacucho area fairly continuously ever since. By 12,200 B.C., they were utilizing wild gourds as dishes and as containers in which to carry things. Five millennia later, nomadic bands still composed of small family groups specialized in pursuing certain game animals such as the llama, deer, and antelope. Shortly after 7000 B.C., guinea pigs, calabash, and achiote (a shrub producing a yellow-orange pigment) made their appearance.

The llama and the guinea pig emerged as true domesticated animals around 5500 B.C. By that time several plants, including quinoa and amaranth—both crop plants distinctive to the Andes today—also would be categorized as domesticated. The stone, wood, and bone tools known to be in use by that time in the Andes and the coastal valleys below indicate that the pioneer Peruvians cooked and prepared a diversified diet obtained by hunting, fishing, gathering, and horticulture.

Although details of the full record are not available, the central Andean region from Ecuador through Bolivia became in pre-Columbian times one of the world's greatest centers for the domestication of plants. The Andean setting, drawing from both the Amazonic and desert sides of the central highlands, accumulated over the prehistoric millennia a very rich domestic plant endowment. The Andean peoples brought under cultivation at least five cereals and five beans, two squashes, thirteen root and tuber crops, twenty-one fruits, five beverage plants, six or more condiments, five fiber plants, at least four narcotic plants, and more than seven ornamentals. Twenty-six other plants grown in the central Andean microenvironments, whose points of origin are still unknown, were pre-Columbian cultigens in both Mesoamerica and the Andean region. As modern scientists have realized, these foods provided the Andean peoples with an extremely sound diet. The potato alone, since it spread worldwide in the post-Columbian exchange between Old and New Worlds, continues to provide a major share of modern mankind's energy requirements.

While the Andean Native Americans also domesticated animals, the continental faunal endowment was less susceptible to domestication and not as varied as that of the Old World. Nevertheless, the ancient Andeans domesticated two large animals, the llama and alpaca, both cameloids, for their wool and meat, and as beasts of burden. They were unable to domesticate the closely related guanaco and vicuña. In domesticating llama, alpaca, guinea pig, and muscovy duck, the Andean peoples achieved markedly more success at this difficult task than did any other Native Americans. Their quantitative achievement in plant domestication stands, moreover, on a par with that of any other peoples elsewhere in the world.

As the ancient Peruvians mastered their Andean food production technology, they passed through a fundamental demographic transformation from small to large groups. They became stable villagers just as did Old World peoples wherever other such cultural revolutions had occurred.*

Around 4300 B.C., village life began in many places in the highlands and coastal valleys. Settlements soon became densely populated, particularly in those coastal areas that had access to maritime food resources nearby. A coastal site known as Huaca Prieta in the Chicama

---

* While much has been made of the possibilities for overseas contacts and migrations, there is very little to substantiate that any such events, however tantalizing or seductive they may appear, were anything but the most casual or accidental. The conclusion that emerges with increasing clarity is that the Native American population developed its cultures independently from the Old World.

How much intergroup contact occurred between peoples in the Peruvian area and those in Mexico and Yucatan one can only speculate. There are some highly suggestive indications that there may have been strong influences passing between these areas at the time of the Olmec societies in Mexico and the Chavín horizon in Peru. Yet details can be discerned only dimly in the ancient remains scattered by natural forces and the vandalism of later peoples. Such conjecture aside, what stands out is the fact that the ancient Peruvians not only mastered the technology of plant and animal domestication on a large scale, but also accomplished this in a natural environment with greater extremes than those of Old World areas where major Neolithic revolutions took place.

Valley was, for example, inhabited around 4,200 years ago by people already gardening. They wove cultivated cotton fibers into fishnets and clothing. They planted squash, gourds, lima beans, peppers, and perhaps some fruits. Clearly they were people whose ancestors had lived in the area a long time. Archeologists have thus far located more than 1,000 places on the littoral, including the fog-watered *lomas* or ridges that seasonally grow an ephemeral vegetation, where Native Americans as early as 10,000 B.C. gathered, hunted, or fished.

After 1800 B.C. two very significant technological changes swept through the local tribal cultures of the area, imposing on each a new cultural similarity with one another and heralding a complex of other changes. The first brought knowledge of ceramic-making and the second spread large-scale maize cultivation throughout the littoral and over the Andean slopes to the upper altitude limit of maize production, around 3,000 meters.

These two major innovations began to modify the landscape in ways that have been familiar ever since. The technique of firing clay to produce hard nonporous containers enabled people to fashion household and ritual pottery in many shapes. To this day, many rural Peruvians cook and carry water and ferment their home-brews in such handmade vessels.

The vast increase in caloric value that the addition of maize brought to the Peruvian diet allowed these ancient Peruvians to survive and prosper as sedentary horticulturists. Once committed to a sedentary life they built homes of stone or bamboo, wood or sun-dried bricks. One coastal housing style known as wattle-and-daub combined bamboo or wild cane stalks and mud plaster; another tied mats woven from split bamboo, cane, or similar materials to a pole framework. These architectural styles have endured, housing the poorest of the Peruvians. Being easily erected, they have also sheltered entire populations however on an emergency basis when an earthquake, flood, or other natural disaster reduced a whole people to temporary poverty. Today, ambitious parties of urban squatters seizing control of lands temporarily shelter themselves in the age-old style of pole-and-mat huts.

While maize cultivation represented a significant new addition to the Andean diet per se, it also enlivened social affairs. If *chicha* drinking did not start among the ancient Peruvians with their first maize kernels, these peoples quickly adopted the practice. *Chicha,* an aboriginal term for maize beer, is a fermented, nutritious beverage with an alcoholic content of two or three percent of total volume. While *chicha* can be produced from quinoa or any number of sugary fruits, ancient and modern Peruvians perfer *chicha de jora,* made from sprouted maize kernels. Once sprouting has converted starches into sugars, this maize is ground, added to water, and heated over a slow, steady fire until fermentation livens the product.

With maize, or at least with *chicha*-making, ancient Peruvians learned ritual drunkenness and associated maize with religion and fertility. Along with their maize, they planted special gourds that could be cut to produce commodious *chicha*-drinking bowls. Almost four millennia later, the peasant properly drinks *chicha* from a special gourd, not forgetting to pour a few drops on the ground for the ancient Earth Mother.

From this time forward, increasingly large-scale, organized trade united desert coastal settlements with those in the Sierra and the rain forest. Cultural interchange significantly improved life in all three zones. Coastal valley gardeners soon cultivated maize, peanuts, cotton, manioc, and hot peppers, all crops apparently obtained from rain forest domesticators. On the other hand, coastal valley dwellers probably learned by this time that they enjoyed a great competitive advantage in intertribal trade, because they could produce or gather salt from pans along the coast and secure good bargains inland where salt was scarce.

Especially on the arid coast, but in the highlands as well, cultivation on any but the most precarious of scales depended upon irrigation. Ancient Peruvian gardeners therefore constructed canal irrigation systems throughout the valleys. They continually cleared away wild brush to make room for larger fields watered from new, larger canals. After taking up maize cultivation, they built terraces in more elaborate scale and pattern than they had ever before. Production areas such as one found in the Chilca Valley followed the irregular, narrow arms of the river basin back into the Andes for many kilometers. Cultivators constructed intricate terracing with dwellings built into the base of many terraced banks. This is not a prime agricultural area, yet over 1,500 dwelling units were found in one 3-kilometer section where the valley measures less than 100 meters wide.

In other words, the ancient Peruvians who took up maize and potato cultivation, and the increasingly sedentary life these high-calorie crops permitted, quickly converted the river valleys into irrigated oases supporting dense human populations. These valleys have remained so ever since. Shortly after the horticultural change, an organized, intervillage polity soon encompassed each irrigated coastal valley from the Andean foothills to the ocean. Prior to 1800 B.C. the social and political systems of the highland peoples also largely coincided with each small cultivated valley. From the latter Sierra village horticultural base, the first large-scale regional culture developed in the north central highlands of the upper Marañon Valley around 1400 B.C. This Chavín culture quickly spread over the area now comprising Ancash, Lima, Huánuco departments, and adjacent regions. The principal sites thus far identified with this first expression of a pan-Andean unity are the temples at Kotosh in Huánuco and Chavín in Ancash. Allegiance, motivation, and dedication were clearly required of many persons in order to construct such strictly nonutilitarian public projects as the massive and complex ceremonial structures at Kotosh and Chavín. These demonstrate that a significant mobilization of great numbers of people occurred in this society at this time.

A distinctive art style decorated the culture's representative artifacts and structures all over central Peru. Considering its origins in the upper Marañon drainage, the tropical features of Chavín's intricate art convincingly demonstrate highland cultural ties with the Amazon basin peoples. The highly abstract and finely executed stonework symbolically employs such tropical animals as the harpy eagle, the cayman, and the feline. Indeed, similarities between the details of Chavín art and that of the contemporary Mesoamerican Olmec culture provide evidence that these two peoples may have shared many basic religious and artistic concepts. The Chavín peoples, like the Olmecs, worshiped sky, earth, and water deities represented in stone images. As well, priesthoods wielding great secular power directed the common people involved in this trans-Andean religious movement as they did in the Olmec society.

The Chavín peoples became the first in the central Andean area to benefit from the development of metalworking, which apparently diffused from Colombia. Golden rings, crowns, pendants, pins, and spoons of the elite rulers found in Chavín-period tombs in Chongoyape on the far north coast attest to this advance. More important however is the fact that maize horticulture, which fostered permanent sedentary settlements, spread rapidly during the Chavín time, allowing this large-scale religious and perhaps political system to hold out as its outstanding social contribution the development of urban-type settlements.

Although the "cult of Chavín" declined around 400 B.C., the impress of its ideas, symbols, and art influenced other cultures for the next 1,500 years. The pattern of religious devotion and pilgrimage established during the Chavín period continued to characterize Peruvian peoples, who maintained high standards of both artistry and artisanry in their production of religious—including funerary—textiles, ceramics, and sculptures. Yet despite this general continuity, numerous regional societies eventually emerged with their own ethnic identities and styles. Nazca on the south coast, Lima on the central coast, Huaylas, Pucará, and Cajamarca in the Andes evolved separate ethnic identities that continued through many centuries.

None of these post-Chavín cultures has so captured the imagination of contemporary scholars as the Moche or Mochica, which emerged around the present-day city of Trujillo. The Moche people built extensive irrigation works, vast temples, and numerous towns in the Virú, Moche, and Chicama valleys. They gardened efficiently enough to dress well, even luxuriously. They walked on cabuya (*Agave*) fiber sandals. Over their cotton undergarments they wore richly woven shirts, kilts for men and skirts for women, and they covered their heads with double-cocked hats. In cool weather, they donned ponchos decorated with large, bright geometric designs. Unlike the classic Greeks who slept under their cloaks, the Mochicas wove blankets of both cotton and llama wool. They laid their heads, moreover, on ceiba-tree cotton pillows. The rich decorated themselves with golden ear plugs and other precious ornaments and jewelry.

The prosperous Moche people showed a distinct flair for artistic realism as well as conventional geometrics. In particular, they utilized their ceramic wares to depict almost every aspect of their lives. This art shows a society governed by priests and rulers heading a highly stratified population of considerable technological sophistication. The Moche, like the Nazca, Lima, and Topara peoples to the south, conquered the inhabitants of neighboring oases and incorporated them into regional, intervalley states that were centrally controlled. Cities grew in most of the major coastal oases throughout this era and also in many highland valleys, continuing the pattern of Chavín times.

These civilized folk lived well in vividly painted wattle-and-daub or sun-dried brick houses, some as high as three stories. They installed louvers under the thatched eaves facing the sea to conduct cool breezes through their quarters.

The hallmark of these coastal nations was the vast ceremonial complex of temple mounds, public squares, and priestly quarters. The largest such monument to religion, called the "Temple of the Sun," rose in the Moche Valley. In the Rímac Valley (Lima) alone, clusters of immense, solid sun-dried brick pyramidal temples, numbering almost 100, dominated the flat landscape. About two centuries after the time of Christ, the temple at Pachacámac in the first valley south of Lima began to attract pilgrims, adherents of a religious cult that was to endure for the next 1,300 years. Oracular predictions like those issued at Delphi in the classic Greek world constituted a significant part of the Pachacámac devotion.

In Moche times, coastal people continued to exploit Pacific resources. Artistic representations leave no doubt that fishermen braved the waves riding astride small reed boats shaped like hobby-horses. Occupational specialization of cultivators and fishermen almost certainly had developed, so that fishermen traded fresh and probably dried fish for horticultural products. Equally important, Moche cultivators and those in other coastal states sailed cargo rafts offshore to

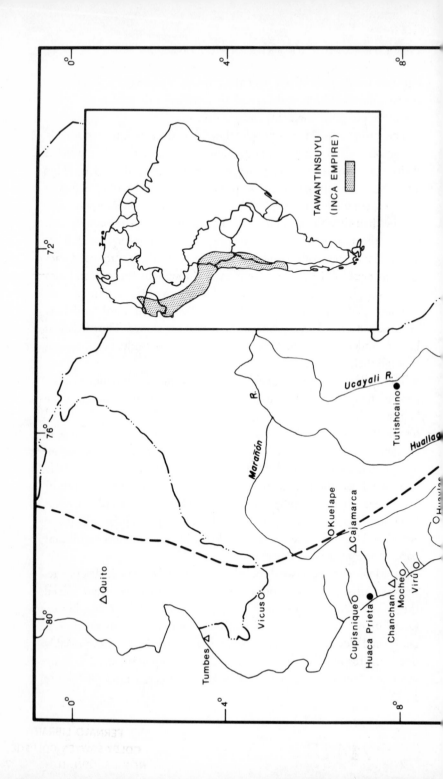

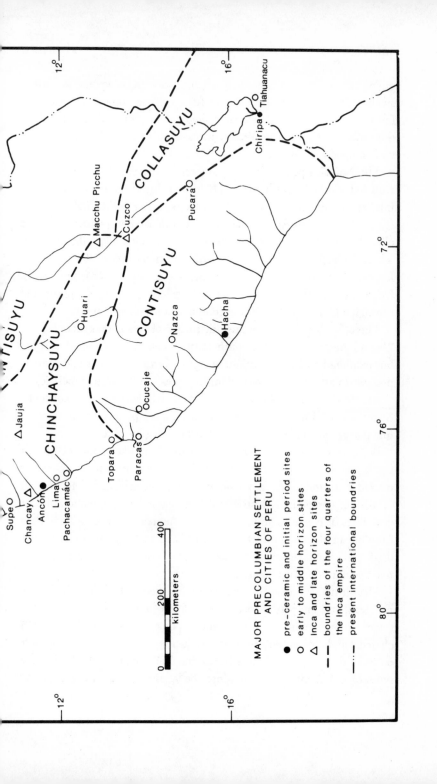

MAJOR PRECOLUMBIAN SETTLEMENT
AND CITIES OF PERU

● pre-ceramic and initial period sites
○ early to middle horizon sites
△ Inca and late horizon sites
— — boundaries of the four quarters of
        the Inca empire
—··— present international boundries

guano islands to haul nitrogen-rich bird manure to spread on intensively cultivated fields—in order to feed a dense population, Mochica
farmers triple-cropped their maize fields. Apparently, they recognized
the problem of declining fertility in oasis soils that had been irrigated
and cropped for centuries.

The Mochica people lived by any terms a civilized life. They were
well fed, clothed, and housed. Their art evinced both a sophisticated
intellectual life and humor. It distinctly portrayed individuals, perhaps
for the first time in Andean history. An authoritarian political-religious
elite that brooked no internal opposition controlled a stratified society.
These Indians were "civilized," certainly in the sense of conducting
large-scale warfare for territory—which is to say for economic ends.
Consequently, their highly stratified society quite likely originated
through a process of interethnic conquests and subordinations.

The other best-known prehistoric society of this period occupied the
Nazca-Paracas area on the south coast. Its culture resembled Moche,
but exhibited a distinctly different style. Nazca craftsmen and women
possessed particular skill at making complex, multicolored tapestries of
great size depicting many aspects of their lives and religious concepts.
Some tapestries measure 7 by 49 meters. Nazca pottery relied more on
fine polychrome painting than on Moche-style sculpting.

Both societies used water vessels with stirruplike spouts of one or
two openings, although these vessels differed in details. As water
poured out from such a vessel, incoming air whistled. Moche and
Nazca entrepreneurs industrialized to an extent the production of vast
quantities of ceramics and cloth. Large numbers of specialists worked
full-time in their manufacture and utilized molds to reproduce hundreds of ceramic vessels of the same type. Today, copyists occasionally
reuse such molds with great effect.

Metallurgy significantly advanced with the use of gold, silver, copper, lead, and mercury. Moche smiths knew how to cast, gild, emboss,
solder, alloy, hammer, anneal, and repoussé. They employed both
charcoal and coal as fuels for furnaces heating to 1,000° that they built
on mounds to capture the sea breeze for draft. Smiths produced many
types of ornaments, wall hangings, bells, and jewelry in addition to

tools. They alloyed copper with tin to produce bronze, which holds a sharp edge better than copper. Mochica smiths evidently mass-produced knives, wedges, blades, and pins.

Thus, with the passage of centuries, each Peruvian region and valley tended to develop its own cultural identity, language, and political system. Occasionally, these units reached eminence, as did Moche and Nazca. Most Andean cultural history unfolded in the context of such regional independence rather than under expansionist empires.

Having lasted for over 1,000 years, the second period of regional autonomy and ethnic development ended in conquest. For two centuries, two apparently separate empires held sway over almost all Peru and Bolivia. During the Moche-Nazca period of cultural and social florescence, there were similar developments in the highlands. Around A.D. 600 the Tiahuanaco people, just south of Lake Titicaca on the high plateau of Bolivia, and the Huari society, near modern Ayacucho, began to expand their nations through conquest. The Tiahuanaco state eventually controlled all southern Peru from Arequipa south to highland Bolivia and Chile. The Huari territory bulked even larger, its rulers conquering both coast and highlands as far north as the Chicama Valley and Cajamarca, and south to the Tiahuanaco frontier.

Urban growth continued only, apparently, within the Huari empire, but many other trends and characteristics already mentioned continued with the stamp of these two special styles. The Tiahuanaco ruins include a large urban and ceremonial complex with enormous blocks of elaborately sculpted and polished stone, the details of which feature deities and reflect to some degree motifs that first appeared during Chavín times. In actuality, little is known specifically of the Tiahuanaco and Huari empires other than that they arose through military conquest and promulgated some sort of state religion. Their obscurity is ironic inasmuch as the principal sites, especially Tiahuanaco, are among the most famous in all South America.

Partly because of these imperial conquests, the number and distribution of Andean ethnic groups are facts still unknown. Alternating periods of empire and regionalism also raise questions as to the interrelationships among numerous Andean ethnic groups through time.

At least two kinds of coexisting patterns may be discerned, each with social, political, and economic attributes and functions.

The perennial genius of Andean culture has been its success in exploiting the full range of natural environment. Because relatively few communities or regional states had full access to all the microenvironments, they developed various arrangements to increase it. An altiplano community could, for example, trade its potatoes or alpaca wool for the maize of a middle altitude village which in turn might pass along coca which it obtained from a tropical settlement. Such trade tended to center around patterns of intermarriage between the trading villages or ritual exchange relationships that endured for generations. In other instances, llama caravans worked their way around a large trading circuit from highlands to coast or jungle.

Sending entire "colonies" of persons from one region into a different zone in order to garden, graze stock, or harvest on a seasonal or even permanent basis may have been more complex and difficult to arrange. In some cases the ability to implant colonies rested upon ancient alliances, and in others upon warfare. All these practices assured the tribe or state of a supply of produce specific to a particular microenvironment outside its area of traditional political control and often among communities of different ethnic groups.

These customs could account for the former widespread distribution of such peoples as Aymara-speakers, whose core territory centered on the very high altitude plateau around Lake Titicaca. Aymara peoples remain second only in size of territory and numbers to Quechua-speakers today, hinting that their pre-Incaic territorial extension may well have stemmed from the Tiahuanaco expansion.

A second pattern of interethnic relations recorded historically in Aymara country obtained elsewhere in the region as well. Spanish officials found the Aymara-speaking Lupaca kingdom still functioning in Chucuito Province on the Peruvian shore of Lake Titicaca in 1567. Like virtually all other highlanders, the Lupaca divided their society into "upper" and "lower" halves or moieties. Each had its own hereditary lord and authority structure. Both Lupaca moieties contained two ethnic groups, Uru and Aymara, the latter outnumbering the former about three to one. The Uru minority lived at every social level in the seven Lupaca provinces, apparently as lacustrine occupational specialists. Ethnic, social, and occupational stratification implies, perhaps, a caste-division of the society, which may have typified Andean states such as Tiahuanaco.

In the Huari empire, numerous regional urban centers developed. The large capital itself stood near modern Ayacucho. Others included Cajamarquilla in the Rímac Valley near modern Lima and cities in the Cajamarca, Motupe, and Chicama valleys in the north. The city of Chan Chan began in the Chicama Valley at this time and the cult of Pachacamác grew to great importance in the Lurín Valley and influenced coastal art forms from Nazca to Chancay. The Huari highlanders apparently placed considerable value on the supernatural powers of the religion whose devotees went on pilgrimage to Pachacamác. They respected it enough to allow it to thrive with a certain independence.

Urban settlement in ancient Peru followed environmental dictates and also highly pragmatic human rules. In the Moche and Chicama valleys, linked by an 80-kilometer canal system that maximized the irrigation potential in this highly productive area, urban settlements were closely tied to the horticultural economy. Thus, towns occupied hillsides above the canal systems or other sites adjacent to but not within irrigated zones. The choice of these sites generally freed urban dwellers from insects and possible floods and, more important, kept essential irrigated land in production.

Such planned cities reflected the political and technological transformation of Andean societies. In early times, once a family erected its tiny stone or pole-and-mat or wattle-and-daub huts near its cultivated land, it evidently gained, rather easily, some sort of property rights. The cities of Huari-Tiahuanaco and smaller towns of later times clearly showed, however, that centralized authority denied villagers the right to homestead where they pleased. Population densities reached such levels as to press upon the resource base, expanded though it had been by large-scale irrigation works, applications of fertilizers, and ocean-fishing. Powerful authorities bent buildings and cities to fit natural configurations, carefully husbanded water, and arranged to dispose of human wastes. As archeologist Richard Schaedel observed, "Pre-Incaic planners provided green space, fresh air and a view."

Massive sun-dried brick and stone constructions made obvious the division of pre-Incaic societies into sharply differentiated social classes. Those wielding power exacted material rewards in the form of mansions, tribute, and personal service from the lower classes of differing ethnic backgrounds.

To hold their dominions together, Huari rulers had to develop a system of interregional communication. Earlier states such as Moche had already constructed roads and trails in their territories. Huari leaders expanded existing pathways and trade routes to encompass their main centers in a pan-Andean network of roads, trails, and bridges. By the same token, warfare had been a frequent activity in pre-Huari times, as numerous depictions of warriors, battles, trophy heads, and weapons demonstrate. The military capacity of regional states was well developed, and the Huari expansion implied that its leaders excelled in warfare and the diplomacy of conquest.

Why the Huari empire collapsed quickly and completely constitutes, therefore, a continuing mystery. Perhaps an inability to organize and communicate, perhaps a natural catastrophe such as a major earthquake or volcanic eruption played a role. The conquered states may have suddenly rebelled and destroyed the empire. Around A.D. 800, in any case, people abandoned Huari cities in favor of smaller towns and villages. With the disappearance of imperial authority, regional cultures thrived anew for the next 600 years. Many apparently represented the reemergence of old cultural traditions that had survived the tests of time and conquest.

Cities have long provided merely one solution to settlement problems in Peruvian environments. Indeed, a preference for living in small towns and scattered rural hamlets is very evident. Usually extensive hinterlands with dispersed populations surrounded towns that served as the economic, social, and probably political centers. In times of imperial political expansion, however, some towns became cities with a truly urban way of life, without direct rural ties, with extreme concentrations of wealth and of power, sharp social class divisions, and ethnic stratification, as well as increased specialization of labor.

The periods of imperial political unification led by relatively small kindreds never seriously altered the basic community structure of the Andean groups founded upon genetic kinship and control of croplands. Repeated conquests coupled with rapid population growth apparently swept away most of the tribal sociopolitical structure that once existed. Instead, posttribal ethnic groups persisted within the states, retaining their basic extended family or even sib social organizations, and exercising a modicum of control over their lands in one way or another. This essential unit of life, survival, and production became the enduring basis of pan-Andean culture. Territorially based kin groups functioned no matter what empires or nearby towns dominated the locale. The rural ethnic groups constituted the wellspring of Andean life because they were based on soundly tested adjustments to the land. How well these ethnic groups could be organized on a wider scale that bridged deserts, mountains, and valleys would become the test of state and empire.

The period of regional cultures led to a great florescence, especially on the north coast. Apparently descendants of the Moche people, the Chimú developed there the powerful Chimor kingdom. Its troops expanded its initial boundaries in the Moche and Chicama valleys beginning around A.D. 1370 to include within a century all the valleys between Supe and Tumbes and adjacent portions of the Andes. Extending for 1,000 kilometers north and south, Chimor was not as large and all-encompassing either in population or in territory as the Huari empire that preceded it long before as an imperial state. The Chimor conquest kingdom nonetheless developed a corps of highly skilled state administrators whom even the Incas were to find very useful.

Chimú artistry in precious metals reached such heights that the Incas moved the best of these smiths to their capital at Cuzco after the conquest of the area in A.D. 1477. Even after the Spanish conquest, the Chimú smiths could be identified in the Inca capital by their distinctive garments. The sybaritic Chimor upper class had so far departed from the peasant origins of its civilization as to have the skilled smiths fashion quantities of ceremonial items of silver-gold-platinum alloy, and other artisans utilized similarly rare materials.

The Chimú people inherited a long tradition of coastal culture first brought to flower by the Moche. They had usufruct of the extensive irrigation system and a full repertoire of technical skills and resources. The God-King of Chimor ruled a castelike society through an elite consisting of nobility, priesthood, and military sectors. These developed an ethnic cohesion that gives the region a distinctive subculture even today.

Several large cities grew in the irrigated valleys under Chimú rule. The principal one, and center of the kingdom, was Chan Chan, covering 20 square kilometers near Trujillo. From the time Europeans first saw it, they were both perplexed and amazed by its structure: towering 7½-meter-high walls surround nine enormous compounds. Many deliberately labyrinthine inner sections were bounded by lesser walls heavily decorated with intricate arabesques of mythical and representational character. Each compound was dedicated to a divine king. When a Chimor king took power, he built his own huge ceremonial section, filled it with the realm's valuables, and lived in it with his court and retinue. When the God-King died survivors entombed him, accompanied by numerous members of his female retinue who were sacrificed and interred with him, apparently to attend to his afterlife needs. Thereafter descendants, perhaps, maintained the great compound as a sacred monument, but the new king constructed his own compound.

Outside the luxurious royal compounds lived a densely settled population of some 25,000 or more persons, sheltered in simple sun-dried brick and bamboo huts. In many respects, these were not unlike today's squatter settlements that surround cities such as Lima. This Chan Chan population consisted of the skilled artisans, technicians, and cultivators upon whose industry the empire depended and whose obedience, loyalty, and reverence were fundamental for the success of the system. The produce of the fields watered by the great irrigation systems laid down almost 2,000 years earlier and developed through the centuries was lavished upon the elite and the divine rulers.

The remains of the empire indicate that Chimor mobilized a large army of commoners in pursuit of power and conquest. As in past epochs, ceramic remains portray battles and their effects: prisoners, victory, trophy heads, and disabled warriors. It is said of the Chimú that they were master organizers and efficient administrators whose success was clearly evident in the extent of their empire. By the time the Incas began their quest for territory and power, the Chimor kingdom was the largest state to oppose them.

On the eve of the Inca empire, each of its basic cultural and economic developments had been experimented with by the peoples of Peru. Abundant precedents existed for conquest states with complex internal socioeconomic and ethnic stratification in Tiahuanaco, Huari, Chimor, and perhaps even Chavín, although it is not likely that the Incas and their contemporaries had any but legendary information about the earliest states. Nevertheless, a cumulative learning process had occurred, and an evolution of social, economic, and political forms may be discerned.

An overriding fact of life in the Peruvian multiple environments is the need to have social and cultural forms that allow efficient and effective utilization of each of the many natural settings in Peru, with all their variations and peculiarities. Before any large-scale society could form, the ancient Peruvians had to bring the numerous microenvironments into sustained, regular use. The domestication of many plants and animals became the key to this achievement, because most of them were evolved as adaptations to a specific zone. The techniques for exploiting all available environmental niches were fully manifest before the rise of the Huari empire. Absolutely essential to sustaining large populations in the coastal valleys—and to a considerable extent to sustaining communities in the highlands also—were large-scale irrigation works, which eventually evolved as the principal method of environmental control. The canal systems built 3,000 years ago are, in many places, still used today. They formed the base for subsequent civilized life.

Prehistoric Peruvians perfected agricultural terracing along with irrigation on the coastal oases and in the highlands. In the coastal *lomas* belt, special terraces permitted plant cultivation at certain altitudes where the moisture from the fog provided sufficient water to sustain the plant life. The inspiration for this system was nature. Early inhabitants made very close observation of the water source of natural plant life on these ridges. Elsewhere, the ancient Peruvians built terraces to take advantage of arable land in even the smallest lots, and canal systems were so constructed as to avoid both undue loss of water and erosion. Use of steep hillsides, remote canyon corners, and places where special soil and altitude conditions prevailed demonstrates a sophisticated knowledge that resulted from centuries of accumulative experience.

Intensive cultivation and the proliferation of large settlements indicate that the pre-Incaic population reached a very substantial size, although it is difficult to estimate what its numbers may have been. Certainly elites mobilized sufficient masses of workers throughout the entire area to construct vast ceremonial and public structures, roads, terraces, and other common facilities. Food production and priestly quality standards for religious goods encouraged increasing occupational specialization among artisans. Horticultural efficiency allowed portions of the state populations to devote themselves to nonfood-producing pursuits. In Moche, Chimú, and some other states, the fabrication of ceramics and textiles reached true cottage-industry proportions. Artisans standardized styles: shops of belt-loom weavers followed a master pattern hung in the sight of all.

The repeated emergence of Andean-area conquest states indicates that some social need other than pure human perversity and ambition for power had to be met. That need very likely stemmed from the very density of Native American populations. As ancient Peruvians pressed increasingly against available natural resources, some larger political power had to resolve disputes over land tenure, water rights, poaching, intervillage relations, and all the other myriad frictions of day-to-day living in densely populated gardening areas.

On the other hand, the persistence of basic forms of kindreds for several millennia indicates an equal if not greater functional utility of extended family structure in the sociopolitical and natural environment of the area. In the highlands, at least, societies divided the village level communities into "upper" and "lower" moieties or halves. Chiefs commonly referred to as *curacas* or *mallku* led social units at each level of the hierarchy up to the kings. *Curaca*ships were hereditary, passing along the male line in some societies and along the female line in others, mostly on the north coast. Chiefs wielded both titular and real power, both spiritual and temporal.

The labor of vassals in the moiety to which each chief belonged supported these leaders. Commoners provided each *curaca* with servants. Local kin groups held often only usufruct rights to horticultural fields. They typically exploited their own and state fields for subsistence and state purposes in either collective fashion or by labor-exchange arrangements. Abundant food and *chicha* accompanied by drum and flute music turned many labor-exchange occasions into festive events.

Although one can now gain but little idea of the many cultures that once existed, it is clear that the stratified societies of both highlands and coast depended heavily upon the intensive labor of hundreds of thousands of peasant villagers. They were tied to the elite in each conquest state through endlessly elaborated kinship ties, ritual obligations, and reciprocal relationships, just as they have been right up to the present. They shared ancestors to be respected and worshiped, labor exchanges to be fulfilled, ceremonies of the horticultural cycle to conduct, and orders from the *curaca* to obey.

Chapter 2 • The Conquering Incas

The cultural evolution of the Peruvian peoples in the millennia preceding Inca dominion endowed the native Peruvians with a complex culture that would make the subsequent imperial state of the Incas far different from the Aztec analog in Mexico. The culture-building processes by which the ancient Peruvians gained sophisticated mastery of their environment produced a civilization that bore a totalitarian flower lasting but a moment. The Incas conquered other peoples, consolidated their domain, and were themselves suddenly subjugated within a single century.

The *Tawantinsuyu,* as the Incas called it, was truly one of the more remarkable conquest states in world history. In many ways it was analagous to those of the Greeks and Romans in their time and place. The Inca empire stemmed in concept and development largely from the work of one man, Pachacuti Inca Yupanqui, the ninth emperor of the Inca state and the first great conqueror his royal house produced. His hereditary line extended back to a legendary demigod named Manco Capac, who founded the lineage and regenerated human life by bringing about, according to Inca cosmology, a fifth world epoch.

The great conqueror Pachacuti seized power in a coup d'état. When in the face of an attack by the hostile Chanca nation, his father, the reigning Sapa Inca, fled Cuzco, Pachacuti led the army against the Chancas, defeated them, and thus gained control over a large segment of the south-central highlands. Incorporating the war-like Chancas as allies and subjects of the Inca state, Pachacuti then set the Incas upon their own plan of conquest. He was able to use the well-organized armies of the Chancas under the command of his own brother. That brother's successes led, however, to his own execution by Pachacuti, who feared loss of control or competition.

Prophetically, the early history of the Incas anticipated the many problems of succession that would plague the royal lineage as well as subsequent elites in Peru. Between Pachacuti Inca's time and the arrival of the Spaniards, there were apparently two orderly successions. In 1471 Pachacuti's mature, experienced son, Topa Inca, succeeded. In turn, his son Huayna Capac assumed the scarlet fringe of the Sapa Inca in 1493. The sudden death of the latter and his heir-apparent in 1524 led to a struggle for the position of Sapa Inca between the half brothers Huascar and Atahuallpa. While the latter won the civil war, the war divided the empire, leaving a servile Quechua peasantry in the countryside and rancorous ethnic enclaves of recently conquered states that still remembered their independent past. In such a condition the mighty empire was itself open to conquest.

The Incas did not achieve their successes by chance. Yet it would appear that their genius lay not in invention, but in organization and will. Not the least ingredient was the force of the leadership not only of the Sapa Inca himself, but also of his numerous subordinates such as the generals who commanded the armies and those who planned and supervised the affairs of the empire. The Incas were, indeed, the beneficiaries of their cultural precursors, whose knowledge they synthesized in forming an empire.

As a conquest state, the *Tawantinsuyu* required programs for managing conquered peoples, particularly those who remained rebellious and unreliable. Where such groups as the Cañaris, Huancas, and Chimú seemed likely to challenge Inca regional authority the Incas acted in accord with the situation. They slaughtered the Cañaris en masse and crushed their state. They infiltrated the Huancas and then sent colonies of reliable subjects to watch them closely. They dismantled the kingdom of Chimor. In conquering the Chimú people and thus the entire north coast area, the Incas not only faced them in battle, but also undermined the authority of the ruler by divisive diplomacy. The Incas then proceeded to carry off everything of value, including the technicians who had made the region famous for its technological achievements. These Chimú craftsmen were put to work in Cuzco and made to train Quechua-speakers in their crafts.

To establish effective control of all conquered groups, the Incas took the children of the ruling classes to Cuzco for training and indoctrination. In short, the Incas were coolly pragmatic, efficient, and totalitarian in their policies toward conquered nations. Their program of forced resettlement, for instance, well illustrates these qualities, even though it was one of the least drastic Inca policies.

In this important technique of conquest, the Incas transformed the ancient concept of ecological colonies, *mitimaes,* or *mitmaq,* which various Andean peoples had traditionally employed to produce crops in different environments outside their home territories, into permanently settled colonies established largely for political rather than economic or environmental reasons. The Incas decreed that certain villages of dependable subjects should go live elsewhere to break up a bloc of potentially restless new subjects such as the Huancas.

Loyal *mitimaes* kept their identity and distinctive dress—sometimes up to the present—and helped to spread the Quechua dialect originally spoken by the Incas and the neighboring groups in the Cuzco area. They contributed over time to the elimination of other languages once spoken from Quito to northern Argentina. Early historic chroniclers continued to report the existence of ethnically distinct populations within larger geographic units. Perhaps forty-four tribal or ethnopolitical groups can be identified in the highlands and another thirty-eight on the coastal oases. Much is known of some such as the Chimú, Chanca, Huanca, Lupaca, Huaylas, Chincha, and Colla, but little knowledge survives about most, including even the languages they once spoke.

The Inca forced-resettlement programs created for historians what came to be a major ethnohistorical paradox as Inca rulers strove to unify the *Tawantinsuyu* under a single political, social, and religious system with one official dialect. From its pre-Inca base of ethnic and cultural diversity then, the Inca empire attempted to move toward a restrictive area-wide standardization of politics, religion, customs, and language. Yet the forced-resettlement programs had the effect of creating a new kind of sociocultural diversity in local areas because both *mitimaes* and the original ethnic groups long preserved many of their differences in outlook, costume, and custom, if not language. Six principal historic Quechua dialects reflect, perhaps, the possibility of that language being imposed on speakers of other tongues.

Political unification, if not cultural, did take place quickly in *Tawantinsuyu*. In addition to those measures earlier mentioned, the Incas placed legions of peasants at the emperor's call, and they limited geographic mobility for commoners not on imperial business. The Inca professional army, headed by generals of noble birth, could draft able-bodied male commoners between the ages of twenty to fifty for service in military campaigns, a feature of Inca rule that continued for most of the empire's history. They maintained order by instilling fear and using force rather than by encouraging knowledgeable participation.

The Incas subdivided the *Tawantinsuyu* into large administrative and classificatory regions. The sudden growth of the empire created a situation that had no recent precedent, yet the problem of governing an extensive area proved to be critical. Pachacuti and his able son, Topa Inca, apparently first conceived the quarters of the empire as nearly equal in size. As the imperial territory grew, however, *Chinchaysuyu* and *Collasuyu* soon became vast. The provincial divisions of the quarters often corresponded to conquered ethnic states. Their distinctiveness was to some extent preserved, inasmuch as residents of the provinces and their towns wore special headdresses, ponchos, etc., so identifying them. Many still do.

The provincial capitals received the prefix title "great" (*Haton* or *Atun*) giving rise to names such as Haton Sora or Atun Huaylas, some of which carry down to the present. Existing Andean social structure split the provinces into "upper" and "lower" halves, although this varied according to population size. These moieties were, in turn, composed of basic *ayllu* units whose members were kinsmen who formed local communities. Everyone including the Sapa Inca himself belonged to an *ayllu*.

The royal Inca nobility, those related to the ruler, formed eleven *ayllus*. They enjoyed numerous privileges and constituted a distinct aristocracy. The Inca nobility's status and conditions diverged increasingly from the life-styles of the great mass of peasants as time passed. They clothed themselves in the finest vicuña and cotton cloth. They wore large, ornate plugs in their stretched ear lobes, a trait that led to their being referred to as the "big ears" by the rest. The Sapa Inca allowed the large majority of the nobles who were not his relatives to share to some degree in both the privileges and duties of royal *ayllus'* members. Although there was some mobility from one noble rank to another, a position once gained apparently became hereditary. Thus, as the rulers of conquered peoples were of necessity added to the ranks of the Inca nobility, the royal lines reached into every valley and village, in the tightly drawn yet "indirect" system of control. The regional nobility was, therefore, perpetuated and aggrandized vicariously through association with the Inca and through real power and material advantage over their subordinates. In exchange for their services, the provincial *curacas*, who managed units of 1,000 persons or more, occasionally received special grants from the Inca nobles or the ruler himself.

His subjects held the Sapa Inca in supreme awe. They could not confront him directly and were reported frequently to tremble in his presence. The elegant clothing he wore was discarded after one use and taboo for others to see or touch. Servants and noble retainers while singing hymns in his honor swept the path before his fifteen-carat golden litter. He was absolute ruler of the largest New World empire, indeed, one of the largest anywhere.

The Sapa Inca selected members of the nobility for higher administrative posts. The Incas broadly divided the population into a hierarchy of decimal units for tax and other state purposes. A chief at each level supervised those below him in pyramidal fashion, grouping subjects in units of 10,000, 5,000, 1,000, 500, 100, 50, and 10. Leaders usually inherited their position except at the lowest levels, but the units were easily classified and new ones added as the population grew. Extensive record-keeping helped maintain administrative controls. Imperial accountants utilized the celebrated knotted cord devices called *quipus,* the Andean version of complicated tallies. Moreover, Inca rulers periodically sent royal inspectors to review local and regional affairs.

Due to the sudden expansion of the domain, the Incas had to create a second rank of nobles to fill the great number of administrative posts created by conquest. The state bureaucracy certainly became vast as the Incas confirmed the continued authority of local rulers and made them lower nobility in *Tawantinsuyu.* Thus, at the height of the empire in 1520, there would have been on the order of 300,000 unit administrators under the Sapa Inca Huayna Capac. Yet this was only part of the governmental apparatus.

The heads of the four quarters, the *Capac Apu,* and the highest ranking chiefs of 10,000 persons made annual trips to Cuzco to deliver tax goods from their regions, report to the Sapa Inca, and give him gifts. Upon reporting, these men might be personally rewarded by the Sapa Inca with *yanas* or slaves, a concubine, or gifts of jewels. As well, the Sapa Inca might grant permission to affect customs and dress of higher rank such as the privilege of eating off golden or silver plates, wearing a particular fringed headdress, sitting on a thronelike stool, being carried in a litter, or carrying a parasol. On these occasions, the chiefs could visit their children whom the Incas held for training and as hostages at Cuzco—about 3,000 of them, or roughly one from each major *curaca.* Obedience and faithful performance of chiefly duties were, therefore, hardly surprising.

Several other social categories enjoyed special privileges associated with highly specialized functions of the state and the royal lineages.

Like nobles, such persons did not pay taxes in the way commoners did. Artisans, craftsmen, engineers, record keepers (*quipu-camayoc*), military officers, smiths, bridge builders, and the like formed specialized classes. Members of the nobility filled the most important of these positions, while a class known as *yanas* or *yanaconas* performed the more routine or specialized tasks. *Yanas* were usually bound to perpetual service in their occupation, and it seems that some people inherited such a classification. The Incas filled the ranks of the *yanas* from the populations of conquered tribes and states, individuals such as Chimú technicians being packed off to Cuzco if their qualifications were in special demand. Although these people often possessed skills of great importance that seemingly must have conferred high status upon them, it has been asserted by some that they constituted a kind of slave class. The position of Chimú smiths, for example, was perhaps analogous to that of literate Greeks in ancient Rome.

The Inca state religion defined the Sapa Inca as a descendant of the Sun. Logically, therefore, the chief tax-exempt group consisted of the priests and their numerous assistants, who presided over a complex religious organization with a ceremonial calendar full of activity. In Inca theology the "sky gods," which in order of rank were the Sun, Thunder, Moon, and Stars, served the creator-god *Viracocha*. Believers thought other supernatural powers resided in special objects and places collectively referred to as *huacas*. This term now refers particularly to the numerous ancient temple mounds that dot the Andean landscape. Hundreds of shrines of varying importance, ranging from the *huacas* in each *ayllu* to the Sun Temples found in provincial capitals and the principal one in Cuzco, formed a hierarchy reflecting the administrative structure.

The Sapa Inca himself participated in the most important ritual events in Cuzco. Priests at the main shrines were also likely to be noblemen with the social rank of priests declining from the Inca city to the peasant village level, where the caretakers of the *huacas* might be old men capable of nothing else.

Inca priests acted as confessors, diviners, and oracles and were frequently consulted by devotees who then closely observed their advice.

People depended on omens and divination to determine specific courses of action and deemed sacrifices essential to propitiating the natural forces. Inca religion most commonly offered guinea pigs and llamas for sacrifice, but human children and even adults were also sacrificed on occasion. "Chosen women" selected from all over the empire on the basis of their physical perfection and intelligence when examined as children attended and served the priests of the state religion. The royal officials sent those selected to special schools for training in the many tasks of maintaining the state religion: as ceremonial assistants, teachers, cooks, weavers, and so on. The Sapa Inca took some of them as concubines and gave others to nobles as rewards for services rendered the state. A woman of high noble birth, much like a Mother Superior in a Roman Catholic religious order, presided over others reportedly bound to eternal chastity in service of the gods.

The priests placed constant ritual demands upon the common people. The Andean calendar was studded with ceremonial observances that reflected the horticultural basis of life. Several days of feasting and dancing observed the June and December solstices. The state church regularly celebrated fertility ceremonies for animals such as the llama and the guinea pig. The annual round of religious and public events in which most people participated to some degree included new moon and harvest festivals for different crops, planting and spring festivals, rites to control the weather and sickness, and celebrations of the rites of passage of adolescents.

The heavy-handed government and general lack of freedom of choice that prevailed may have made essential the psychological release provided by ceremonies and festivals. Yet Inca ceremonial activities also had the effect of socializing and training the populace in the beliefs, values, and responsibilities the elite demanded. The constant round of ritual needs and requisites provided rationales for much of the work undertaken and set a series of recurrent goals to be met in one's daily activities.

This is not to say that people did not enjoy themselves or that all life was grim or mechanistic. The religious festival calendar offered many opportunities for drama, pageantry, and music. Musicians played compositions in a pentatonic scale on dozens of kinds of pan-pipes and flutes, accompanied by drums and rattles. In Inca times, as in many places now, work in the fields or on communal projects was accompanied by music and dancing. Indeed, martial songs and chants urged on the Inca armies. Andean pre-Columbian music survives today in modified form as popular "country" music. The ample ceremonial calendar also testifies to the high level of productivity that prevailed in the Inca state. Production permitted a lavish expenditure of time, work, and resources on festivals.

Beneath all these ruling social strata lived the great mass of people, most of whom could be classified as peasants. Living in their *ayllus* throughout the vast imperial territory, they formed its most essential ingredient as food producers, army conscripts, laborers for all public works and seemingly limitless human resource pools, from which special classes of persons could be selected for particular needs. They paid food, goods, and services to the empire, which lacked money. Each *ayllu* had to attend the fields dedicated to supporting the Inca, the nobility, and the officials of the state religion, in addition to cultivating its own subsistence fields. One obtains an excellent sense of the agrarian foundations of the Inca empire from the following account by one of the best Spanish chroniclers of Peruvian Indian life, Father Bernabé Cobo:

> "In the lands assigned to Religion and to the Crown, the Inca kept overseers and administrators who took great care in supervising their cultivation, harvesting the products and putting them in storehouses. The labor of sowing and cultivating these lands and harvesting their products formed a large part of the tribute which the taxpayer paid to the king . . . The people assembled to cultivate them in the following way. If the Inca himself . . . or some other high official happened to be present he started the work with a golden *taclla* (spade) . . . and following his example, all . . . did the same. However the Inca soon stopped working, and after him the other officials and nobles stopped also and sat down with the king to their banquets and festivals which were especially notable on such days.
>
> "The common people remained at work . . . each man put into his section his children and wives and all the people of his house to

help him. In this way, the man who had the most workers finished his *suyu* first, and he was considered a rich man; the poor man was he who had no one to help him in his work and had to work that much longer. . . ."

Thus social and political rank, and wealth were explicitly demonstrated in ceremonial fashion. The land commoners cultivated for themselves was divided, like the rest, into basic units that the *curacas* annually assigned to each family according to its needs.

The foodstuffs peasants harvested from royal fields, along with woven goods made from the wool-clip of royal flocks, passed to official control. Bureaucrats stored these commodities in ubiquitous government warehouses that are today readily seen in many places. Such stores supported all state-sponsored activity: the army, construction crews, priesthood, the royal house and nobles, *yanas,* and others performing state service. Royal stores could also be used in case of local emergencies for any of the commoners and officials sometimes distributed surpluses to needy areas. Great llama and alpaca flocks were managed in the same manner in the high plateau regions, particularly from Cuzco south.

In the absence of money, the other obligation levied on the commoners was service in the *mita* or labor pool. All taxpayers had to work a prescribed number of days annually to run the households of local leaders. Each taxpayer could be called up by his *curaca* to work on imperial or local projects at any convenient time, through a draft of men between twenty to fifty years old. In this manner, courvée labor built and maintained irrigation canals, roads, and bridges; exploited mines; provided messengers and servants; carried burdens through each district; constructed temples and other public buildings; and made specialized regional products for noble and ceremonial use. Inca exactions kept people busy and fixed their residence in very sedentary horticultural or pastoral settlements. Peasants might travel only with their *curaca*'s permission.

The government reached down into the villages to manage daily life in other affairs, too. The *curaca* performed marriage ceremonies, for example, in an annual public gathering when he supervised the pairing of young people. Preceremonial steps toward marriage permitted young men and women to test one another and allowed some parental influence on choices.

Life in the *Tawantinsuyu* was marked by features whoşe effect on the populace was similar to that brought about by conditions in Europe. Elite power largely fixed the place of commoners in society, although certain luck could alter one's status. Commoners discharged an endless round of obligations to the state, tilled the fields of the nobility, Inca, and state church, and provided all manner of services to the lords before whom they had to show respect, awe, and humility.

The net result of such institutions, encompassing the daily activities of all commoners, was not only to keep them under the tightest possible control and well occupied with activities sustaining the state, but also to bind them into compactly organized local units with clear identities, leaders, and land, distinctive dress, social, and religious lives. This pattern organizationally related them to, yet isolated them from, the Inca's subjects elsewhere.

The societies of different valleys, towns, and *ayllus* tended to be endogamous insofar as commoners were concerned. The nobles took wives and concubines from wherever they wished or the state dictated, although even they traveled from province to province only on orders.

At its greatest size, the *Tawantinsuyu* covered an area of 984,200 square kilometers, twice the size of Spain or equal in area to Spain and Italy together. Its perimeter stretched from what is now the Ecuador-Colombia border to the Bio-Bio River in central Chile, including all highland Bolivia and northwestern Argentina. *Tawantinsuyu*'s maximum extension came during the region of Huayna Capac, who ruled for almost thirty years. That this vast area over 4,000 kilometers long could have been held together in a single system without any means of communication except runners was truly a feat equaled by few other empires in world history. One may surmise that the totalitarian character of the Inca conquest state was a major factor in both its subjugation and governing.

Essential to such an empire of conquered peoples was swift communication. The Incas accelerated movement of runners and troops by constructing smooth-surfaced roads through the Andes. Anyone who knows the nature of Andean terrain and contemporary problems in transportation can only regard the great road-building achievements of the Incas and their predecessors as truly outstanding. A network of graded, often stone-paved and walled roadways ran to all important places from Cuzco, and connected intermediate points, for an estimated 15,195 kilometers. Hundreds of bridges spanned rivers and chasms. The most interesting of these crossed the Apurimac River in the southern highlands with a 60-meter span. Maintained until the end of the nineteenth century, it became known in literature as Thornton Wilder's *Bridge of San Luis Rey*. The chronicler Estete, who accompanied Hernando Pizarro to Pachacamác, described other bridges such as one crossing the Santa River at Huallanca, Ancash. This bridge consisted of two suspension spans hung side by side, one for nobles and one for commoners who paid in kind to cross it. Pizarro and his men used the span for nobles, and "their horses passed without difficulty." The people of Huaylas District continued to maintain the Huallanca bridge until 1919, when the central government finally erected a steel span at the site. This pattern of dutiful fulfillment of community obligations set long in the past, including the use of ancient building materials and techniques, continued and still continues in many places. The Andean terrain requires now, as it did in Inca times, that constant repairs be made on roads by village work gangs, so this continues to be a major community occupation.

The Inca system, so much indebted to ancient Andean experience but also a product of authoritarianism, showed signs of evolving toward a new social system. The *yanas*, for example, were increasing greatly in numbers and, assigned as they were to serve nobles, epitomized the sharp class or even caste differences. The nobles and state functionaries consumed the economic and social surplus, living in luxury—a fact that drew chronicler comments and conqueror emulation. The commoners who constituted over 90 percent of the population lived a spartan life of hard work. True, this vast peasantry was cared for in its basic needs. The *curacas* saw to that by distributing land use-rights even in the *ayllus*, granting favors to those who worked well, and, in general, handling other affairs firmly. The harsh if provident Inca nobles nonetheless won little political loyalty from the ethnic peasants. Defense of the *Tawantinsuyu* against domestic insurrection and enemies on its borders fell increasingly upon an imperial standing army.

Clarity of administrative obligation and loyalty were essential to such an empire of conquered peoples sustaining an increasingly distinct nobility. Yet Huayna Capac sowed seeds of confusion when he developed a northern administrative center at Quito (Ecuador). In his later years Huayna Capac preferred life there to living in Cuzco, as legend has it because Quito was the home of his favorite wife. Jealousy and competition developed between the nobility of these two distant places. Then a War of Succession rent the *Tawantinsuyu*, weakening from within the empire that faced no really threatening Andean enemies. As he won that eight-year struggle, Atahuallpa could not suspect that beyond the seas lay other empires populated by zealous men impelled by a limitless desire for wealth defined as silver and gold and for power over other men.

Chapter 3 • Peruvian "Conquest Culture," 1532-1572

Santiago! The Spanish war cry echoed off the walls of the royal buildings around the square of the Inca city of Cajamarca on the evening of November 16, 1532. In less than two bloody hours, Francisco Pizarro and 167 companions seized effective control of the *Tawantinsuyu,* slaughtering several thousand Inca nobles and troops, with cannon and war horse, sword, and lance. The Spaniards captured Atahuallpa, the son of Huayna Capac who had just won the War of Inca Succession. Astonishingly, within a few years after Cajamarca, an amazingly small number of Spaniards replaced the *Tawantinsuyu* with colonial political, social, and economic institutions that would endure essentially unchanged for centuries.

The very rapidity with which Spaniards successfully imposed a "conquest culture" on the *Tawantinsuyu* highlights how alike in some respects Spanish colonial and Inca colonial cultures were in 1532. The easy substitution of a Spanish elite for a Native American elite meant that the Spaniards had themselves developed a "conquest culture" well adapted to the task of ruling by seizing power from a wealthy, auto-

cratic Native American imperial lineage dominating masses of peasant horticulturists. Pizarro's conquest of the Inca empire benefited not
only from the forty-year experience Spaniards had in subjugating other
New World states, but also from the evolution during the long Spanish reconquest of the Iberian Peninsula from the Moors of a distinctive
"conquest society" within Spain.

By the fifteenth century, Spanish Christians had come to regard
themselves as a "chosen people" engaged in a religious crusade in the
Mediterranean basin. This fanatic psychology led to the expulsion
from the Iberian Peninsula of Moors who would not accept baptism as
Christians. In the critical year 1492, moreover, the Spaniards also expelled from their homeland its large Jewish population. Spaniards
naturally transferred to their new American conquests many of the
Peninsular institutions and customs that had developed during their
earlier religious crusades at home.

Basic differences between the Peninsular reconquest and the subjugation of Native American peoples quickly forced Spain to modify
Peninsular conquest culture in the New World. New conditions that
demanded institutional changes included the sheer population size of
Native American states and the geographic distance of the New World
from Spain. By the time Pizarro's men set foot on Peruvian soil, Spaniards had already carried out many innovations in their overseas institutions in the course of conquering the Caribbean islands, Mexico,
and the Isthmus of Panamá.

The moment Spanish conquerors decided to rule and exploit the
native populations in the Caribbean, they realized that Peninsular conquest culture could not totally cope with the conditions of New
World dominion. Not only did the native peoples of the Americas
greatly outnumber the population of Spain, but the New World also
bulked vastly larger. Thus the new colonial enterprise demanded that
the Spaniards live among Native Americans to maintain Spanish
sovereignty and to rule the teeming population through a new "conquest culture." This followed Iberian models closely, however, so no
historian should seek to defend the thesis that the Indian frontier in Hispanic America generated a more democratic society than

the homeland on the Peninsula, as has been asserted with regard to North America.

The distant overseas location of the New World demanded further Spanish cultural change. Spain was not a great maritime power in 1492. That technological deficiency forced the Spaniards to compensate in terms of institutional flexibility in the Indies. The Spaniards improved Peninsular colonial institutions to create a class of social, economic, and political mechanisms with no precise equivalents in Iberia.

In addition, by the time Francisco Pizarro led his private army into the *Tawantinsuyu,* the biological Columbian exchange between the Old and New Worlds was already well advanced, to the advantage of the Old World. The great smallpox pandemic that reached Mexico in 1519 decimated the population of *Tawantinsuyu* in 1524. It probably more than halved the peak imperial population and left in its wake an Inca War of Succession that opened an easy path to the Spanish conquerors. It also set in motion a crippling depopulation trend among Andean region Indians that would endure, apparently, for two-and-a-half centuries.

Because of the relationship between disease mortality and the absolute number of persons in a given population susceptible to infectious epidemics, the first introduction of each Old World disease—smallpox, measles, whooping cough, bubonic plague, typhoid, influenza, malaria, and yellow fever—tended to exact its largest human toll. Consequently the loss in absolute numbers evidently was greatest during early colonial times. The imperial Inca population that had been pressing hard against natural resources ranged perhaps around 32,000,000 persons about 1520. It dropped to less than 16,000,000 after 1524, and continued to decline with succeeding disease introductions to probably 5,000,000 individuals by 1548.

Thus, when after several years of exploring and probing the Pacific coast of South America, Francisco Pizarro landed in the *Tawantinsuyu* near Tumbes early in 1532, several key factors had already combined to allow Pizarro and his Spanish coconquerors to seize Inca power rapidly. One key to the situation was the horrible death of the Sapa Inca

Huayna Capac during the smallpox plague of 1524, at the apogee of his military and civil power. His crown prince died in the same epidemic, leaving the empire not only demoralized but disoriented as well. Atahuallpa, offspring of Huayna Capac and a Quito wife, fought Huascar, son of Huayna Capac and a Cuzco wife, for the emperor's scarlet fringe. Their contest so splintered authority that Pizarro never faced more than a fraction of the prepandemic might of the *Tawantinsuyu*. The Inca army never unified to engage the Spaniards and large field forces remained uncommitted to imperial defense.

In contrast, the motley force of conquerors assembled in Spain and Panamá by Francisco Pizarro and Diego de Almagro evinced total commitment to its purpose. Members of the expedition represented a cross-section of Spanish overseas conquest society, acting with decision under the stern hand of Pizarro. Of the 168 conquerors present at Cajamarca, 21 percent came from Extremadura, 20 percent from Andalucia, and 19 percent from Old and New Castille. Most had emigrated, in other words, from poverty-stricken Peninsular provinces. The largest single contingent, some 8 percent, came from Pizarro's home town, the city of Trujillo, and reflected the prevailing preference for one's genetic kinsmen and coresidents. A quarter of the men at Cajamarca claimed noble blood, and as many as 30 percent may have been literate, so they were not representative of the Peninsular population. Some 3 percent, including the expedition's chaplain, Valverde, may have been recent Jewish converts to Christianity. The members of the expedition included 7 percent former white-collar workers, 8 percent merchants, and 13 percent artisans, demonstrating how gold-fever cut across social status groups.

Significantly, Francisco Pizarro also obtained royal permission, three years before he undertook Peru's official conquest, to add fifty Negro slaves to his 1529 expedition. Evidently he was well aware of the attrition in Native Americans already well underway. Consequently, a Black man became the first "Spaniard" ashore at Tumbes when Pizarro landed his force on the soil of the *Tawantinsuyu*.

The invaders from the Old World appeared strange and exotic to the natives of the *Tawantinsuyu*, lending them a certain psychological advantage. The Spaniards also enjoyed a tremendous technological superiority over Native American armament which greatly added to their psychological advantage, with particular effect in face-to-face combat. When the two forces met at Cajamarca, 37 percent of the Spaniards were mounted on imposing war horses hung with noise-makers and armor.

The Spaniards could bring to bear nonhuman energy on a scale that no Indian could possibly match. At Cajamarca they possessed, in addition to war horses, the further advantage of firearms, including cannon. Thus, the disparity in numbers between the conquerors and their Inca opponents was not nearly as large as it seemed.

Even when the Indians overcame their fear of horses and guns, the Spaniards still held a distinct edge in hand-to-hand combat. They wielded very high-quality steel swords—often the justly famous Toledo blades. Inca clubs, maces, or halberds simply could not match the steel sword or saber. Native American projectiles, whether arrows or spears or sling-thrown stones, could not penetrate metal or mail, so armored Spaniards ran little risk in battle.

The psychology of the Inca approach to the unparalleled circumstance of invasion by bearded men with skins both lighter and darker than any Incas had ever seen played another key role in this conquest, as it had in the earlier Aztec reception of Spaniards. The Inca rulers traced their ancestry to a deified predecessor who was reputedly also bearded and light-skinned. The Inca elite's image of its own ancestry clearly influenced Atahuallpa at first in dealing with the strange new beings. Nevertheless, one surely cannot conceive of the contender Atahuallpa ordering his litter-bearers to carry him right up to Pizarro and his men in the provincial city of Cajamarca had he not thoroughly expected to receive obedience and respect as heir and member of the sacred royal lineage. Atahuallpa regarded the Spaniards as either supernatural, or at least honorable and honest men.

In fact, Pizarro and his Spaniards were only too mortal. Greedy for riches such as the precious metal litter that bore the Quitan contender for the imperial throne, they also felt contempt for any non-Christian, regardless of exalted rank. Thus the psychological orientation of the

Spaniards and the Inca leadership upon initial contact helped to set the stage for the decisive hours in the later afternoon of November 16, 1532. The Spaniards immediately seized the initiative. From that moment on they never looked back, as Pizarro and his followers went about substituting themselves for the Inca ruling nobility.

The hostage Atahuallpa perceived by the end of 1532 how greedy the Spaniards at Cajamarca were for silver and gold. He sagaciously attempted to buy his freedom with royal treasure, but failed to discern the duplicity of the Spaniards. Atahuallpa lacked, after all, any previous experience with Europeans to serve him in his hour of need. The quantity of precious metal collected for Atahuallpa's ransom staggered the 168 Spaniards at Cajamarca. Gold alone filled a room 22 feet long by 18 feet wide to a height of 9 feet. Silver filled a smaller room twice. When they melted most of the artistic creations, the Spaniards divided up 13,420 pounds of 22½-carat gold and 26,000 pounds of silver. This treasure bulked three times greater than Cortez's spectacular garnerings from the Aztec capital in 1521. At fluctuating current prices for precious metal bullion, the Cajamarca ransom was worth on the order of $30-50 million in gold and $1.5-2 million in silver. The present value of the unmelted artistic works is incalculable.

To the Cajamarca ransom, the now enlarged conquistador task force soon added an even greater treasure looted from the public buildings of the Inca capital of Cuzco, further supplemented with precious metals from administrative cities throughout the *Tawantinsuyu*. In mid-1533 Pizarro allowed twenty men to hurry home to the Peninsula with their sudden riches. Some conducted royal bullion to the Spanish court. Others acted as Pizarro family stewards. All recruited reinforcements by stirring Peninsular gold-fever.

While gold was a prime motivation in bringing people to Peru, the key to Spanish colonial rule in the Andean region lay in rapid substitution of Spaniards for members of the Inca royal *ayllus*. This process met with astonishingly little resistance. A nearly total transfer of power occurred between a few hundred men within less than half a decade.

The Inca nobility of the eleven royal *ayllus* that exercised absolute power over the teeming imperial populace appears to have numbered no more than about 500 individuals at the time of the conquest, although it could well have been more numerous prior to the devastating smallpox pandemic. The great mass of Indian peasants who could have acted as a major force were not motivated to defend in battle the interests of the numerically small group of Inca overlords.

When Manco Inca, the leader of the Neo-Inca state, besieged Cuzco and the Rímac Valley in 1536, a few hundred Spaniards and Indian allies were able to defend themselves successfully. By that time, the Neo-Inca forces even used horses, captured Spanish swords, and hardened, copper-tipped lances. The crucial difference appears to have been that the Indian masses took little part in the struggle. Commoners served either Spaniards or noble Incas as personal servants, burden-bearers, grooms, and so on, but a very small elite group apparently did the decisive fighting. This parallel between the overseas Spanish conquest state and the Inca conquest state tremendously facilitated transition of sovereignty from one small elite to the other.

Peninsular culture provided ready models for many aspects of New World conquest culture, but Spain created many new, purely colonial institutions to deal with the Indians. Queen Isabella signed in 1503 a decree authorizing New World colonial authorities to grant not lands, but a royal trust termed *encomienda* to successful explorers and military leaders. The sovereign piously charged the trust holder or *encomendero,* with converting his heathen Indian charges to Christianity. Isabella's precedent would haunt occupants of the Spanish throne during most of the colonial era, but it constituted a fundamental component of Spanish New World conquest culture. Conditioned by Peninsular experience, Spaniards in the New World constantly sought to convert *encomienda* grants of power over Native American populations into title to the lands these people occupied. Officially, however, an *encomendero* had only the power and duty to exact tribute for the crown and personal service from Native Americans while carrying out the duty to Christianize them. He was not given the land on which his grant of Indians lived.

The *encomienda* had been authorized for nearly thirty years when

Pizarro began his conquest of the Incas. He was thoroughly familiar with the conquest institution as it had already fully developed in Mexico, Panamá, and the Caribbean. Consequently, licensed by the crown to conquer and govern Peru and appointed its governor, Pizarro granted Indians to some of his mercenaries.

As Governor, Pizarro began to reorganize Inca territory by founding special Spanish municipalities, sometimes in existing Native American settlements, sometimes not. Spaniards who settled in such municipalities became citizens thereof charged with their governance. Pizarro legally established the first colonial municipal government at Piura in 1532 even before going to Cajamarca. He placed forty settlers in charge of the Peruvians inhabiting the Chira Valley where aboriginal Piura was located. The forty citizens of Piura became Peru's original *encomenderos.* The ease with which Piura peasants transferred their allegiance from Inca rulers to Spanish *encomenderos* would indicate that the Inca power elite had generated no strong loyalties in the old Chimú kingdom cultural area. It also portended what would happen in many other ethnic enclaves in the *Tawantinsuyu.*

After spending some eight months at Cajamarca, Pizarro marched south to Cuzco. He paused en route to leave a garrison of half a hundred men at Jauja, capital of his Chanca allies. Formally converting Cuzco into a Spanish city, Pizarro also granted nearly 100 *encomiendas* to his principal followers, who became its founding citizens. He also awarded grants of Indians to the new citizens of the Jauja municipality, but they would soon migrate to the Rímac Valley near the Pacific coast. In this fashion, the basic pattern of colonial land tenure was set by the time Pizarro finished his *encomienda* distributions.

How that happened may be seen in a list of what one of the *encomiendas* that Pizarro assigned to himself later paid his Mestizo daughter each trimester: 300 pairs of rope-sole and 100 pairs of another type sandal, 60 halters, bridles, cinches, and hobbles; 20 lariats, cargo packs, and large *Agave* fiber sacks; 6 *Agave* fiber horse blankets; 25 woolen dresses; 15 skirts, shawls, blouses; 2 woolen cushions, 1 woolen mattress, and 10 dresses made from finely spun wool. These utilitarian items were produced in two *obrajes:* colonial factories where

Indians wove standardized products for tribute on Spanish upright looms.

From their "trust" populations, the *encomenderos* soon exacted, extralegally but effectively, household supplies as well as personal service. Spanish *encomenderos* also demanded that their tributaries shift their tribute or "gifts" increasingly from purely Native American products to Old World commodities. Indian peasants perforce learned to cultivate Old World plants, although they proved to be slower to incorporate them into their own diets than to grow them for tribute. *Encomenderos* required their tributaries to grow chickens and render tribute or make propitiary "gifts" of fowl and eggs, as well as grains. Thus they established a pattern of Indian production of animal protein with virtually no consumption thereof. Peruvian peasants learned to herd the rapidly increasing cattle, goat, European swine, and sheep herds without slaughtering animals for their own consumption, save with permission of the local *encomendero* agent—a Spanish employee or Indian *cacique*—for special festive occasions. So a pattern of peasants seeking favor and placating powerful overlords with "gifts" of hens and eggs emerged early and still endures today.

While Spanish *encomenderos* lived on rural production, they resided in towns. A Spanish municipality consisted of much more than an urban settlement. It formed the original basic administrative jurisdiction of Spanish colonialism in Peru. The urban settlement became the capital of the municipal territory. As one condition of their grants, the *encomenderos* dwelt in this municipal capital. Their households very soon included their Spanish wives plus Indian concubines, Negro slaves and Indian servants, Spanish relatives, supporters, and hangers-on. Another condition required the *encomendero* to remain active in the colonial militia, ready to arm himself and mount his ever-ready war horse when called to the flag. *Encomenderos* acted as the government of city and hinterland. Notaries and lesser bureaucrats helped them to keep records in proper Spanish language and form. Spanish legalism did not decrease overseas on the Indian frontier; if anything, it increased.

Municipal authority extended far out into a rural territory that reached as far as the border of the next municipality. Thus the social and political functions of the Spanish municipality tended to merge in many ways not seen in more modern governance. The power of the municipal authorities, originally citizen—*encomenderos* forming the colonial elite, extended throughout the territorial jurisdiction, making them socially supreme.

Spanish *encomenderos* spread around the former Inca empire to live in roughly two dozen headquarters cities. Their reorganization of Incaic administrative space was greatest in shifting power to coastal settlements because they preferred them over highland centers favored by prior Inca nobles. The Spaniards soon abandoned Incaic Huánuco, for example, to construct their own colonial administrative city, renamed León de Huánuco, at a lower altitude.

New settlements such as the new Huánuco followed a standard city plan specified in royal decrees, in contrast to either Native American or Peninsular settlements. Inca Pachacuti had deliberately constructed Cuzco as a commodious imperial capital, and by the time of Spanish conquest it already centered upon an open square, which the Spaniards readily adapted to their colonial city specifications. With numbers of skilled builders available from the dense Indian population of the Cuzco Valley, the eighty original Spanish citizens easily converted Inca temples to Christian churches. They similarly converted Inca palaces into colonial government buildings or personal mansions. Inasmuch as the Incas had laid Cuzco out with splendid streets to facilitate ceremonies, the colonial laborers readily straightened thoroughfares around fairly square blocks so that Cuzco soon conformed to the prescribed colonial city plan. Still, it retained a distinctive Incan style because colonial builders typically utilized Incaic foundations and masonry, which remain today.

Nevertheless, Francisco Pizarro fundamentally reoriented Inca society and polity away from the Andean heartland toward the Iberian Peninsula when he established his second Peruvian capital at Lima. The first site chosen for the capital had been Jauja, located due east of Lima in the highlands. Pizarro was forced to reconsider this choice when his erstwhile partner in conquest, Diego de Almagro, founded

Quito and later Trujillo. Almagro's acts were theoretically intended to counteract the intrusion of the Guatemalan Governor, Pedro de Alvarado, in late 1534. The arrival of the rival colonial governor, wealthy from his share of Aztec spoils but eager for more, forced Pizarro to seek a capital near the sea for political and strategic reasons. Alvarado's approach by sea demonstrated that Pizarro would have to retain close ties and the legal backing of the Spanish crown if he were to uphold his supremacy in wealthy Peru. That required overseas communications via the Panamanian Isthmus.

Thus Pizarro founded Lima, City of the Three Kings, on January 6, 1535, in the lower Rímac Valley near Pachacamác which had been so important in preconquest Peru. Because of political pressures, he acted hastily in terms of his still-limited knowledge of *Tawantinsuyu*'s geography. His relocation of the capital at Lima, only 12 kilometers from the aboriginal fishing town of Callao on the Pacific coast, placed Peru squarely in the European colonial pattern. Lima faced the sea with its back to the Andes and the Inca capital of Cuzco. This act marked a conceptual reorganization of space and power that was new in the Andean experience.

From the moment of its founding, Lima assumed institutional primacy among Peru's municipalities, although it lagged for a while in population. Pizarro endowed it, following crown policy, with municipal land, settled literate citizens with secondary school educations there, began erecting buildings designed for the capital of the realm, and assigned lots for *encomendero* mansions. Because Pizarro's forces included Italians, Greeks, Africans, and a potpourri of bureaucrats and adventurers, Lima started as a multiethnic, cosmopolitan settlement. Indeed, prostitutes plied their trade in Lima no later than 1537, antedating by a decade the first religious order for women established there.

Lima also became the clearing-house for exporting the riches of Peru to Spain, an event that had more significance than was immediately apparent. When the Incas conquered the north coastal Chimú kingdom, they shipped vast quantities of Chimú treasure to Cuzco. As the Incas had seized Chimú accumulated capital, so the Spaniards, in their turn, seized Inca accumulated capital, but a vital difference between Inca and Spanish seizures of assets from conquered populations lay in pre-Columbian circulation of treasure within the area and post-Columbian export from the area. From the moment Pizarro authorized the first veterans of Cajamarca to return to Spain, the colonial pattern of exportation was established. With the establishment of Lima and the expansion of the prehistoric facilities of the Callao fishermen, the pre-Columbian highland cities decayed. In focusing upon the vice-regal city of Lima and the unquenchable desires of Spain, colonialism insured that all Peru would become progressively more beggarly, even while perched upon its literal as well as figurative throne of gold.

Significantly, Peru's first vehicular road connected Lima to its port of Callao in the 1540s. The use of carriages remained, however, extremely limited because horses could not haul them over the elaborate Inca roads designed for pedestrians, to whom slopes did not matter.

Encomendero households quickly replicated the major patterns of Peninsular Christian family life, significantly varied by concubinage with Indian women and actual harem-keeping by a few *encomenderos*. Strongly imbued with Iberian values concerning the fundamental importance of family and lineage, *encomenderos* struggled to pass their power and privilege on to their heirs. Less than 10 percent of the Peruvian *encomenderos* remained unmarried by the time colonial institutions solidified around 1570. Following Spanish Christian models in form, many *encomendero* households formed cradles for the creation of the new Mestizo race generated during the Columbian exchange.

Within each municipal capital, great *encomendero* families set the social pace and style for the whole society, just as had the noble Inca families they replaced. Spanish *encomenderos* made Spanish women heads of their official households for the most part, but retained their Indian mistresses. Conquest society thus began with the distinction between the "official" wife with ecclesiastical and legal sanction, and the often equally stable union with the mistress in the "little house" or "down the street" that survives to the present time. As "official" female household heads, however, Spanish wives of *encomenderos* could and did enforce their standards of cultural behavior in many spheres of life.

Few Spanish wives ventured to the old Inca capital or other highland settlements. Many powerful Spaniards married Inca noblewomen of the royal *ayllus*, thus assisting the development of Quechua-Spanish bilingualism and setting a language pattern for the highland dominant group that still endures. The Spaniards in the Andes acquired a subtle dimension of power by becoming bilingual themselves while keeping the Spanish language mostly secret from Native Americans.

The process of Inca linguistic unification remained far from complete at the time of the Spanish conquest. The Spaniards continued to spread Quechua, however, by using it as the language of rural commerce, religious proselytism, and provincial administration. The only other language to survive spoken by substantial numbers of people was Aymara, used by the peoples of the *Collasuyu* in the Titicaca lake basin and their scattered *mitmaq*.

Spaniards organized a conquest society more complex than either its Peninsular or Incaic antecedents. Because the Spaniards remained culturally Iberian, they tried to adhere to the quite meticulous distinctions between social ranks observed in Spain. Yet relative social placement on the Peninsula underwent striking alterations during the formative colonial period in Peru.

Francisco Pizarro, for example, quickly legitimized his Mestizo children by Inez Huaylas Yupanqui, a daughter of Huayna Capac. His legitimate half-brother Hernando married Inez's and Francisco's Mestizo daughter Francisca in 1552. Their offspring passed into later generations the title of Marquis de la Conquista, which the grateful Emperor Charles V had granted to Francisco. In other words, Hernando's marriage to his Mestizo niece consolidated the Pizarro family fortune and lineage. Hernando erected the largest mansion on the square of the Spanish city of Trujillo and emblazoned it with sculptures of enchained Incas and busts of Francisco, Inez, Francisca, and himself. Other Spanish or Spanish-Mestizo families that remained in Peru purchased noble titles, building up a considerable colonial nobility.

The destinies of the other men of Cajamarca ran the full gamut of success and failure. Francisco Pizarro was assassinated in 1541 by the Almagro faction among the conquerors. Open civil war among the Spaniards wracked the colony until 1548 when Gonzalo Pizarro, who had attempted to set himself up as "King of the Realm of Peru," was captured and beheaded in Cuzco. In all, 14 percent of the Cajamarca veterans died in the civil wars between 1537 and 1554, almost four times more than had died during the conquest itself. Almost a fifth of the original conquerors died in Indian rebellions. Of those who survived, half chose to remain in Peru, while the rest, mostly those of higher social rank, returned to Spain. Of the repatriates, nine out of ten returned to their homelands and home towns to consolidate or capitalize upon their good fortunes. Those with connections and family prestige succeeded. The ones who were originally poor and of low social condition failed, and many of them, embittered, chose to return to Peru.

Generally speaking, those who remained in Peru fared well, obtaining numerous high colonial positions, holding vast *encomiendas* and enjoying the high status that would probably have been denied them in Spain. In the colony they constituted a kind of unique and very exclusive club of men bound together by adventure and experiences no one else could duplicate. Nevertheless, few great fortunes survived in Peru. Only the descendants of Gerónimo de Aliaga still hold title to the original property of their forebear on the Lima Plaza de Armas.

The conquest society immediately developed its own independent criteria for social power and distinction, on the same bases as pioneers in other New World areas had. Peruvian Spaniards made seniority of settlement in the colony one of their fundamental criteria of social prestige and position, alongside traditional patterns derived from Peninsular society. Thus, *encomenderos* who participated in the capture of Atahuallpa possessed seniority and position above those who came later. Those who occupied Cuzco achieved the next greatest seniority, other conditions such as actual Peninsular nobility being equal.

Colonial conquest society generated a long series of ethnic distinctions of social place that the reconquest had not generated on the Peninsula, particularly because of the rapid rise of the racially mixed new populations. First of all, native-born Spaniards thought in quite a Peninsularcentric manner that "blood" deteriorated with geographic distance. In other words, genetic Spaniards born on the Peninsula thought they retained all the qualities that they associated with Spanishness. These Peninsulars termed those Spaniards born in the colonies *criollos,* or Creoles, and considered them inferior to themselves. The phrase *"a la criolla"* came into use to denigrate Creole behavior, which was viewed as always lacking some vital ingredient.

Patrilineal Spanish Christians viewed the roles of conqueror and colonial governor as male activities. Most Spaniards who sailed from the Peninsula to the New World were male. From the earliest period after the Columbian voyages of discovery through colonial times, only about 10 percent were women. This unbalanced sex ratio naturally fostered unions between Spanish men and Indian women, as nearly every writer on Spanish colonialism has noted. Thus the New World conquest society produced from its beginnings a new Mestizo racial group constituting a major phenomenon of the biological Columbian exchange.

By the time Pizarro's forces entered Peru, miscegenation had been underway long enough for a number of Mestizos born in the Caribbean Islands and Panamá to accompany the Spanish conquerors of the Incas. The Peruvian Spaniards who had not already formed liaisons with Panamanian, Nicaraguan, or island women apparently soon made them in Peru. With their strong sense of social hierarchy, Spaniards found Inca noblewomen attractive as both wives and concubines, thus bringing a disproportionate quantity of Inca genetic traits into the Peruvian Mestizo population. Naturally, the Mestizo children born even immediately after the conquest did not reach maturity and begin to reproduce until about 1552, when they materially accelerated the pace of growth of the new and distinctive racially mixed population that eventually would become numerically dominant in republican Peru.

We see in retrospect that the growth of the Mestizo population was of great demographic importance in all the colonial territories. Where

European and Native American contact was most intense the destruction of the local population with its lack of resistance to Old World diseases was unabated. In Peru, certain Old World afflictions such as malaria and yellow fever caused much higher mortality at elevations near sea level than at higher Andean altitudes. Consequently, the Spaniards witnessed the heavy depopulation of many of the rich coastal valleys. They then imported African slaves to attempt to replace the Native American manpower lost in the epidemics. The slave trade therefore acquired an importance in Peru like that in the Caribbean lands.

Spanish New World conquest society also created a new social place for Black slaves imported from Africa, or from Spain or the Azores Islands. Bishop Bartolomé de las Casas, early clerical champion and protector of Indians, actually advocated massive importation of Black slaves into New World lowlands to perform manual labor in order to spare the Indians. Consequently, slaves drawn from many parts of Africa learned the Spanish language, even to communicate with one another, and rapidly learned certain cultural traits of their masters. Many Blacks, in spite of their legal slavery, occupied a cultural niche between the white elite and the Indian subject population. Spanish masters often used Black slaves to carry out punitive measures against Indians. As a result, the latter came to fear Blacks as much as Spaniards, especially in highland provinces such as Cuzco. For the most part, however, slaves were concentrated in the coastal oases, especially the Rímac Valley. By 1554 colonial Lima's Black population numbered over 1,500 and was rapidly growing.

The Old World diseases also opened the way for many another Old World component of the Columbian exchange. Human pressure on the irrigated land base sharply decreased, proving quite convenient for Spaniards who began to plant wheat, other small grains, wine grapes, olive trees, sugar cane, and Old World vegetables. Negro slave or Indian tributary crews cultivated the vacated lands under Spanish supervision. Spaniards energetically pursued the profits to be made by rearing and selling horses during the immediate postconquest period, and all sorts of Old World livestock at slightly later dates. This kind of biological reorganization of New World life progressed very rapidly after 1532, so that by the time Viceroy Francisco de Toledo began molding colonial institutions in 1569, a colonial ecological pattern had been firmly established.

While such mundane processes were underway and passed largely unnoticed, the erstwhile conquerors were engaged in complex and vicious maneuvers in their struggles to gain power in the rich kingdom. Traitorous acts and assassinations were commonplace. Francisco Pizarro survived less than nine years after the decisive two-hour encounter with the Inca emperor Atahuallpa and troops at Cajamarca. His dispute with his partner Diego de Almagro over the question of who controlled Cuzco produced a bitter civil war. After the Pizarro faction defeated and executed the elder Almagro, his Mestizo son and partisans continued the political-economic struggle. Pizarro died on the swords of the Almagro partisans in 1541.

At that time, the king's first viceroy in Mexico was only six years into his masterful conversion of Cortez's private enterprise conquest into a royal colony. The Spanish monarch may have remained unsure of the ultimate success of transferring the European model of viceregal governance to the New World, or simply have lacked the right man to send to Peru. In any event, after Pizarro's assassination the crown dispatched a royal commissioner to pick up successfully the reins of royal authority. Then Crown Prince Philip II, acting for his father Emperor Charles V, sent the first viceroy to Peru.

Arriving in Peru to enforce the 1542 New Laws of the Indies (which, on paper, materially lessened *encomendero* privileges and power), Viceroy Blasco Núñez de Vela set off an *encomendero* revolution. The first viceroy brought the first king's magistrates to establish the *audiencia,* or royal court. Disembarking at Tumbes on March 4, 1544, they went overland to Lima to establish a royal legal system in the colony. Thus the crown overrode the 1529 contract with Pizarro that prohibited lawyers from practicing in the new conquest state. This royal action imposed the Hispanic cultural pattern of enthusiastic litigation upon colonial Peru and its republican successor.

Francisco Pizarro's younger brother Gonzalo, outraged by the New

Law reforms, led conquerors against the king's personal representative. They defeated the royalist contingent and killed the viceroy. The revolutionaries frightened the *audiencia* magistrates into naming Pizarro the king's governor of Peru, thus carrying out Peru's second coup d'état (counting the bloody seizure of Atahuallpa at Cajamarca in 1532 as the first) after the arrival of the Spaniards. The revolutionaries envisioned persuading the Pope to name Gonzalo Pizarro king on grounds of royal Spanish mistreatment of Peruvians.

In this crisis the president of the *audiencia,* Pedro de la Gasca, assumed the leadership of royalist forces. He proved to be more persuasive than had been the rigid first viceroy and managed to rally sufficient military strength to defeat the revolutionaries. He executed Gonzalo Pizarro in 1545, along with a large number of key followers, thus ending the prospect of an independent Peruvian kingdom. The royal *audiencia* and its presiding magistrate thus must receive the credit for finally establishing royal authority in Peru after almost twenty years of strife.

The royal idealism on behalf of Native Americans expressed in the New Laws died in the civil wars. Pedro de la Gasca and his successors found it necessary, in the grim reality of Peruvian conquest society, a society based upon exploitation of Native Americans, to reward over 218 key members of the royalist army, many of them belated turncoats from Pizarro, with the very *encomiendas* he was able to expropriate from rebel partisans. Thus royal hegemony required the sacrifice of royal idealism and perpetuated the *encomienda.*

The crown hoped to continue de la Gasca's restoration of royal rule by transferring the very able Antonio de Mendoza from New Spain to Peru as its second viceroy, but he died in 1552, less than a year after taking command in Lima. The third viceroy, Andrés de Mendoza, Marqués of Cañete, arrived in 1556 and finally established the European viceregal government during his six-year term.

The full imposition of royal authority placed royal officials in all regions. The most important colonial representatives of direct rule were *corregidores* appointed by the viceroy to head *corregimientos,* or provinces, following the Iberian administrative model. The *corregi-*

mientos eventually numbered fifty-two. These jurisdictions divided the viceroyalty into much smaller units than the less than two dozen original municipalities. The crown endowed the men appointed as *corregidores* with vast powers to levy tribute, regulate the actions of *encomenderos* and other Spaniards, legislate, preside over criminal and civil law suits, chair meetings of the town councils known as *cabildos*, when they were present in one of the Spanish municipal capitals, and exercise the *repartimiento*, or state monopoly of selling goods to conquered Indians.

Spain paid its *corregidores* very low salaries. Yet they served in regions remote from Christian civilization, where they frequently suffered from cultural shock, altitude sickness, or *verruga*, an insect-transmitted disease endemic in lower Andean valleys. They had to wrest their compensation from the Andean peoples. In the consequent exploitative system, Indians usually played the role of thoroughly cowed, submissive subordinates, in order to avoid punishment and diminish abuse. Thus the seeds of graft and corruption quickly sprouted as part of the conquest culture.

Charged with overseeing provincial government, the *corregidor* worked with the authorities of each municipality, headed by a mayor and council. Municipal citizens—Spaniards—occupied these and lesser municipal offices. Because of the advantages such posts offered, Spanish subjects actively sought them, usually by purchasing appointments from the king or the viceroy. Continually pressed for funds, the Hapsburg monarchs resorted to the sale of colonial offices to raise money. Having paid considerable sums for their offices, municipal officials and *corregidores* typically set out to make good on their investments. They did not, therefore, look kindly upon viceregal supervision of their affairs. Very early in the postconquest period, provincial factions formed around the *corregidor* and his cronies, on the one hand, and the surviving *encomenderos* on the other. The clergy gravitated between these groups with both sides perceiving the viceroy as a threat.

Caught between the upper and nether grindstones of provincial forces vying for power were the lower castes—Indians and Mestizos. The latter directed their energies toward finding social places in the

colonial structure that reflected a Peninsular disdain and outright fear
of their growing numbers. The Indians struggled to survive multiple
layers of exploitation. They began to comment bitterly among themselves about the affluence of the *corregidor*-clerical or *encomendero*-
clerical alliances, relative to their own condition. The Quechua and
Aymara highlanders developed ways of expressing these feelings of
alienation that survive to the present. When government technicians
recently urged members of one highland community to buy sleek,
pure-bred Merino sheep, the peasants expressed their evaluation of the
animals as too expensive to maintain with the comment that "They
look as though they eat like Christians."

Although the *corregidores* represented centralized authority, several
aspects of colonial social structure fostered a resurgence of regionalism.
The *corregimientos* themselves coincided with preconquest environmental zones with distinctive ethnic populations. Only a small number
of key Spaniards lived in the far-flung administrative towns, for *encomenderos* reached a maximum of only about 500—an almost one-to-
one replacement of Inca nobles—and the *corregidores* numbered a
tenth as many. The Spanish sense of social hierarchy kept these Spaniards living in towns. Consequently, Spain's conquest state relied
heavily upon indirect rule of peasant masses through hereditary Indian
leaders. Thus conquest culture hardly disturbed Native American continuing identification with a *terruño,* or little homeland.

To an unknown extent, preconquest distinctions between different
ranks of Indian leadership disappeared in a colonial category of "tribute chiefs." Spaniards referred to them by the Caribbean term *cacique*
or the Andean term *curaca.* These Indian authorities bore the principal responsibility for exacting tribute from the peasant for the *encomenderos* and the crown.

The colonial *curacas* organized the periodic tribute-paying expedi-
tions from rural areas to the urban residences of *encomenderos* and
royal officers. Expedition members carried tribute in kind. Once in the
cities, they lived in shanties on suburban lots of the *encomenderos* or
crown lands and carried out their assigned tasks. *Curacas* played a
middleman role between the Spanish elite and the Indian mass, and

they experienced more frequent face-to-face contact with Spaniards than did any other group of Indians. As a result they became the first Indians to learn to speak Spanish, to be permitted to learn to read, write, or adopt Spanish styles of dress; some even came to bear arms and ride horseback. Most *curacas* descended from regional kings and powerful chiefs conquered during the latter phases of Incaic imperial expansion. One significant consequence of this situation was renewed sociocultural regionalism. The crown maintained the authority of these local Indian leaders who in turn maintained relatively peaceful and efficient exploitation of Native American masses with little direct Spanish help. Thus indirect rule by Spain meant, if anything, a weaker drive toward cultural unification of Andean populations than had Inca indirect rule.

Influenced by pious Christian ideals and advised all too often by courtiers who had never seen the New World, Spanish monarchs decreed measures that in many instances expressed high ideals in impractical policies. Thus the crown itself very soon established a strong tradition of colonial governance characterized by legislative idealism bearing little functional relationship to the social and economic reality of the provinces. Colonial officials conducting day-to-day governance of the Peruvian peoples also pushed hard and constantly for pragmatic goals requiring Indians to alter their behavior. While *encomenderos* resisted the New Laws of the Indies of Charles V, they later united with the crown representatives to impose a *Pax Hispánica,* to implement the colonial city planning laws, to demand that Indians attend Mass, pay tribute, labor in silver and mercury mines, and render other forms of personal service. Conquest culture and colonial rule thus imparted a look of cultural uniformity to many aspects of life throughout old *Tawantinsuyu,* like Inca rule before it.

At the same time, Hispanic culture itself contributed to the growth of a new Andean regionalism. The conquerors displayed their attachment to Peninsular home towns by naming new settlements and renaming Indian ones for Spanish cities and towns. They even dressed "their Indians" in the lackey and peasant clothing of Extremadura, Andalucia, and other Spanish regions. Those Spaniards who stayed in

the colony to become its prestigious pioneer European settlers transferred their psychological commitments to a significant extent to the
towns and valleys where they finally settled. Their offspring developed strong emotional commitments to their *terruños,* areas where they
were born, rather than to such an abstract entity as the Peruvian kingdom. Thus Hispanic and Indian cultural themes of attachment to
one's birthplace reinforced each other.

One enduring consequence of Spanish policy was a considerable
preservation of cultural influences from the prehistoric Chimú kingdom. Unlike the Incas and Spaniards, the Chimú reckoned descent
matrilineally. Indirect rule recognized the matrilineal principle in north
Peruvian chieftainships for much of the colonial period. This meant
that female leaders performed duties there that male leaders carried
out elsewhere in the colony. Such female preponderance in indirect
rule became not only a symbol of the cultural distinction between the
northern peoples formerly contained in the Chimú kingdom and other
Peruvians, but a principal factor in maintaining the cultural and social
distinction between northern and southern Peru.

In parallel ways, Spanish indirect rule fostered other regional differences. Seeking dissidents within the Inca empire during the conquest such as Cortez had used to good advantage in conquering the
Aztecs, Pizarro early accepted offers from the Huancas of the Mantaro
Valley to serve as bearers for the Spaniards marching on the Inca
capital. Subsequent indirect rule returned to them a degree of independent action, save warfare. Consequently, the Mantaro Valley in
the central highlands followed a distinctive regional course of colonial
development. These prime examples suffice to illustrate the origins of
the cultural regionalism strongly manifest in modern Peru.

Peruvian conquest society functioned in terms of a variety of occupations and skills either not present in Inca society or considerably
changed. The vast bulk of the peasants, of course, remained agricul-
turalists and many pursued settlement specialties such as blanket-
weaving or pot-making on a part-time, seasonal basis. The emergent
conquest culture greatly expanded the variety of full-time occupations
beyond *Tawantinsuyu* levels. While the Spanish need for notaries to

draw up legal documents may have replicated Inca dependence upon the *quipu-camayoc,* the need for paper was new. The conquest society soon wrote so many documents that it supported full-time parchment-makers in Lima.

The castelike hierarchy of conquest society resulted in a qualitative separation in medical treatment. Spaniards and culturally Spanish Mestizos patronized European physicians and employed household remedies of mostly European origin, although many Indian elements gained a place in the latter.

Pre-Columbian medical practitioners in ancient Peru had successfully performed surgery as difficult as trepanation—removing skull bones to relieve concussive pressure on the brain. Such high-order skills disappeared after conquest, probably because the doctors were put out of business by fanatic colonial Christian priests. With the most sophisticated aspects of their preconquest culture lopped off in the colony, the Indians necessarily fell back upon local curers with few advanced skills who relied heavily on herbal remedies and curing rituals that provided patients with needed psychological support.

Although Pizarro's private army and the others involved in the conquest lived to a large extent off the Native American populations they encountered, the Spaniards were often too culturally rigid to adapt completely to the foods, clothing, and other resources of the New World. Iberians in the viceroyalty sought to duplicate Peninsular lifestyles. The conquerors relished grape wines and distilled alcoholic beverages, wheat products, beef, pork, mutton, chicken, and other familiar Mediterranean foods and flavors. They also cherished the feel of Spanish silks and the effect of military finery while on campaign. An economically powerful group of merchants accompanied, in the European style, the conquering armies to satisfy the demand for such luxuries by importing them or training local people to produce them. These merchants soon settled in the Spanish municipal capitals alongside the powerful *encomenderos.* In their shadow, petty trade became the occupation of Mestizos and Indians.

Spanish households required retinues of slaves and servants, the latter drawn from the *encomiendas.* Spanish wives saw that the Black slaves and Indians were trained in Peninsular customs as much as possible. The Iberian kitchen was copied, along with clothing styles, which were subject to sumptuary laws that kept Indians from wearing "gentleman's dress." Spanish women played a major role in converting servants to Roman Catholicism. Priests nevertheless carefully segregated Spaniards from Blacks and Indians in their celebrations of the sacraments. Indeed, new baroque and rococo churches became largely the domain of the Peninsular or Creole Spaniards and selected Mestizos. The rest of the people attended services, often in their "own" chapels and only at special times in the main churches, a custom that has carried forward into the present century in many areas.

The servant population, Black or Indian, received training to enable it to satisfy the wants of colonial rulers. Members of these groups learned to make silk stockings, shoes, buttons, and tailored clothing, all innovations in *Tawantinsuyu*. Milliners, collar-makers, and button-makers became numerous in the main cities.

Demand for another half-dozen skills came from the same wealthy group that sought luxurious Spanish-style housing with tile roofs, balconies, and great doorways. Cabinet-makers, screw-makers, lock-makers, brick-makers, plasterers, masons, tile-makers, and chair-makers catered to those with money. Very likely some preconquest masons, stone-cutters, plasterers, and painters managed to shift from part-time specialization while gardening for subsistence, to postconquest full-time labor. Indians and slaves worked under Spanish architects to fit new mansions with doors and often balconies produced by Spanish carpenters in Peninsular styles derived from the Moors. In spite of the demand for Spanish artisanry, Spaniards remained reluctant manual workers, so those who did work with their hands quickly trained Blacks and Indians in Old World skills to make up for the deficit in Peninsular artisans, and to move themselves into entrepreneurships.

Because most Indian peasants did not have a working knowledge of the Spanish language, they could not learn or understand many aspects of Spanish culture. Yet such people quickly acquired some Spanish implements and developed the skills to use them. One of the most important was the Andalusian style (really ancient Egyptian) ox-drawn plow, which Indians adopted in many but not all regions. Iron bars, shovels, and hoe blades superseded bronze in those areas where *encomenderos* supplied them.

Half a dozen more occupations opened up for Native Americans in overland transportation using Old World domestic animals and technology. Certain strategically located communities specialized soon after the conquest in running pack-trains. Olmos Indians, for example, specialized in moving cargo by mule over the road from the northern port of Paita to Lima. Lima and other Spanish municipal capitals developed small corps of artisans to service the transport network. Native Americans became blacksmiths as well as silver- and goldsmiths, farriers, and saddle-makers. Indian farmers along pack-train routes planted alfalfa as a cash crop to be sold in the form of pasture-privileges to passing muleteers. Other Indians continued to serve as rapid overland messengers, called *chasquis,* although not as efficiently as they had in Inca times.

Spanish specialization did not, in one respect, expand the Incaic range of occupations in conquest society. No Indians, to speak of, entered the Spanish Catholic priesthood even though, as fanatic Christians, Spaniards included Roman Catholic priests in practically all their activities, even in their private armies and retinues. Friar Vicente de Valverde, for instance, played a key role in Pizarro's treatment of Atahuallpa. Very early the pattern of the Spanish priesthood was set whereby the 350 or so priests who took up residence in Peru by the 1560s served the Spanish population far more than they attempted to convert the Native American masses. Most priests soon attached themselves to the urban households of the wealthy *encomenderos,* either directly or as curates of parish churches endowed by the Spanish elite to serve urban Spanish congregations. Some priests worked for *encomenderos* as missionaries to the tributary Indians for whose conversion the *encomendero* was responsible. Priests and *encomenderos* alike, however, appear to have defined such ministers more as personal chaplains to the *encomendero* families than as missionaries. The Roman Catholic church in Peruvian conquest society was an elitist institution for the Spaniards, not a strongly apostolic one.

Even members of the religious orders who first reached Peru preferred the richly endowed semimonastic life in the urban centers to the more demanding, Spartan existence required of those attempting the conversion of culturally alien Native Americans. The leader of the first group of Augustinians to enter Peru in 1551, for example, arranged the marriage of his sister to a wealthy *encomendero* who thereafter endowed the order with a fine house and a regular income.

By 1550 the Mercedarian, Franciscan, and Dominican orders had sent priests into Peru. Jesuits arrived in 1568. Spanish urban residents recruited priests about as rapidly as they arrived, establishing a pattern of urban concentration of clerics unaltered to the present day. Lima could boast a pious orphanage in the 1550s, and St. Andrew's Hospital for Indians from 1561. Yet no really significant missionary effort appears to have been made among the Indians prior to Viceroy Toledo's and Archbishop Toribio de Mogrovejo's final definition of colonial institutions in the 1570s and 1580s. Only the *caciques,* whose duties as agents of indirect rule brought them into contact with Spaniards, developed an interest in becoming Christians. They probably did so under occasional pressure from *encomenderos* or crown representatives. Many did seek baptism, adopted Spanish names, and in some cases learned to make a rough signature and perhaps to read.

In other words, Christian conversion did not constitute a primordial motivation for the conquerors of Peru, whatever the personal formal devotion of Father Valverde and his colleagues. The Peruvian conquest culture emphasized the search for gold and silver wealth, power, and a sumptuous, sometimes even hedonistic, secular life.

With the suppression of their public rituals, the Andean masses were left to their own religious devices for forty years and more, depending upon their geographic location. The Spaniards immediately suppressed Inca state religion, and interdicted the major pilgrimage to Pachacamác. Quite likely they did not themselves realize that Inca religion was only recently imposed upon devotees of a number of regional cults. Once conquest suppressed Inca worship without promptly replacing it with apostolic Christianity, regional believers reverted to earlier religious patterns. In many areas relatively free from resident

Spanish supervision, Indian priests continued to lead peasants in aboriginal ceremonies. Where Spanish clergy were more active, peasants fell back upon family-centered forms of aboriginal belief. They resorted more to magic than to organized religious ritual for lack of priests trained in the sophisticated doctrines and rituals of aboriginal religions. Peasant religion focused then as it does now upon matters important to peasants: fertility amulets, which were quickly transferred to Old World domestic animals as well as Andean ones, rogation ceremonies, and the like.

As the Columbian exchange progressed, conquest culture rites practiced by Indians in peasant settlements began to exhibit more and more similarity to religious customs and preoccupations practiced concurrently in peasant Spain. Andean religion was largely concerned with the annual cycle of life: personal life crisis events such as birth, marriage, and death, and events of the agricultural calendar. Larger celebrations revolved around more cosmic happenings recounting mythical origins, conquests of barbarians, and so forth. Precisely the same concerns and commemorations preoccupied provincial Spain. Other similarities can also be found in the "little cultural traditions" and beliefs relating to sickness, witchcraft, evil eye, bad airs, and spirits. Most Spanish conquerors came from small towns or villages; more than half were plebeians. They and many who followed participated in numerous village and regional versions of Roman Catholicism and its Mediterranean antecedents, and they actively transferred many of these practices to Peru. The rich, glittering fabric of intense Peruvian Catholicism today reflects two fundamentally diverging streams of devotional development initiated in the immediate postconquest period. On the one hand, the first rulers of Peru and their heirs sponsored and attended the solemn *Te Deums* and High Masses in the cathedral churches of the established state religion. Especially formal are the rituals in Lima's cathedral, the seat since 1548 of an archbishop and frequently a cardinal. On the other hand, the peasant masses make the streets of provincial towns and villages pulse with their joyous, often humorous celebrations, processions, and burlesques of European conquerors.

The importance and irresistible character of these periodic events is revealed in an incident that took place during the Spanish conquest. Returning from an exploratory trip to the oracle at Pachacamác, which still functioned under the Incas, Hernando Pizarro stopped at the mountain town of Jauja. There he hoped to confront the Inca general Chalcuchima, whom he hoped to dupe into captivity like Atahuallpa. Pizarro was surprised to find a huge festival in progress. Apparently the secular activities accompanying the religious observances so tempted the Spaniards as well as the Inca army that both forces joined in the festivities for five days of fun and revelry. Afterwards, neither side felt like a confrontation. The pattern of community celebrations was, in any event, very firmly established prior to Spanish conquest, and as subsequent events show, proved to be an enduring one.

Had the peasantry not managed to preserve its ability to laugh and make fun of the solemn overlords, it would have gone mad mining the treasure troves of the Andes. Awed by the unprecedented riches they gained by sacking Inca palaces, temples, and storehouses, the conquerors only slowly turned their attention to the ores. Prospectors did fan out through the new colony, however, probably always led by Indian guides acting under duress or seeking personal advantage in the new social order. By 1542, Spaniards learned of auriferous deposits in Carabaya Province in southeastern Peru. A gold rush ensued. A similar rush occurred at the same time in the Quito region.

The ore discovery that shaped colonial Peru came in 1545, when Spaniards learned of a virtual mountain of high-grade silver ore at Potosí, in upper Peru (modern Bolivia). Spaniards promptly began to drag Indians in chains from their homes to the hot shafts in the Potosí mines. If a conscripted native died, the greedy Spaniard was likely to sever body from head with his saber rather than stop to unlock the shackles which linked groups of men to chains to keep them from fleeing. As soon as Pedro de la Gasca defeated Gonzalo Pizarro to end the civil wars, he prohibited this abuse of the Inca *mita*, but his orders were written on "wet paper," as Spanish puts it. Within a few years Peru poured into Spain's royal and commercial coffers a stream of refined silver that revolutionized the power and price structure of Europe, and would eventually finance the Industrial Revolution.

An innovator in New Spain worked out a colonial "patio process" for recovering silver from its ore. This required mercury to mix with the ore to combine with the silver for later washing out. That converted the Peninsular Almaden mercury mine into a major source of income for the Spanish crown. The state monopolized the sale of mercury, and was able to calculate the royal tax on silver in terms of the quantity of mercury sold to miners for its extraction. In 1563 Peruvian miners freed themselves from the high shipping cost of importing Almaden mercury. Spaniards finally learned from Indian guides the location of the Huancavelica mercury deposits that provided preconquest cosmetics for high-born ladies. With the discovery of silver and mercury mines of major magnitude, the pattern of later colonial life took shape.

Peruvian conquest culture evolved very rapidly from New World Spanish conquest culture worked out in the Caribbean, Mexico, and Panamá. Brawling conquerors fighting over various spoils carried this pattern further here than anywhere else in the New World, to the point of actual civil war. Twenty years passed after the conquest before royal authority was established and *encomendero*-dominated conquest society became a colonial one. Then Spain wielded power directly through royal representatives and indirectly through Indian *curacas* and a few locally selected municipal officers. Spaniards, Indians, Black slaves, and the new Mestizo races shared many common traits of conquest-colonial culture, yet continued to differ along regional, ethnic, and linguistic lines in spite of the operation of the cultural Columbian exchange. It took a powerful viceroy finally to forge a colonial culture and institutions that could survive the corroding effects of stagnation, greed, and corruption.

Chapter 4 • Classic Colonialism, 1569-1700

Arriving in Peru six years after the discovery of the Huancavelica mercury mine, the fifth Spanish viceroy, Francisco de Toledo, carried out the definitive colonial reorganization of Andean civilization. His wide-ranging policies, by establishing patterns of social, economic, and religious action that would endure for most of the remainder of the colonial period, fundamentally influenced the later post-Columbian exchange in the region also. During his 13-year tenure, Toledo set up a new type of Native American officialdom, one that strengthened direct Spanish rule and increased crown revenues, yet individually answered to local populations and their interests.

He accomplished what he did by spending more time in the Sierra personally inspecting the viceroyalty than did any other viceroy. Consolidating the authority that Pedro de la Gasca and the Marqués de Cañete had won for the crown, Francisco de Toledo firmly established viceregal authority. He conquered the Neo-Inca state in 1572. Thereafter the monarchy was able to dispatch viceroy after viceroy with no significant local opposition until the wars of independence 250 years later.

Two patterns of viceregal selection bear emphasis here. The Hapsburg monarchs, following the precedent of the always money-short Emperor Charles V, often sold viceregal and other colonial offices to raise funds. This meant that viceregal and other royal offices in Peru had to be obtained in Spain by Spaniards and that viceroys acted as personal representatives of the throne. Peruvians, even powerful and ennobled Creoles, found themselves excluded from the highest vice-regal offices. In addition, the royal representatives overseas worked intently, if not primarily, with the goal of recouping and expanding the personal fortunes with which they had bought their positions. Likewise, those native Peruvians who obtained lower royal posts also came to treat these positions as almost personal property, obtained for the purpose of increasing one's personal wealth.

From Pizarro's founding of Lima in 1535 until the surrender of the royalist army in 1824, some forty-seven persons headed the Peruvian government for an average tenure of six years each. The Hapsburg kings appointed twenty-seven viceroys between 1535 and 1705 of whom a third had been viceroys of New Spain promoted to Peru. Others had served on the Council of the Indies or the Royal Council, and 70 percent were noblemen when appointed.

While Toledo strove mightily to centralize power and institute direct viceregal rule, after Toledo's time the viceroys and other chief executives and magistrates in Lima seldom ventured out of the capital city. They were content to rule Peru through a colonial bureaucracy, to the extent that Lima's writ actually ran in the provinces. They knew that no colonial chief executive could achieve full direct control of Peru from Lima, that no bureaucrat bound to his desk in the capital city looking overseas to Spain could even know the realities of life in the Andean highlands where most Peruvians lived. But they cared little about provincial life as long as the mines produced enough to satisfy the king and the Indians peacefully paid their tribute. At the same time, provincial peoples in Peru perfected during the long years of colonial *Pax Hispánica* a wealth of cultural patterns that neutralized to a considerable extent the impact of capital city dictates, satisfying instead local needs.

Some of the Toledan reforms fostered regionalism. Toledo evidently recognized the environmental and ethnic bases for the provincial divisions the Incas employed, so he largely returned to them in establishing boundaries for *corregimientos*. In this way, Toledo organized a provincial level of direct administration below the viceroy, under the responsibility of a *corregidor* in each jurisdiction.

Toledo also struck at the *encomenderos* and their conquest society control over municipal governments by prohibiting them from holding local offices. This measure did not, however, immediately terminate *encomendero* power over municipal affairs, inasmuch as Pizarro had under color of his contract with the crown appointed many perpetual municipal officers and the latter, contrary to the interests of the crown, had formed a self-perpetuating corporation whose members chose their own successors. Early in Philip II's reign, which began in 1556 after Emperor Charles V abdicated, the new king began openly selling the post of government notary on the Peninsula. By 1559 Philip had expanded this policy to the Caribbean islands, and he extended it to Peru in 1565. Thus, by the time he sent Francisco de Toledo to Peru as his viceroy, the latter knew the need for offices to sell. The Toledan prohibition, which commenced a long struggle for primacy between Peru's Spanish pioneers pursuing autonomy and the crown seeking cash, got its impetus from the need of the crown for income through the outright sale of municipal offices therefore, more than from the principle of direct rule.

Colonial municipal government called for a number of officials in each jurisdiction, so that the potential income to the crown from auctioning off these positions loomed large, even though each office might be sold for the lifetime of its purchaser. An *alcalde* headed the municipal government, presiding over meetings of the *cabildos* or councils and carrying out numerous ceremonial as well as ordinary administrative duties. Four or more *regidores* served on the *cabildo*, depending on the rank of the settlement—a matter also determined by royal decree. Keeping municipal records required scribes; law enforcement called for constables known as *alguaciles*, and other functions had their *mayordomos*. Iberian custom and royal policies demanded that municipal officials reside in the municipal capitals, so those who purchased their positions from the king perforce became citizens of their new jurisdictions, in contrast to the noncitizen Native Americans within it. Peninsular natives enjoyed distinct advantages in bidding for municipal offices, yet auctions were also announced in the affected municipal capitals, where some Creoles were able to perpetuate their control of municipal offices.

Even after Toledo excluded *encomenderos* from municipal offices, those powerful Peruvians who had already acquired this status—through inheritance from conquerors, royal grants, occasionally by purchase—continued to collect tribute from the Indians. The economic power conferred upon *encomenderos* by tribute collection appears overwhelming from a modern perspective. For example, Juan de Mori received an *encomienda* in 1550 from Pedro de la Gasca. A citizen of new Huánuco, Mori annually received from the Indians of Conchucos Province 2,500 pesos in gold or the equivalent in silver, the produce of 1,518 hectares in wheat, maize, barley, and potatoes; 30 sheep; 12 kilograms of candle wax, 30 hogs; 130 chickens and 15 pairs of grouse every four months. Every Friday throughout the year this *encomendero* was to receive 20 eggs. Tributaries brought him 25 donkey-loads of salt annually, 10 of them for the viceroy, augmented by 25 wooden beams not less than 20 feet long; 100 *Agave* stems of similar length; 25 troughs and trays; 6 chairs; 20 cutting-boards; 25 wooden plates and bowls. Every four months the tributaries carried to the *encomendero's* household 40 pairs of riding sandals and riding tack, rope, woolen sacks, whips and pack straps made from *cabuya* (*Agave*) fiber. The grant also provided that twenty-five Indians were to herd the *encomendero's* animals on his own land and in Huánuco. Another dozen served as burden carriers. Forty more planted and harvested 15 hectares of wheat and maize for the *encomendero's* household use. Four of them were also carpenters and potters for seasonal work in their specialties. The *encomendero* was to provide these forty married men with land to cultivate to raise their own sustenance. Juan de Mori's trust required him to provide a priest for the spiritual guidance of these Native Americans, and they had to supply the clergyman with maize, potatoes, hogs, chickens, sheep, eggs, firewood, *chicha,* and anything else he might need.

The economic resources such tribute placed in the hands of some 500 *encomenderos* kept them social and economic peers if not superiors of most royal officials who purchased royal offices in the colony in an attempt to make fortunes in a few years. *Encomendero* control over the peasants was supervised, at least in theory, by the *corregidores* who reviewed the work of all officials within their areas of jurisdiction. Other officials, such as notaries and scribes, judges and inspectors, aided the basic power hierarchy in running public affairs. Peninsular-born Spaniards usually filled these posts. They directed the activities of those Indian authorities involved in lower-level direct colonial rule.

During his personal inspections of many provinces Viceroy Toledo found a conquest society firmly based upon the power of these *encomenderos* and the hereditary tribute-chiefs of pre-Incaic ethnic groups. He attributed the deplorable state of the Native American masses at this time to excesses by the *encomenderos* and the *curacas,* and to the absence of proper Christian indoctrination. He therefore began by reordering society at this Indian level.

Most of the peasants, Toledo discovered, inhabited small dispersed hamlets and family farmsteads scattered over the Andean slopes. To govern them better and to facilitate missionary efforts to convert them to Christianity with a relatively small number of priests, Toledo recognized, they had to be more concentrated. One of Toledo's most significant reforms of conquest society, therefore, called for Indians to settle in new towns and villages following the physical plan laid down in royal decrees. Toledo's orders brought into existence hundreds of new colonial settlements called *reducciones,* conveniently located in flat valley bottoms but often, as it turned out, on sites subject to deglaciation disasters such as floods and avalanches. These settlements followed the colonial grid-pattern plan, which formed a checkerboard around a central square where the church and the municipal office were erected.

Viceroy Toledo reiterated earlier royal decrees that prohibited Spaniards from living among Native Americans. This meant that the local governing personnel of the new *reducciones* consisted of Indians. Just as Toledo struck at *encomendero* power, he attempted to put an end to *curaca* power. He prohibited hereditary *curacas* from holding local offices. Toledo's scheme allowed only priests and *corregidores* among Spanish officials to deal with Indians personally or through their lieutenants, and his ordinances charged these officials with law enforcement and litigation.

In 1575 Toledo established a new system of Native American local governance made up of officials drawn from the Spanish municipality with the Spanish titles of mayor, councilman, and the like. He did allow the bisecting Andean moiety divisions to carry over. Adult members of Indian communities convened on the first day of each year to select two sets of officers for the year. In colonial settlements with populations greater than eighty, each moiety selected one mayor and two councilmen. One constable served the entire community. A scribe or *quipu-camayoc* had to be a permanent official because of the skills necessary to the office. After attending New Year's Mass in the Spanish town where the *corregidor* or his lieutenant resided, newly elected Indian officials humbly received Spanish staves of office from the *corregidor* or his surrogate and entered immediately upon their duties.

The Spaniards brought with them from the Peninsula their custom of symbolizing public office with wooden staves, a custom that soon carried over to colonial Native American as well as Spanish municipal officialdom. Lower-rank Indian leaders became widely known to their fellows collectively as *varayoc*. This term is appropriately half Spanish and half Quechua. Spanish *vara* means "staff" and Quechua *yoc* means "bearer." Local artisans charged with carving the staves of office for the *varayoc* developed, if Spanish officials did not design them, distinctive styles of staves, ranging from tall, massive silver-banded clubs around Cuzco to slender wands topped with a small metal cross in the Callejón de Huaylas.

These Native American colonial officials quickly became ubiquitous leaders of indigenous communities. They organized their fellows to carry out the basic physical labor of maintaining the colonial economic

infrastructure. They managed all local affairs, but especially the cleaning and repairing of irrigation canals vital to all subsistence, streets
and roads, bridges, shrines and chapels, and public facilities of all
kinds. As the lowest ranking officers of the colonial hierarchy, local
mayors marshaled the workers in turns to fulfill their draft labor obligations in the *mita,* a system adopted by the Spaniards from the Incas.
They saw that the populace kept Christian religious observances and
also dealt with minor disputes and litigation.

Toledo's system of colonial governance failed to displace the hereditary chiefs as quickly perhaps as he expected it to when he enjoined
curacas (and Spaniards) from interfering in community selection of
varayoc. Still, this new form of local government proved to be one of
the most pervasive as well as enduring colonial institutions, under
which the largest number of Peruvians lived for the longest time.
Although constitutionally abolished during republican times, it still
endures in attenuated form in many places. Hundreds of rural communities annually select their mayors, councilmen, constable, and inspectors in the manner Toledo prescribed, even preserving the moiety
structure in many areas. These officials, known variously as *varayoc,*
alcaldes, alcaldes pedaneos, regidores, alferezes, or *alguaciles,* still carry
their venerated, silver-adorned staves of office as they go about their
duties. Their surviving functions retain, however, a strong orientation
toward religious observances and reflect a ritualistic, hierarchical social
structure inherited from the Toledan ordinances.

Toledo also laid down rules of procedure to be followed in Native
American selection of local leaders. These were designed to secure
more-or-less free elections. Predation by local interests seeking to exploit peasants for their own benefit repeatedly compromised the integrity of the prescribed electoral process. The *corregidores,* the very persons responsible for protecting Native American interests in colonial
legal theory, actually headed the list of manipulators. Priests, *encomenderos,* and *curacas* all played influential roles in corrupting the
ideal system, particularly as great haciendas with large serf populations
developed in the Sierra.

In the contest for colonial control, those seeking advantage kept Indian officials well stocked with alcoholic beverages to ease their endless rounds of church-sponsored festivals and rituals of office and to encumber them with debt. Non-Indians secured the selection of Native Americans who would be obedient, subservient, and acquiescent. Thus the end result saw the leaders of Native American communities often serving as errand boys for the dominant local Spanish groups. The powerful colonial interests that used them regarded Indian officials with bemused paternalism at best. Yet in limited ways they functioned as cultural shock-absorbers between exploiters and exploited.

A typical basic premise of leader selection within the Native American community came to be that no one wanted to serve the Spanish master. Moreover, the honor of being a royal official, even at this low level, obliged the *varayoc* to feast his peers. This was particularly true in those Indian settlements where Spanish priests demanded that *varayoc* sponsor the festivals celebrated in honor of the local patron saint and those on the major holy days. Clearly, not every peasant family could afford to provide a *varayoc* in a given year. Only those families who had stored surplus food and goods and were able to borrow from many relatives and ritual kinsmen could afford the "honor" of having a senior male serve as a leader. The dominant group could impoverish an uncooperative Indian for life by manipulating his premature selection as a *varayoc*.

Despite the ambiquity of the role of local leaders, positions such as native mayor were the only avenues for community status recognition and prestige open to Indians. The pattern became so firmly established that families competed for the honor of providing a *varayoc*. In the rigidly hierarchical colonial society, serving Peninsular masters, however reluctantly, brought some crumbs of reward from one's village peers.

As life-long residents of their settlements, the *varayoc* remained firmly embedded in their extended families and regional subcultures. However honored they might feel by appointment to local offices, the *varayoc* placed local indigenous interests—family, *ayllu*, and *terruño*—ahead of Spanish interests. When a colonial official called for a courvée labor force or *mita*, the illiterate *varayoc* could easily "misunderstand" the verbal message and arrive with fewer than the number of workers demanded, come days late, or omit friends and family from the levy. Thus the *varayoc* found some freedom to favor their own families or *ayllus* in apportioning work and a limited compass for avoiding bureaucratic demands by playing to the hilt the "dumb childlike Indian" role.

When dominant group interests did not intervene, local selection of *varayoc* became a matter of coaptation; that is, incumbent *varayoc* usually picked their successors. They knew which families could afford the "honor" and which could not. Near the end of the year the outgoing *varayoc* walked through the settlement carrying bottles of distilled cane alcohol, calling formally on good prospects or cornering them on the paths to their fields. The *varayoc* offered the prospect a drink, and he who downed a slug of cane alcohol thereby ceremonially signified his acceptance. Subsequently, the Spanish official in the administrative town had but to ratify the selection of the outgoing *varayoc* by ceremoniously handing staves of office to the drafted-volunteering incoming leader, usually at New Year's Day Mass.

The financial burdens of a year in such office could plunge a leader's family into debt for a decade or more. In contrast to the political and social differentiation leadership gave, *varayoc* service functioned as a powerful economic leveling device among Indian families. That fact was not lost upon families of incumbents hunting for replacements in little societies characterized by an absolute scarcity of desirable goods. In such closed systems, families accurately perceived their share of the scarce benefits as varying with the shares held by their peers, and they acted out of envy to keep everyone at approximately the same economic level. Such invidious competition simplified the Spanish task of economic and political control over the more numerous subject populations.

The different official leadership positions came to constitute a set of sociopolitical ranks with strong religious responsibilities and sanctions. Indian community leaders ascended through the set of ranks as they aged and as they accumulated sufficient wealth to afford to discharge official responsibilities for another year. By faithfully fulfilling their duties in lesser offices they gained higher ones. They could obtain the blessing of the local priest with whom they worked closely—an external and supernatural sanction for the power they exercised while bossing their fellows.

Once a Native American held for a year the *vara* of the senior local office, he graduated, as it were, into an informal council of elders. Toledo contributed in his ordinance a provision for the eldest local residents to vote first when electing their mayors, councilmen, and constables. Aboriginal social models honored aged persons. Thus everyone in the community honored its experienced elders, conceding them many marks of respect. The elder joined other veterans of the never-ending struggle to lighten the colonial burden. The council of elders discussed local issues, advised the *varayoc* in office, admonished the young to observe the rules of decent behavior and effective kowtowing to the Spaniards.

Viceroy Toledo created this new type of Indian leadership in order to diminish the still great powers of conquest culture tribute-chiefs and eventually to replace them. Even under the *encomenderos,* Andean *curacas* had been able to maintain to an amazing extent the Incaic economic infrastructure. Under early indirect rule, they managed to mobilize work forces for many purposes. Judging from records of communications in the hinterland, the *curacas* mobilized work parties to maintain portions of the Incaic stone road system, suspension bridges, and even the storehouses between major Sierra population centers. They also satisfied *encomenderos* by appearing with the demanded work parties of proper size at the tribute-payment season in urban centers. They even hired laborers out to Spaniards who did not command tribute labor.

After Toledo reformed the tribute system to assign tributary labor to the mines and textile mills, and created a new set of Indian officials, the continuing decline in the total numbers of Indians due to disease and abuse further inhibited *curaca* ability to turn out men for traditional work. Moreover, many Inca roads became progressively less relevant to the colonial economic pattern, although they continued in use throughout the colonial period. New roads to expedite movement of specie from Potosí to Callao might have been built, but Spaniards introduced Peninsular carting technology only in the coastal valleys. In the Andes they used pack trains led by Spaniards and often conducted by culturally flexible Indian, Negro, or Mulatto muleteers. Donkeys, mules, and horses required little more than an Indian footpath, slightly widened on steep mountain slopes.

Yet the hereditary *curacas* possessed the ability and cultural value in Spanish eyes to survive, in spite of changing economic patterns and Toledo's assault on their power. First of all, the titles, privileges, and functions of many Inca nobles and authorities survived into the colonial period. Respectful of royalty and title, colonial officials continued to trace and recognize the Inca royal lineage and to award it special status. A good example of such recognition was the high social status of the Cuzco Indian noble José Gabriel Condorcanqui, who led an uprising under the name Tupac Amaru II on the eve of the war of independence.

Fortunately, the actual structure of colonial governance outside the viceregal capital can be reconstructed not only from the records of the dominant group, but also from at least one major record left by an aged eyewitness to the transition from conquest to colonial society. This was *don* Felipe Guamán Poma de Ayala, a bilingual Quechua and Spanish-speaking Indian. He enumerated in a petition intended for the crown, the rank, privilege, titles, and responsibilities of Native American functionaries. Not surprisingly, he saw them replicating the Incaic provincial hierarchy virtually to a man.

At the top of colonial governance of Indians survived the chief descendants of the Sapa Incas to whom Spanish officials granted some *encomiendas,* rights to wear Spanish clothing, carry arms, ride horses, be schooled and addressed as *don* or *doña*. These terms of address assumed great social importance in status-conscious Peru and are still a trait that forms a key element in interpersonal relations. These descendants of Incas collected tribute for the Spanish king who, in turn, kept their positions hereditary. Their powerful but ambivalent position aligned them closely with the *encomenderos,* who also collected tribute from the peasants and were descended from the conquerors of the Inca *ayllus*.

At a second level of Indian governance survived the descendants of the provincial heads of the administrative quarters of the *Tawantin-suyu*, the *Capac Apu*. While they held no *encomiendas*, they also collected tribute and supervised those of lower rank within their regions, enjoying many of the colonial privileges noted above. They ranked as noblemen. Below them came the paid "gentlemen" chiefs known as *curacas* or *caciques* who served as heads of districts of 1,000 tribute-payers. This was the Incaic *waranga* rank, also entitled to address as *don* in colonial society.

Incaic principles still organized lesser ranks. The *mandón mayor*, literally the "big boss" in charge of 500 tribute-payers, ranked highest among those who paid tribute. Such Indian officials in their colonial capacity as *varayoc* were the principal mobilizers of labor for the *mita* and other work demanded by *encomendero*, *corregidor*, and *curaca* alike. "Big bosses" did not inherit their positions, nor were they or their wives entitled to be addressed with the terms of respect. Other subordinate Indian officials were termed *mandoncillos* or "little bosses." They included the mayors of villages charged with responsibility for 100 tribute-payers and those responsible for 50, 10, and 5 tribute-payers. The lower an official stood in the hierarchy of power, the more specifically Indian were his cultural traits. Guamán Poma's drawings subtly show that the people in the lowest three positions wore a combination of Spanish and indigenous clothing, whereas the higher ranks sported only Spanish attire. Guamán Poma saw them all as serving Spanish interests and being corrupted by them.

Some hereditary *curacas* perceived the cultural trend of colonial society. They translated their surviving power into terms understood by both Spaniards and Indians while they continued to wield social and political power as surrogates of the *encomenderos* or crown representatives. With money, farsighted *curacas* added to their land grants by purchasing properties from the always impoverished crown. Such *curacas* insured that their descendants would control blocs of one of the major sources of Peruvian wealth and prestige: grazing and agricultural lands. They achieved such predominance in local Native American affairs as to enable their descendants to continue to exact economic tribute and/or social homage up to the present time.

Even though Toledo did not succeed in abolishing *curacas*, his reorganization of peasant Indian labor obligations did effectively weaken them. That reorganization fostered subsequent regionalism because Toledo designated inhabitants of specific territories to pay the tributary labor tax at specific mines. Thus he defined regions within which major exchanges of population and products occurred to the exclusion of other regions. Toledo perpetuated the preconquest principle of subjects laboring for the state, instead of introducing the European principle of their paying cash taxes. Thus he established the most infamous feature of classic Spanish colonialism and its most deadly dimension, after Old World diseases, for the Peruvian Indians.

The most difficult duty of lower officials was always to mobilize laborers for the *mita*. The drafted laborers or *mitayos* faced such common forms of labor as the *mita de plaza*, or courvée labor, and the *mita de obraje*, or work in the textile mills, with much less fear than the deadly *mita de minas*. The *mita de plaza* involved general weekly service in Spanish towns—construction, maintenance, street cleaning, and cobbling. Frequent earthquakes that destroyed urban buildings brought additional *mita de plaza* levies.

Work in the textile mills demanded regularized labor under factory conditions for work days beginning at 7 A.M. and ending at 6 P.M. The *obrajes* met fixed and rigid production schedules aimed at fulfilling the tribute and profit-seeking demands of the *encomenderos*. In pursuit of these goals, each of the dozens of mills in the *corregimientos* assigned adults and children alike to spin wool, card, dye, and weave on the new Spanish upright looms quickly introduced to Indian weavers who also used their traditional belt-looms. The mills often possessed dormitory and living arrangements, including a jail for recalcitrant workers. Children from nine to sixteen years of age worked on the premise that they needed to learn a useful trade. Growing pastoral estates, often owned by *encomenderos* or other Spaniards with official positions, produced wool for the mills. In addition to cloth, these turned out cordage, sacks, blankets, gun fuses for the blunderbusses in use, and shoes and leather goods.

A wide variety of persons and institutions owned and operated these enterprises. In theory, all produced goods to meet tribute requirements. *Encomenderos, curacas,* parish priests, bishops, judges, Jesuits, Mercedarians, and Dominicans operated *obrajes.* Some ran benign mill regimes. Others waxed ruthless in pursuit of personal and corporate profit. Being poorly paid by customary standards, provincial officials of all sorts anticipated recuperating salary deficits with what they could skim off such operations. Kickbacks and under-the-table arrangements became the norm.

Even before Philip II began to sell colonial offices, his father Emperor Charles V had already instituted a high income tax of 50 percent, the *media anata,* on the salaries of viceregal employees. That rate of taxation rather clearly implied an underlying assumption that royal appointees acquired sufficient profit beyond salary for the levy to be tolerable. In sum, the whole colonial system inspired graft on a huge scale that the rather puritanical Inca nobles initially must have found unimaginable. All the graft skimmed from every colonial office ultimately came from the sweat, tears, and bleeding fingers of Indians.

The *coup de grâce* for hundreds of Native American communities throughout the Sierra came not from the local forms of *mita,* but from work in the mines under the *mita de minas.* This required individuals to spend long periods away from their homelands and literally worked thousands of Indians to death. By the time Pedro de la Gasca gained control of Peru for the crown, the mine draft was too firmly established for his later pious prohibitions to take effect. Spanish entrepreneurs continued the horrors of Potosí where working conditions killed two of every three Indians forced to work the deposits. The Spaniards went on chaining groups of *mitayos* together to prevent their escaping en route to Potosí.

Viceroy Francisco de Toledo's regulation of the *mita de minas* endeavored to reform the truly horrendous Spanish abuse and wastage of Native American peasants. Toledo's ordinances set a general pattern and rules for most of the colonial period until Bourbon representatives undertook new reforms near the end of the eighteenth century. Toledo authorized royal officials to draft for mine labor from one-fifth to one-seventh of the *hatanrunas*, men aged eighteen to fifty years. Those legally drafted had to perform some task at the mines for a year. According to Toledo's ordinances, they were not to be required to work more than about 620 kilometers from their residences or to be worked "unreasonably." The Spaniards benefiting from the labor draft were to pay *mitayos* the local wage and the cost of their travel.

In practice, those rules Toledo promulgated to protect the *mitayos* were almost totally ignored or were bent to serve the special interests of greedy mine owners and operators. To them what mattered most was that Toledo legalized the forced draft of Indian labor, for in one respect, Spanish miners resembled Spanish *encomenderos:* both personally abhorred manual labor; Spanish "miners" owned ore veins, but Native Americans worked them.

The continual application of Toledo's relatively well-intentioned rules to Sierra life and labor had disastrous consequences for the Indian population. The *mita de minas* compounded the lethal effects of epidemics, famines, and other calamities killing Native Americans. The fact was recognized at the time, yet little was done to change or halt the pernicious effects that were clear to most observers.

The two most infamous examples of the mine draft are those that furnished the Spanish monarchy with its greatest Peruvian revenues. Potosí came first, but its silver production boomed after 1564 when Spaniards began to exploit the Santa Bárbara mercury ore deposits at Huancavelica in central Peru. These mines made the viceroyalty the richest and most important area in South America for two centuries. Toledo ordered the Santa Bárbara mine leased to a miners' guild. Royal officials contracted with members of the guild to produce mercury. A governor with extraordinary authority supervised both mines. Each year the regime established by Toledo assigned 1,800 *mitayos* to work at Huancavelica and 13,500 at Potosí.

To what degree the *mita de minas* influenced the Indian population trend can only be estimated, but the effect must have been great. If the labor quotas were adhered to at all closely, about three million men worked in these two mines alone over a 200-year period. The "mine of death" of Santa Bárbara drew its forced labor from a wide area in the central Andes from what are now Junín, Lima, Huancavelica, Ayacucho, Apurimac, and Cuzco Departments. South of this recruitment area, Indians went to work at Potosí, with those traveling from Cuzco walking 1,000 kilometers, a trip of several months. This assignment usually resulted in the migration of the entire household of the *mitayo,* including animals, abandonment of village lands or their reassignment to others, and a sojourn of a minimum of one year at the mine. Although the obligation legally required only about one-half year's work, the fact was that production requirements imposed by management forced a man to employ helpers, often his wife and children, to meet them, or go into debt, or both. Rarely could a worker discharge his obligation in one year's time.

Once at Potosí, the peasant found that he worked in the most primitive and dangerous conditions. Mechanical and other technological devices used in Europe at the time lightened no labors at Potosí. Brute force extracted ore from ever-deepening shafts. Rather than install proper and convenient entrances and exits to the shafts, mine owners determined that they could save time and obtain greater production by having *mitayos* remain in the mine. So for five straight days miners ate, slept, rested, and worked in the shafts. The life span of an Indian miner under such conditions was equivalent to about three years.

As the total Native American population declined, the labor allocations became progressively more difficult to fill, so conniving colonial authorities accelerated *mita* turns from the legal seven-year intervals to shorter and more frequent ones. The cumulative effect over time was devastating to Indian communities, producing a chain of consequences of utmost importance in altering the character of colonial society.

Toledo's forced labor decrees left Indians only a choice between evils. One choice meant living as tributaries of the crown. Those who did so paid their tribute in the mines such as Huancavelica or Potosí, a form of killing labor that demanded long travel and probable death. Those making this choice who survived often obtained royal recognition of their communal land and water rights. They closed ranks against outsiders to become a more socially isolated and corporate community.

Recognizing the lethalness of the *mita de minas,* many Indians chose logical ways to escape its deadly burden. The *mita de minas* was levied only upon the natives of a particular locality and not upon outsiders. Thus leaving one's *terruño,* or native land, became an important technique for escaping the labor exaction. Colonial policy produced massive population shifts with profound social and economic consequences.

The Indian migrant found few options open. Many who moved attached themselves to powerful Spanish or *curaca* households in the cities and towns to exempt themselves from the *mita* through permanent servitude. Others found urban refuge as artisans or in service occupations. The disease mortality rate in coastal settlements ran very high, but labor there was far less exacting than in the hot shafts of Potosí or the near certainty of mercury poisoning at Santa Bárbara.

Indians unable to reach or stay in a town could remain independent but tribute-paying peasants, or opt for survival in serfdom on the growing number of estates controlled by avaricious, newly landed aristocrats. Many Indians chose to strengthen the already prevalent pattern of patron-client socioeconomic relationship. The new landlords purchased lands, sometimes directly from the crown and at times from *encomendero* descendants short of cash. They also seized lands of depopulated Indian settlements and employed devious means to acquire Native American property wherever possible. Such encroachments on aboriginal lands continued throughout the colonial and even during the republican period until 1969.

In spite of such pressure upon Indian communities, many managed to survive into the present century. Sheer geographic remoteness of many hamlets tucked away in high altitude valleys well removed from the seats of colonial officialdom and its exploitative interests enabled some Native Americans simply to "lie low" and be ignored. Various monarchs granted titles to hundreds of Indian communities, which thus preserved their land bases. These titles augmented the power of the local Indian officials established by Toledo's 1575 ordinance and bolstered the integrity of many communities.

The expansion of Christendom failed to keep pace with the rapid geographic explosion of New World conquest society. Although the conquerors destroyed Inca state religion when they took Cuzco and terminated such things as the Pachacamác pilgrimage, Roman Catholic priests proved to be slow to take up the monumental task of truly converting the native population. As one viceroy put the state of affairs in 1583, "this land was founded upon greed and vested interest and this is what they always worship." Not until after Toledo's civil and economic reforms did a new Archbishop of Lima, Toribio de Mogrovejo, undertake parallel reforms of ecclesiastical life on the king's direct orders in 1581.

The general state of the Peruvian Roman Catholic church had reached such pass that Archbishop Mogrovejo subsequently achieved sainthood, in part because of his quarter-century long struggle to reform the church. Significantly, three of his Peruvian contemporaries also achieved sainthood for their exemplary acts during this period of reform. Two are well known internationally: St. Martín of Porres and St. Rose of Lima. Of the other two, St. Francis Solano and St. Toribio Mogrovejo, only the latter sainted archbishop retains much popularity in Peru today.

Saint Rose and Saint Martín both were born and lived in Peru's primary city, Lima. Born in 1586 soon after Archbishop Mogrovejo initiated basic reforms in the church, Rose followed what might be labeled a classic if agonized path to sainthood. This beautiful Creole chose the holy life-style of earlier Spanish women and retreated from secular life into monastic hideaways. Rose distinguished herself by her persistence in the face of resistance from female superiors of organized convents in the Lima of her day. She eventually became a *beata* of Saint Dominic, spending long periods as a recluse. She often beat herself with a chain, fasted, or ate potatoes prepared with bitter herbs.

Rose of Lima was profoundly influenced by the story of St. Catherine of Sienna, who had by divine grace received a wedding ring from Christ, which remained invisible to everyone but her. Rose's vision had Christ say: "Rose of my heart, be my wife." She persuaded her relatives to have a ring made for her bearing those words in Spanish. Her confessor placed it on her finger on March 16, 1617. She died on August 24th of that year at the age of thirty-one.

Born in 1579, Martín's rise to sainthood was entirely different. As Rose was to provide many Creoles with an intercessor, Martín filled a similar role for Lima's Mulattos and Blacks, the servants and slaves who constituted about half of the capital's population. Born poor, Martín was a Mulatto who became a lay brother in a Dominican religious institution in his native Lima. He accepted whatever menial tasks he was assigned by the socially superior priests; as a nurse in the monastery infirmary he became famous for healing the sick and miraculously making plants grow. The "priest of the poor," Martín interceded for them, wrangling funds and favors from the wealthy and powerful, including the viceroy, to support his charities, among them the rescue and education of orphans abandoned in the city.

When Martín died in 1639, he was a figure of tremendous appeal for a mass of oppressed, low-born Peruvians resigned to little if any upward social mobility during this life while hopeful that things would improve in the hereafter. Thus Martín found a sympathetic legion of devotees in Peru, and devotion to him spread steadily beyond Peru, leading to his belated beatification in 1837. Finally, when the Roman Catholic hierarchy intensively reexamined its position relative to the Black populations in both Africa and the New World, Pope John XXIII canonized Martín of Porres in 1962. That international popular devotion to Martín had outstripped official recognition until the "people's Pope" acted, highlights the populist nature of the social values Martín symbolizes.

Most important of the quartet of Peruvian saints in accelerating the rate of cultural change among Native Americans, Archibishop Toribio Mogrovejo wielded the most power within the church during his lifetime. Born in 1538, he was the son of a city councilman in Mayorga in León, and a cousin of Juan Mogrovejo, one of the men of Cajamarca. Toribio graduated from Salamanca in religion and law, and had served as Inquisitor of Granada, before he arrived in Lima in 1581.

Unlike his predecessors, this energetic cleric repeatedly visited remote congregations in the vast archdiocese, dying during a final visitation at Zaña on the north coast in 1606. Before his death, Toribio had already established a firm reputation as a miracle-maker. Archbishop Mogrovejo's greatest miracle was reforming the greedy Peruvian clergy and setting in motion the conversion of Native Americans to Christianity.

When Mogrovejo landed, he carried the king's explicit orders to hold an archdiocesan church council, so he convened the bishops of his jurisdiction on August 15, 1582. After much tribulation the council carried out in the religious sphere what Viceroy Toledo had accomplished in civil affairs, in the judgment of Peruvian Jesuit historian Rubén Vargas Ugarte. Among its acts, the council of 1582-83 allocated 3 percent of the income received by endowed clerics and councils to finance a seminary, which Archbishop Mogrovejo was finally able to start in 1591.

Meanwhile, during his time-consuming, physically exhausting inspections of his archdiocese, Toribio confirmed tens of thousands of new Catholics and admonished priests to work diligently to convert the Indians and to learn to speak the native languages. Archbishop Mogrovejo's pastoral visits to his archdiocese resembled Viceroy Toledo's inspection of Andean provinces. This endeared the archbishop to his Christian flock, but set an example few of his successors emulated. Indeed, the church establishment disliked Mogrovejo almost as much as the common people, especially the Native Americans, adored him. According to popular belief, he cured the sick at his touch, besides bringing sweet water from barren rocks. Today his name, Toribio, is commonly still given to peasant children in northern Peru where his impact was great.

Most priests remained much less sympathetic to the Indians than did their archbishop. A priest's half-brother who assisted many other clerics, chronicler Felipe Guamán Poma, left graphic clues as to what went on during the great period of conversions in his devastating sketches of hypocritical clergymen. He showed them whipping Indians in parish textile mills, accepting bribes, fighting amongst themselves, fathering dozens of illegitimate Mestizo children, gambling, and conniving with other exploiters of Native Americans, *curacas, encomenderos, corregidores,* and their servants. Guamán Poma concluded harshly that "Actually, the poor Indians are disappearing in this kingdom because of the priests."

Five years later, Antonio Vázquez de Espinosa, himself a priest, visited Lima. He described the Dominican convent there as "sumptuous," hung with paintings by a famous Seville artist, gilt walls in the three naves of the temple, sacristy treasures worth over 300,000 ducats, and over 250 friars. The Franciscan convent housed over 200 friars; their church also was gilt despite their vows of poverty. The Augustinians had a merely "splendid" convent for 150 friars "in the best part of the city" with a "magnificent" temple. The Mercedarians were just finishing their church when Vázquez visited Lima, but he characterized its main chapel as the best among all the convents. He found over 200 Jesuits in the city.

These urban and provincial extremes in the Peruvian church existed within a decade of the death of the reforming archbishop. With hundreds of priests in richly endowed convents in viceregal Lima, one can only imagine how difficult Mogrovejo must have found it to stir the comfort-loving priests to grapple with the difficult chores of learning Indian languages and teaching Christian doctrines to uncooperative heathens. If provincial priests exploited their Indian charges as severely as Guamán Poma described their doing at the end of Santo Toribio's archepiscopate, how much worse they evidently treated them earlier!

A major mechanism of colonial expansion of the great tradition of Roman Catholicism in Peru was the development and spread of localized fusions of Hispanic and aboriginal beliefs and practices. Religion as practiced in the valleys, towns, and hamlets as opposed to the priestly formality in Lima, Arequipa, Trujillo, and other centers of Hispanic hierarchical influence, reflected the immediate concerns and predilections of people who were not living at the center of the national society. To a great extent what the provincial people did mirrored what general colonial policy and interpretation called for. On the other hand, most people had no access to the sites of major ritual activity, such as the resplendent cathedrals and churches of the cities. Indeed, thousands of rural settlements seldom saw clergymen, so their residents followed local lay religious leaders who developed their own versions of what they perceived as Christian practice.

Conquest culture also saw active attempts by conquistadors to transplant the customs of their home districts in Spain. The saints of Andalucia, Extremadura, and Castille found new homes: the Virgin of Guadalupe, Virgin de los Remedios, Our Lady of Mt. Carmel, St. John, St. James Major, and many others. Particularly important in Peruvian Christianity became veneration of the cross and crucifix on May 3d in celebration of the Invention of the Holy Cross, and September 14th for the Exaltation of the Holy Cross. Even today, in hundreds of places devotees carry in elaborate May 3d processions the crucifixes known as *Taita Mayo* ("Father May"). Likewise, on September 14th local religious activists in many settlements still take down the often massive hilltop crosses, carry them to the local chapel for blessing, and then reerect them.

The miracles missionaries described and the miraculous acts of faith recorded in Peru itself served to heighten Peruvian anticipation of such events. The cultural, social, and physical stresses under which provincial peoples lived during the colonial era precipitated strong human needs to revitalize the spirit and sense of identity, both individual and communal.

These circumstances in community after community generated long-enduring local identification with particular miraculous events and experiences. A typical event took place in the village of Huaylas. A lone donkey carrying a great box arrived mysteriously at the church door. After a time, people grew curious and opened the box to discover a striking painting of the Virgin of the Assumption. The bishop deemed it a miraculous occurrence and sent both village priest and painting to Rome where the Pope reportedly gave it his blessing, designating the Virgin as the new patroness of the town.

This continuing process personalized the saints and symbols of European Christianity and fitted them into local world views and contexts. Thus in many villages, a tree growing naturally in the form of the cross often inspired devout persons to drape sacerdotal sashes around the symbolic trunk and branches and even to etch the figure of Christ more clearly than it appeared in the tree's natural contours. Christian symbols would be seen in the natural configurations of rocks or mountains and so became syncretized with native religious symbols.

While most such events are minor and their festivals occupy only a few people, some have attained immense popularity and thrive as established cults with full approval from the church hierarchy. Many of these Peruvian additions to the Christian calendar relate specifically to the catastrophic earthquakes, tidal waves, and avalanches that have on the average of every ten years since 1533 smitten sections of the coast and the Sierra. These events have given rise to a large number of "disaster saints," fusing Christian and aboriginal concern with natural catastrophes.

In Cuzco, the earthquake of March 31, 1650, for example, demolished much of the colonial city and its churches. A crucifix survived and became a figure around which the population rallied and subsequently developed a strong sense of dependence, praying for the intercession of God to protect and secure them from the effects of tremors and quakes. The crucifix became known as "Our Lord of the Earthquakes" (*Nuestro Señor de los Temblores*) and was designated Cuzco's patron. Similarly, on the north coast at the heart of the old Chimú kingdom, the earthquake of February 14, 1619, gave greater meaning to the Virgin of Perpetual Help (*Virgen del Perpetuo Socorro*) in Huanchaco, a fishing village suburb of Trujillo. The annual procession of *"la del Huanchaquito"* has become a large-scale popular festival drawing hundreds of pilgrims.

Arequipa, located on the slopes of an active volcano and subject to frequent eruptions and quakes, named St. Genaro, the patron of volcanoes, as its patron saint following the eruption of Ubiñas volcano in 1600. After a disastrous earthquake in 1687, however, Genaro was replaced by St. Martha, who was considered more efficacious. Her procession still occurs on July 29th each year.

By far the most important of these holy figures is that of Our Lord of Miracles (*Nuestro Señor de los Milagros*). The popularity of this holy figure and its great festival parallels that of the preconquest Inca Pachacamác oracle and pilgrimage. In addition, the "Nazarene" as He is often called, was and continues to be the special subject of devotion and holds the same appeal for millions of Peruvian Blacks, Mulattos, and Mestizos as does St. Martín.

The largest probably and most popular cult in Peru today, that of Our Lord of Miracles, is a major cultural and spiritual legacy of colonial times. Colonial policy precluded Blacks and Indians from even entering the sumptuous parish churches and the cathedral of Lima. Largely converted to Christianity, many Angolan and other slaves sought to emulate the Spaniards by forming their own sodalities. They created a rustic chapel in one corner of a mule corral in an area of Lima first occupied by former residents of nearby Pachacamác. There, an unknown artist in 1651 painted a crucifixion scene on the chapel wall that survived a disastrous earthquake in 1655, even though the tremor brought the cathedral and churches of the city tumbling to earth.

The slaves called this miracle to the attention of other residents of the city. Before long, devotion to the New Lord of Miracles spread among members of the city's other ethnic groups. The clergy decided that God had indeed given a sign, and they quickly incorporated the crucifix into the formal ceremonial calendar of Lima. In 1671, Viceroy the Count of Lemos commissioned an artist to embellish the painting with background figures. Since then it has purportedly remained as it was.

October became the month for special annual devotion to Our Lord of Miracles. In addition, since 1655 devotees have frequently taken replicas of the painting on procession to quiet the shaking earth. The lay groups formed to care for the image and to carry the litter functioned to integrate the Black population of the city into its religious life. The major sodality to care for and bear the image was and is largely made up of Blacks and Mulattos. Today it is one of the most powerful lay organizations in Lima, owning apartment houses and other properties. Whether members of this sodality or not, devotees wear purple habits, dresses, capes, ties, or armbands each year during October, the "purple month." Pilgrimage has grown so large that hotel rooms in Lima become almost impossible to obtain during October, when central city activity is virtually paralyzed by processions of 200,000 persons.

Major earthquakes tumbled Roman Catholic churches to the ground in Peru in major cities forty-two times during the colonial era. The typical Peruvian temple has, consequently, been reconstructed at least two or three times. Today's elegant church buildings date, therefore, largely from the eighteenth or nineteenth century, or from even more recent refurbishings.

The nearly constant process of church rebuilding brought about significant artistic consequences. A distinctive Andean style of tower construction diffused widely to city churches, for example. Framed oil paintings on linen (or colonial cotton) sometimes survived earthquakes better than the walls where they hung and could often be rescued before walls collapsed. Frescoes and elaborate architectural plastering typically shattered during even a minor earth tremor. The colonial new rich recognized the snob value of oil paintings. Wealthy colonial patrons supported, therefore, the development of no less than three major circles of somber religious painters in the Peruvian viceroyalty. One emerged, as might be expected, in silver-rich Potosí. A second developed in the old Inca capital of Cuzco. The third arose in Quito. These represented the urban extreme, however; the vast majority of Peruvian churches were simple rural chapels built and maintained by local worshipers too poor to afford any but the cheapest adornments.

Not all the pilgrimage festivals important to Peruvian Christians originated in response to natural disasters: some stem from exemplary devotion. Some hereditary Indian *curacas* after their conversion deliberately fostered Native American devotion to Christian saints as a strategy for maintaining their control and rank over the peasant masses. Such appears to have been the origin of the devotion of the Virgin of the Candelaria at Copacabana. As Roman Catholic priests recount the events, Viceroy Toledo regarded the conversion of the dense Indian population in the Lake Titicaca region as having been forced and consequently of little value for controlling the population.

Alonso Viracocha Inca, governor of the *Aransayas,* founded a sodality at Copacabana to foster Indian conversion to Catholicism after a statue of the Virgin of the Candelaria was brought to Copacabana on February 2, 1583. The fame of the miracles attributed to this statue spread over the high plateau, stimulating a large regional pilgrimage still of great importance in southern Peru and northern Bolivia.

Another aspect of Peruvian conquest culture that took hold as Andean Native Americans converted to Christianity was that of the ritual kinship system of Roman Catholicism. Indeed, ritual kinship became a major colonial contribution to modern Peru. The multiple stresses of Mediterranean life—wars with infidels, natural disasters including earthquakes and volcanic eruptions, epidemic disease, and the frequent accidents of rural farm life—had long led to Catholic emphasis upon ritual kinship. Even though extended family ties remained very strong, disasters could and did repeatedly orphan children. The church insured that they would remain in its congregation by providing them with godparents responsible for rearing them within the church in the event that their parents could not or did not. The man (*padrino*) and woman (*madrina*) who agreed to become godparents (*padrinos*) of a godchild (*ahijado*) when it was baptized bore primary responsibility in this respect. On the Peninsula, parents typically strengthened social ties for their children within their extended families by recruiting godparents among their own prestigious kinsmen.

The very nature of Spanish colonialism both altered the godparenthood pattern (*padrinazgo*) of ritual kinship in colonies such as Peru and gave it even more importance in the conquest culture of the colonial New World than it had originally had on the Peninsula. The selective and relatively small-scale migration of Spaniards to Peru meant that colonial Spaniards could seldom select ritual kinsmen from their genetic kinsmen who remained in Spain. Consequently, colonial Spaniards necessarily turned to nonkinsmen for godparents far more frequently in the colonies than they had in Spain.

A concatenation of factors further fostered this pattern in Peru. The adventurous Spanish migrants to the colonies, forced to choose unrelated godparents, often did so with more than half an eye to insuring the future temporal as well as spiritual welfare of their children. In other words, Spaniards remained culturally oriented toward lineage as the fundamental extension of personality, even when their children were legally viewed as illegitimate offspring of an Indian mistress. They sought, therefore, godparents who were better off than themselves in power and/or wealth, hoping that such godparents would improve the social status and economic well-being of their godchildren.

Conquest society and its colonial sequel fostered a shift in emphasis from the godchild-godparent (*padrinazgo*) aspects of Roman Catholic ritual kinship to the parent-godparent (*compadrazgo*) aspect. In addition to establishing a fictive relationship between godchild and godparent, the Catholic sixteenth-century tradition also created strong bonds between the godparent and the parent. They became what Englishmen of the period called godsibs (*compadres*) recognizing a sacred bond established by church sanction. Godsibs (root of the English "gossip") spoke and acted respectfully toward one another and could be trusted more than other people in an extremely individualistic, atomistic society. Thus, through its religious function and authority the *compadrazgo* system both confirmed and secured new bonds of friendship and dependence between conquerors and later Spanish official and powerful colonial families that developed in the New World.

The church imposed doctrinal restraints on secular relations between godsibs like those between genetic brothers and sisters. Thus, in addition to whatever sensuous pleasure a Spaniard might gain from Indian mistresses, the children of these alliances allowed him to forge socially important ritual kinship ties with genetically unrelated peers and superiors, not only for his offspring through *padrinazgo* but for himself through *compadrazgo*. Those superiors who stood by baptismal fonts while priests christened their godchildren thus consolidated and even expanded their own social power. They became patrons who granted this favor to clients, exacting allegiance in return.

As Christianity spread among Peru's declining Indian population, observant Native Americans noted the social utility of ritual kinship in a conquest society. When the *curacas* converted, powerful Spaniards typically acted as their spiritual sponsors, and often allowed the new Christians to adopt their names. The ritual kinship relationship brought the native leaders quite explicitly under the protection of powerful clerics and *encomenderos*.

When *curacas* persuaded their followers to convert, they naturally acted as ritual sponsors or persuaded Spaniards to do so. Thus the conquest cultural pattern formed patron-client relationships across the ethnic barrier. As colonial policy promoted sale of European goods to Indians, the latter even found themselves caught up in patron-client relationships with the *corregidores* forcing merchandise on them. The ritual kinship system provided a ready vehicle for establishing patron-client ties that were exploitative yet reassuring and at times rewarding.

The Indian might have to sell his horticultural surplus and livestock to his godsib at less than market price, but there was no other "market." In turn, the merchant-official to some extent protected his Indian godsibs from other rapacious Spaniards or Mestizos and provided a form of credit in a cash-short economy to pay the head-tax. This was the sort of economic exploitation routinely practiced by Spanish *corregidores* and others in a hurry to make a fortune and return to Spain.

Colonial society developed several other variations on Mediterranean ritual kinship besides its expansion to reinforce patron-client relationships. The small number of Spaniards in Peru relative to the Indian masses meant that priests themselves acted as spiritual sponsors of new Christians more frequently than they had done in Spain. Expanding on the idea, the Andean peoples found more than a dozen occurrences during one's life cycle to acquire ritual kinsmen.

The dogmatic demand for godmothers when combined with the scarcity of Spanish women in Peru—especially Spanish women residing in or near the Indian districts—may have given a rather small number of truly devout Spanish women disproportionately great influence on colonial Catholicism among the Indians and Mestizos. The demographic situation of Spanish women had other consequences. Spanish women were concentrated as spouses of Peru's most powerful men, especially during the earlier colonial period when precedents and patterns were being set. The high social status of these few women encouraged them to play autocratic patroness roles before a lower-class Mestizo, Black, and Indian audience. This traditional female role also combined attributes such as pity and compassion that led these women to generate a characteristic pattern of periodic distributions of material charity to the poor. That pattern did not even begin to alter until the first groups of middle-class young women graduating from the Peruvian National School of Social Work founded in the 1930s began applying rationalistic values.

By 1613, colonial exploitation had already left its marks on the population. The eleventh man to claim the title as "Vice-King" was thirty-six years of age, having previously served King Philip III in Spain and Mexico in the same capacity. He was named the third Marqués of Montesclaros and had the proper high standing as a Peninsular nobleman. He presided over a lavish court in Lima, which was the center of social life on the South American continent. The city bulged with royal officials of every level and with holders of *encomiendas,* many of them descendants of the original grantees. Also on hand were wealthy merchants and financiers capitalizing on opportunities for great profits in the Lima trade created because Spain channeled through the city commerce with its South American possessions.

Such individuals operated at the highest social and political levels and left numerous documentary traces for the historian. There was, however, another more populous Lima at the opposite end of the social scale. That was the city of Indians, Blacks, Mestizos, other low-caste foreigners, and mixtures of these peoples. Indians were in theory assigned to an *encomendero* who collected tribute from them on behalf of the king. All were subject in theory to the detailed regulations set forth with regard to their rights and duties. Indians and their racial correlates could not, for example, dress like Spaniards of noble and high-class standing, such finery being the mark of gentlemen and their ladies. Moreover, they were denied the use of horses and the right to bear arms. Often their *encomenderos* required them to dress in a specified livery that indicated not only their tribute grouping, but also at times their occupational specialty. Such dress still survives, and today is considered a major index of "Indianness."

Yet information about the true condition of this population is scant, making very informative a census of the Indians of Lima taken in 1613 by a scribe, Miguel de Contreras, on the viceroy's order. Brief census descriptions indicate the patterns of dependency and patronage, the relation between urban residence and rural origin, the chiefs and *encomenderos*. Above all, the census fixes people of the Indian castes as possessions of the colonial elite. The bare details of life, simply translated from the census report, tell us much about life behind the upper-class scene—that is, in the slum alleyways of Lima. Typical entries read:

"In the house of don Gerónimo de Aliaga, an Indian girl, Inés, was found, 12 years old, who said she was a native of Huaraz, orphaned and who did not know who her *encomendero* or *cacique* was . . . and that she was brought up in said house of Aliaga.

"In the house of Dr. Alberto de Acuña, Judge, lives an Indian named don Juan Payco Chacaca, native he said of the town of Huaura of the *corregimiento* of Chancay of the *encomienda* of doña Elvira Verdugo, widow of Captain Sancho de Rivera, and his *cacique* is don Berbabé Caxa of the *Ayllo* of Begueta and of the *ayllo* Chacaca whose *cacique* is said don Juan who is 25 years old; married to an Indian named Leonor de Acuña, native of the town of Nazca and who does not know her *cacique* because she has been brought up in the house of said doña Elvira Verdugo since she was a nursing baby; and she is of the *encomienda* of don Pedro Gutierez de Mendoza, citizen of this city; she is 26 years old and they have three children. . . . This man is an embroiderer by trade and wears Spanish clothes and haircut and has always lived in the house of his *encomendera*.

"Field hand, married. . . . In the other house is another Indian

who calls himself Miguel Caruabilca, native of the town of Great
Huaylas, and his *cacique* is don Cristóbal Bilcarima, and the *encomendero don* Francisco de la Cueba. He has been in the city about
20 years and is a field hand 37 years old. He is married to Juana
Chumbi, native Indian of the town of Guamantanga, province of
Canta and her *cacique* is don Rodrigo Rupaychaya and *encomendero*
don Martín Pizarro; she is 36 years old and has no children. They
have as property these houses in which they live and two Black
slaves, one Esperanza and another Leonor.

"In the street that goes from that of Mr. Dr. Arías where Juana de
Montoya lives in the house of Captain Xacome de Quesada a woman
was found in his service who was branded on the forehead who said
she was named Francisca de Quesada, a native Indian of Portugal of
the town of Pigo and is a slave of her master . . . she is married
to a Mulatto slave of the same master . . ."

This census, although certainly incomplete because Contreras complained about absenteeism and was held up by a festival, is highly
rewarding. It shows ancient Lima not as a remote colonial outpost be-
fogged by its *garua,* but as a veritable crossroads of humanity. The
cosmopolitan population that filled the pages of the castes included
"Indians of China of Manila" (Philippinos or perhaps overseas Chinese in their second foreign land), the "Indians of Portuguese India"
and "Indians of Japan," and Native Americans from all parts of Peru,
Chile, Ecuador, Mexico, Panamá, and the Chiriguano tribe. With
them in every condition were Black men and women from Angola and
other African countries and tribes. A few were married to "Indians"
while still others apparently belonged to Indian masters.

The total population of Lima was 25,167. Of this number, Blacks
and Mulattos constituted almost 50 percent, and it is clear that the
viceregal capital remained largely slave and Black throughout the colonial period. Spaniards reportedly comprised about 47 percent of the
people recorded, with Indians and Mestizos making up the rest. The
fact that the latter were grossly underrepresented in the census indicates that many were already "passing" in order to avoid classification
as tribute-payers. Migration to the city also constituted an important
device by which Indians escaped the demands of provincial *caciques*

and *encomenderos* eager to press them into tribute-paying roles, and the *mita de minas*.

This migrant population reflected peculiar characteristics produced by colonial Peruvian conditions. Although 71 percent of the provincial migrants were under thirty years of age, few children were recorded. Several factors created that anomalous demographic situation. To begin with, this early seventeenth-century population suffered a very high infant mortality rate. The sex ratio stood at an abnormal 204 men to every 100 women. Only 40 percent of the adults seemed to be mated. Lower castes had a most unstable social life.

Sheer underenumeration, a persistent problem in all censuses, surely accounts in part for the reported dearth of youngsters. Contreras's remarks reveal that he had difficulty finding people and that many claimed ignorance of their masters, ages, and other matters. These urban Indians had already developed proven defenses against colonial bureaucracy, just as they had in rural areas against landlords and *encomenderos*. The main defense was ignorance, a familiar recourse for members of subordinate ethnic groups seeking to maintain some modicum of control over their affairs in an oppressive multiethnic colonial state.

In any event, once Viceroy Francisco de Toledo gave definitive form to basic secular institutions, the really outstanding feature of Spanish domination of Peru became its stability. True, the number of Christians increased after Archbishop Toribio de Mogrovejo reformed the conquest-culture church, and their quality improved after local saints appeared. True, new and old Christians either joined in devotion to disaster saints or turned anticlerical. True, Mestizo numbers grew rapidly while Indians continued to decline. Still, these changes occurred so slowly as to seem almost imperceptible, so that the patterns Toledo established characterized Peru in 1700, and many survive today.

Chapter 5 • Rebellion and Reform
Under the Bourbons

At the beginning of the eighteenth century, Spain experienced the trauma of a change in her ruling dynasty. The last Hapsburg to occupy the Spanish throne died in 1700. In 1701, a grandson of King Louis XIV of France succeeded to the Spanish throne. After a war over this succession, the House of Bourbon reigned until Napoleon Bonaparte marched through the Pyrenees and forced Charles IV to abdicate in 1808. French and Italian influences on Spain after 1701 replaced Austrian and Flemish ones.

The dynastic change brought with it some changes in the Spanish colonial policy on Peru. Beginning in 1704—the last Hapsburg viceroy died in 1705—the Bourbon monarchs appointed the first of seventeen viceroys they would name. The men they picked were of marked personal achievement far oftener than had been the selections of the Hapsburgs. Only 47 percent of the Bourbon viceroys had inherited titles, compared with 70 percent of the Hapsburg viceroys. This and similar Bourbon efforts to improve colonial administration often met with limited success, however, because by the eighteenth century the colonies moved with a momentum of their own.

That phenomenon may be noted in the characteristics of the viceroys themselves. No fewer than 71 percent of the Bourbon viceroys came to Lima through the royal bureaucracy, having been promoted from lesser New World posts. None came from service as viceroy of New Spain, however, as had often happened under the Hapsburg kings. By 1705, New Spain had surpassed Peru in wealth and importance, while Peru had become a problem.

The history of the famous Huancavelica mercury mine under Bourbon dominion demonstrated one of many ways in which colonial dynamics proved to be more powerful than royal policy. From the very beginning, private interests had vied with the crown for mercury proft. Corruption ran rampant, especially in the guilds managing production, and malfeasance became a permanent part of the system. Santa Bárbara's production vastly diminished over two centuries. The Almaden mercury mine on the Peninsula could deliver mercury to Lima at less cost than could Santa Bárbara. The mercury content of the Peruvian ore had fallen, and it was difficult to obtain *mitayos*. In 1758, in a final attempt to save the mine, the king appointed a stern, able, and astonishingly honest governor who proved beyond doubt the extent of the infamy.

Governor Antonio de Ulloa earned the hostility of Viveroy Manuel de Amat y Junient when he refused to pay the customary ten to twelve thousand peso a year kickback to the viceroy. Ulloa's appointment in 1758 also interrupted a traditional practice by which magistrates of the royal *audiencia* of Lima rotated the Huancavelica governorship among themselves, making each judge wealthy in his turn.

At the local Huancavelica level, Ulloa's attempt to enforce contracts and rules earned him the enmity of the establishment. By insisting upon social unity, Ulloa further outraged local "society" when he initiated the celebration of the coronation of King Charles III with a joint parade of Spanish troops, citizens, townsfolk, and Native Americans. Three years later, when Ulloa ordered Spanish troops to practice with Mestizo companies, they rejected the order. The viceroy supported the mutinous troops, of course. The new king failed to support Ulloa when he most needed royal backing. Bitterly disappointed, Ulloa resigned after six frustrating years of having struggled against the combined forces of Peruvian colonialism. It seemed evident to him that the regime lay virtually beyond reform or redemption. Subsequent Bourbon reorganizational attempts in 1784 to replace the decadent provincial administration of the *corregimientos* with intendants bore out his pessimism.

Still, it was the Santa Bárbara ore body itself that played the key role in Peru's downturn. The number of Native American deaths from mercury poisoning had always been in reverse proportion to the quality of the ore mined: the better the ore grade, the deadlier the mines. Thus those Indian laborers who opened the Huancavelica "mine of death" mined high-grade ore that was so poisonous that even the families of the miners felt the ill effects. As well, working conditions were so incredibly bad that Spanish officials admitted that the mine was a living hell. Viceroys testified indirectly to this fact by frequently commuting death sentences passed on Indians and assigning them instead to work in Santa Bárbara. When the ore grade declined, the health of the miners improved. From 1730 to 1760, a period after there was a large drop in mercury content, the population of Angaraes Province, a principal supplier of *mitayos* for the mercury mine, doubled. This rate of increase far exceeded the Peruvian pattern at that time and was the result of fewer deaths from mercury poisoning and minor improvements in working conditions. That this biological index of change occurred before Ulloa arrived at Huancavelica indicates the extent to which Peruvian social and ecological dynamics outweighed royal powers.

If standard sources of information about Peru's colonial population are to be believed, the number of Indians declined throughout most of the period of Spanish sovereignty. By 1792 viceregal officials could count only 608,894 Indians. Even taking into account undernumerated rural Native Americans, depopulation had been dramatic. A few scattered analyses of local population trends suggest, on the other hand, that Indian numbers reached their nadir sometime during the late sixteenth or early seventeenth century. If so, it took a long time for the survivors to build up large rural peasant populations again.

The Spanish and Mestizo population trend ran directly counter to the Indian one. Although they consistently said they intended to return to the Peninsula, many Spaniards remained in Peru after founding Creole or Mestizo families. The number of Spanish immigrants never changed its minority status. Thirty years before Independence, Peru contained only some 136,000 to 140,000 Peninsular and Creole Spaniards. By that time, the viceroyalty contained nearly twice as many Mestizos, 245,000. The long colonial process of miscegenation between Spaniards and Indians had produced the new Mestizo race— a major result of the post-Columbian exchange of genes, plants, animals, and germs. Colonial census figures show the Mestizo population of Peru as doubling every 26-year generation from conquest to the eve of Independence. Paradoxically, such a high rate of growth is typically associated today with the effects of modern medicine when first introduced in Third World countries. Furthermore, eyewitness accounts of infectious epidemics and endemic diseases provide evidence that it was not a change in the environment that led to the growth of the Mestizo population, because mortal dangers faced all Peruvians from birth to death from whatever cause. Thus, the very high rate of Mestizo population growth argues that the first generation and succeeding ones displayed truly remarkable hybrid vigor.

Mestizos also benefited, perhaps, from genetic resistance to smallpox, measles, and other Old World diseases, a resistance that Native Americans lacked. By the same token, the incorporation of African genes into the new gene pool may have introduced such characteristics as sickle-cell immunity to malaria—a significant survival factor in coastal valleys.

Peru imported slaves throughout colonial times. By the 1790s, over 41,000 free *castas*—the colonial term for persons of mixed ancestry— were enumerated in the viceroyalty whereas the number of slaves barely surpassed 40,000. In other words, Mulattos formed marital unions with various types of Mestizos, creating on the coast especially a Caucasoid-Amerind-Negroid hybrid. The Peninsular elite socially stigmatized such persons, arguing that they were cursed with the worst features of all three original groups in behavioral terms. They were, however, probably biologically blessed with the disease resistances of all three.

Despite a common belief that Negro slaves were imported principally to replace the dying Native American population for field work in the coastal valleys, no less than 44 percent of all slaves enumerated in Peru in 1792 lived in Lima Province. Granting that some of those slaves worked truck farms near the viceregal City of the Kings, most worked in Lima itself. The percentage of the population in other major cities that was Black and enslaved was insignificant at the end of the eighteenth century: almost 4 percent in Trujillo district, 3 percent in Arequipa, and only one-half of one percent in Cuzco. The social and economic base of the viceregal capital city continued to rest, in other words, on Black labor. In contrast, the official enumeration showed Arequipa with a greater Spanish population than Lima, 22,207 to 18,209. Arequipa contained the greatest concentration of Spaniards in Peru and they took tremendous pride in their "racial" purity.

Viceroy Francisco Gil de Taboada's 1792 census showed that only a small percentage of the total population was truly urban, and that most of that was Spanish or Black. The five most urban districts in the viceroyalty were Lima, Cuzco, Arequipa, Trujillo, and Huamanga (Ayacucho). Together they contained only 16 percent of the enumerated population of just over one million persons, and even within these districts were nonurban areas.

The colonial period population growth of Lima alone seemed impressive compared with that of other cities. The census of 1796 showed that Lima had a population of 52,627, which constituted 5.8 percent of the total population of Peru. It had taken 182 years for the population to double since 1614, indicating the slow pace of growth. Arequipa, the second largest city, contained 36,431 persons or 3.5 percent of the total. Cuzco's 24,842 inhabitants comprised only 2.2 percent of the total, while Trujillo mustered 11,908 residents or 1 percent of all Peruvians. Peru was about 12.5 percent urban by the mid-1790s.

Colonial Lima, with its Callao port, became the same type of primate city that Alexandria, London, Manila, Djakarta, Bombay, Bangkok, and Cape Town have been with respect to their interior hinterlands in parallel colonial and mercantile situations. When Pizarro founded the City of the Kings in 1535, he insured that Peruvian society ever after would differ from Inca imperial society. The Incas made their capital at Cuzco the conceptual umbilicus of the universe. Lima turned colonial Peruvian eyes away from the Andes toward Spain for social, economic, and political leadership and toward the Christian holy places for religious inspiration. The Lima-Callao area became the main center of European cultural behavior, social forms, and artifacts imported to Peru. Many Creoles nonetheless preferred the clear, warm mountain air of Arequipa to the chilly *garua* of Lima. Others chose to settle in the highlands above mosquito range, which were healthier areas than Lima and Callao, the two latter marked by malaria and yellow fever epidemics, typhoid, and other fevers frequently renewed by shipboard transmission.

As viceregal capital, Lima automatically possessed an institutional complexity greater than that of any other municipality in Peru. In 1779 the professor of geography and mathematics at the University of San Marcos, Cosme Bueno, inventoried the principal cities of the realm. He found that Lima was endowed with 106 public and ecclesiastical offices and public facilities, while Arequipa had only eighteen, Cuzco fifteen, and Trujillo nine. Lima held, in other words, 58 percent of the kingdom's social and political institutions, a realistic measure of its degree of privilege and dominance over the provinces.

The colonial primacy of Lima was further strengthened as a consequence of royal concentration of power in the viceroy and his court, which replicated that in Madrid. The viceregal court included the chief representatives of all other colonial institutions, such as the *audiencia* and the church. The Peninsular and maritime orientation of such royal representatives further strengthened Lima. Such Spaniards literally turned their backs on the Peruvian provinces, with which they dealt only in the most perfunctory ways or in times of crisis. Their thoughts frequently dwelt on Spain; their eyes watched for the ships calling at Callao.

In a colonial system led by Spaniards whose loyalties and interests lay overseas, provincial cities could never become more than lesser versions of Lima. So poorly were they regarded that a common sentence passed on Spaniards and even those members of the Mestizo population provoking official displeasure or charged with committing crimes might be exile five or fifty leagues from Lima for terms of months to years. Ica, Pisco, Huánuco, and Huancavelica often received exiles from the viceregal capital, although those convicted of serious offenses were usually shipped to that far outpost, Chile.

Only exceptional viceroys or official inspectors ever visited the provinces for anything save emergencies. The great Francisco de Toledo (1569-81) actually preferred life in the Sierra to that of the capital, but recognized colonial geopolitical reality. Later, the Count of Lemos, Pedro Fernandez de Castro (1667-72) journeyed to southern Peru while putting down a rebellion in Puno, leaving his wife in Lima for five months as acting vicereine. Most viceroys, in contrast, spent their entire terms in Peru without traveling more than a few leagues from the City of the Kings. The Bourbon viceroys maintained the pattern established by the Hapsburg representatives and even reinforced it by further improving the physical appearance and conveniences of Lima. Even since independence, the colonial pattern has characterized Lima officialdom and Peru's upper classes. Both the bureaucracy and the social elites of modern Peru continue to denigrate the provincial residents, their needs, and their culture. Thus sociopolitical centralization of the Spaniards in Lima played a key role in fostering regionalism in the provinces, where the principal population centers of Arequipa, Cuzco, and Trujillo came by late Bourbon times to regard Lima as an adversary.

Throughout colonial times, the Roman Catholic clergy continued to prefer the low-altitude coastal valleys to the rigors of the Sierra. The Spaniards in Arequipa evidently enjoyed family life, commerce, and recreation on the sunny slopes of *El Misti* volcano, while many persons in foggy, multiethnic Lima retreated into convents. By the end of the eighteenth century, the capital city contained more clerics by far than any other major center, no less than 15 percent of all those counted in 1796, followed by Trujillo on the north coast with 7 percent. Monks and nuns lived in even greater urban concentrations, with a majority of all nuns, 55 percent, in Lima; Arequipa had 15.5 percent, Trujillo 12.4 percent, and Cuzco only 6.3 percent. Inasmuch as the clergy carried on nearly all formal education in the viceroyalty, schools inevitably followed the concentration of clerics in Lima. This generated "educational migration," which has characterized Peru ever since.

Clerics and royal officials significantly ritualized life in Lima and even in other Peruvian cities. The viceregal bureaucrats and church prelates dominated social activity. Masses, processions, *autos-de-fé*, and the arrivals and departures of ships constituted the most frequent public events taking place in Lima's Plaza de Armas, the great churches, and the Callao roadstead. For such occasions, officials paraded in full finery with badges of rank and office and were often treated to fireworks or bullfights. The streets of Lima presented a striking contrast to this display. Although some streets were cobbled, most were dirt, and all were littered with refuse.

The populace frequently cringed in fear of impending disasters. Great earthquakes periodically visited enormous destruction upon one and all. The largely wattle-and-daub housing of the city often went up in flames from kitchen mishaps of slaves and servants. Reading diaries of the times, one is also surprised by the frequent references to murders and other violent acts that apparently occurred at all levels of the society.

Residents also awaited with anxiety the moves of British, French, and Dutch pirates who sometimes lurked offshore to ambush treasure fleets or attack coastal settlements. To protect Lima from such attacks, the Hapsburg Viceroy the Duque de la Palata constructed, beginning in 1685, an immense defensive wall with thirty-four bulwarks around the city. Ships brought not only immigrants and officials, cargo and news, but also seaborne dangers. Every craft that tied up at Callao threatened to renew the cycles of smallpox, influenza, plague, or yellow fever to add to endemic gastrointestinal infections that killed half of the newborn and many adults annually.

Because of the continued need for rebuilding in the wake of fires and earthquakes, the capital usually teemed with construction activity. This pattern greatly aided the thirty-first viceroy, Manuel Amat y Junient, in changing the physical face of Lima. Ruling the kingdom for fifteen years in one of the colonial era's longest reigns, Amat began to give Lima physical and social characteristics that have endured until today. When he arrived in Peru in 1761, Lima was still recovering from the disastrous 1746 earthquake, and Amat introduced some European innovations in urban technology into the rebuilding process. He had public lighting installed on the main streets, permanently altering the character of Lima's daily routine by lengthening the evening hours of recreation outside the home. Amat stimulated the construction of Lima's first cockpit in 1765, and three years later ordered the Plaza de Acho bullring erected. The populace was already addicted to the Spanish tradition of bullfighting, first performed in Lima in 1541 by no less a figure than Francisco Pizarro. The custom in Lima as elsewhere prior to Amat's time, however, was to stage the fight in the Plaza de Armas. For that reason, few embellishments were to be found in the central squares of Lima and many other cities until bullrings were built. Later Amat refurbished the parks of the city, and he even built a promenade to amuse his mistress in Rímac *barrio,* just outside the city walls. Encouraging Lima's most popular devotion, Amat directed the construction of a church for the painting of the Lord of Miracles. He reportedly even worked as a carpenter on the project.

Every improvement Amat made in Lima in emulation of King Charles III's urban improvements in Spain served to make the primate city even more attractive to both overseas and domestic migrants. Simultaneously, Amat contributed mightily to Peruvian centralization by significantly widening the gap in elegance between Lima and the provincial cities.

Coupled with the events of Amat's reign came an intensification of Creole intellectualism, marked by the appearance of a new periodical, the *Gaceta de Lima,* and the growing activity of literary circles. Bookstores did a brisk business. With the cafes, they constituted favorite elite meeting places along the newly lighted streets. Amat sponsored and then guided through considerable reforms of the ancient Uni-

versity of San Marcos. After Charles III expelled the Jesuits from his
dominions in 1767, the viceroy successfully redeveloped its curriculum.
With royal approval, Amat established a university library using books
left by departing Jesuits. He revitalized the examination system, the
selection of professors, and then election of the rector, who became for
the first time a full-time, paid administrator. The musical comedy
theater enjoyed great popularity, and cafes filled with growing numbers of affluent middle- and upper-class Creoles, Peninsulars, and even
Mestizos.

Indeed, the popular heroine of the Lima stage at the time was
Micaela Villegas, known in history and opera as the vivacious "Pericholi." Amat proceeded to enliven Lima's social life shortly after his
arrival by beginning a long-lasting affair with the Mestizo actress, provoking scandal and delight in Lima circles.

The Creole spirit of Lima, with its own subculture and style that
had matured through the years when Lima dominated not only Peru
but all South America, shone forth. For many persons, the *Pericholi*
represented the "perfect *criolla*"—bright, coquettish, and *viva* or ready
to take quick advantage of her opportunities. Thus, a Mestizo came to
personify the first well-defined Creole behavior-type, and this type has
continued to distinguish Lima's culture.

By Amat's time, the social and cultural amalgam revealed in the
1613 Lima census had evolved into an established lower class whose
social roles were thoroughly stereotyped. Popular opinion designated
black slaves and freemen in particular as exponents of a "light-
hearted" way of life that featured its own style of music, forerunner of
the *marinera* later identified as a discreet national style. Black cooks
were already preparing their special *"criollo"* cuisine, which to this
day is much sought after and preferred in Lima. Capital city subculture stereotyped occupational roles: Mestizo street vendors, charcoal
sellers, and lamplighters, Black servants and slaves shielding clergymen
with umbrellas, and so forth. In this milieu, the Sierra Indian felt
foreign and uncomfortable—a "rube among city slickers"—lacking the
urbane social graces and styles.

Thus colonial social hierarchy generated a coastal and especially

Lima Creole subculture. Servants and slaves created a distinctively Peruvian pattern under the noses of Spaniards too preoccupied with the Peninsula to worry about cultural process in Lima, if they were even aware of it.

Some freedom of inquiry and expression for Peruvian Creoles and Mestizos emerged only late in the colonial era, through the voices of José Baquíjano, Hipólito Unánue, and others in the newspaper founded in 1791, the *Mercurio Peruano*. The concerns expressed in its columns contained their own provinciality. While their words spoke of the Indians and the abuses of the colonial system, the authors really continued to be occupied with expanding the power and privileges of the Creole urban classes. The strong, vocal, self-styled "liberal" intellectual establishment that emerged at the end of the last colonial century remained intimately involved with the direction of Peruvian governance for the next two generations. Their actions however served elitist Creole interests rather than broad, popular goals.

While the late Bourbon viceroys increased sociopolitical and economic centralization in Lima, Indians in various provinces provided abundant evidence of their dissatisfaction with colonial conditions. The defeat of the Neo-Inca state by Viceroy Toledo's forces in 1572 ended organized Indian military resistance to Spanish political control of Peru. Only later in the long colonial period did parts of the Sierra population rise up in arms. Typically small in scale, such uprisings involved at most a few thousand utterly frustrated peasants striking out at the nearest colonial targets. Spanish authorities usually found such outbursts easy to put down, partly because of their geographic and temporal isolation one from another.

Still, Spanish fears, perhaps fed by guilt, led to rumors in Lima in 1666 that Indians planned to burn the city. Authorities mobilized troops, but found no real evidence although they had eight Native Americans hanged. Again in 1675, a capital city scare and suspicion of British agents who had supposedly gained Indian allies led to the hangings of three Indians. The twentieth-century fear psychosis that Sierra migrants to the shanty-towns around Lima would rise some dark night to slaughter members of the urban elite in their beds evidently had already become established by the latter half of the seventeenth century.

The known rate of serious, spontaneous, violent Indian protest against colonial abuses accelerated during the Bourbon period of sovereignty. That could be taken as evidence that Indian life was improving, in view of historic analyses of social revolutions showing them to occur when the socioeconomic situation is being ameliorated. In 1737, a *cacique* named Ignacio Torote in the Pangoa area of the upper rain forest led his Indian followers in armed campaign against Christian missionaries. He preached a holy war of extermination of those emissaries of Western civilization and maintained some kind of tribal force hostile to colonial rule on the rain forest frontier.

One notable Mestizo leader of a Native American millenarian peasant movement, Juan Santos Atahuallpa, for various reasons failed to gain the attention that the later Mestizo rebels Mateo García Pumacahua and José Gabriel Condorcanqui received. Juan Santos was a man of exceptional experience for his place and time. Born about 1710, he served as an acolyte for the Jesuits in Cuzco. He learned Spanish and Latin in addition to his native Quechua. As a young man, he had the opportunity to travel to Spain, Africa, and possibly England, as the servant of a Jesuit, returning to Cuzco before 1740.

Then, Juan Santos suddenly left Cuzco in 1742 and proclaimed himself the direct descendant of Atahuallpa, whose name he appropriated. Santos and some of his family moved into the high jungle area in Central Peru where the Franciscan missionaries active among the Campa, Shipibo, and other tribal groups of the area expressed alarm upon his advance. Soon Santos Atahuallpa had indeed successfully gathered a revolutionary force of converted Indians and frontier Mestizos, driving out the missionaries, and taking over a large region. His intent was to recapture all Peru, throw out the whites and their Black slaves, and reestablish the Native American realm. Wearing Indian clothing and grooming himself in aboriginal style, Santos Atahuallpa carried a crucifix and preached his own version of the Christian scriptures.

His followers considered Santos Atahuallpa divine, and they faithfully fought off numerous attempts by the viceroy to retake the area. While Santos Atahuallpa never succeeded in moving his revolution-millenarian movement into the Sierra, he nonetheless remained free until his death in 1756.

Born of the cultural and social conflicts that engulfed the Andean peoples, Juan Santos Atahuallpa's movement exhibited a powerful strain of nativism with which the culturally Hispanic Mestizos and Creoles could muster little sympathy. His jungle allies were the feared and despised tribal peoples collectively and derogatorily called "chunchos" by the rest of Peruvian society. The movement resembled latter-day "guerrillas" in its political strategy, but it lacked their urban intellectual connections. Santos Atahuallpa initiated a millenarian movement that achieved striking practical success, even though it was limited and temporary.

The Indian condition in Peru continued to deteriorate under the legal extortions of corregidores. Resentments roused by the repartimiento, which forced Indians to purchase inferior goods at inflated prices, set off in 1776 a wave of violent protests. Viceregal regular troops easily defeated 2,000 rebels in Arequipa who included members of the colonial militia organized during the Seven Years' War. Royal officials nipped in the bud a planned Cuzco revolt by hanging two leaders. Yet insurrectionists assassinated hated corregidores and other colonial officials in various central Peruvian provinces. In Huánuco, for example, Indian violence continued for several years under Mestizo leadership, driving out the corregidor in 1777 and preventing tribute collection. The preponderance of firearms in the hands of the Spaniards and the royalist Creoles and Mestizos, however, relegated such provincial violence by Native Americans "armed" with slings and clubs into the category of isolated protests.

The enlightened Spanish monarch Charles III had already acted early in 1776 to find out why Peruvian revenues were falling and social unrest rising. Following his earlier successful policy of sending special inspectors clothed with extraordinary royal powers to New World colonies, Charles appointed José Antonio de Areche as inspector of Peru. While many inspectors successfully carried out significant reforms on the scene, Areche's appointment backfired. Reaching Peru in 1777, he entered into a contest for power with the viceroys.

In 1779 Inspector Areche imposed a new "voluntary contribution" on the non-Indian colored castes to help support the colonial militia. A registration of potential contributors, termed a "census," roused bitter resentment among Mestizos, Mulattos, free Blacks and 'all other free castes except Indians. They saw themselves being treated like the subordinate and despised Native Americans by crown tax policy and rebelled in at least a dozen cities.

When, for example, Areche's representative met with colonial militia leaders of non-Indian colored castes in Lambayeque to arrange their registration, the Black leaders wrote a protest petition to the viceroy. The Lambayeque Blacks kept their militia posts through viceregal inaction, and thus provided a model for other colonials seeking to inhibit official taxing power.

Whatever the specific combination of resentment over the *repartimiento* and outrage over the new "contribution" exacted from Mestizos that may have motivated him, José Gabriel Condorcanqui led the next and largest protest. He rebelled in 1780, quite likely for both personal and ideological reasons, assuming the name "Tupac Amaru II." This Mestizo was apparently a legitimate descendant of the Inca royal house, inasmuch as the Spaniards so recognized him, with the title of Marqués de Oropesa. Consequently, he held a position of considerable local power in Tinta, one of the outlying provinces of Cuzco. Bilingual, Condorcanqui dressed in Spanish style and associated largely with Spanish priests and officials in the region. In 1777, Condorcanqui journeyed to the viceregal capital to present to the attorney-general petitions on behalf of indigenous communities asking that they be exempted from the Potosí *mita de minas*. Inspector Areche refused to act on grounds that Condorcanqui brought no proof of abuse of which the Indians complained. The blunt Sierra Mestizo then prepared a memorial extending the petition to all inhabitants in his Tinta Province, but his uncourtliness won him no backing. He spent a year in Lima making futile representations.

Returning to his province in the latter part of 1778, Condorcanqui found peasant protest clearly brewing in the Cuzco region. During the following year or so, he evidently conferred with compatriots and ordered his own thoughts and emotions. On November 4, 1780, José Gabriel Condorcanqui, after celebrating Charles III's birthday with the local *corregidor,* took him prisoner and began a major revolt against abusive colonial rule. Announcing his continued higher loyalty to the Spanish king and Catholic faith, Tupac Amaru II had the *corregidor* dressed in a Franciscan habit and executed in the public square of Tungasuca before an audience that included over 200 Spaniards and Mestizos. A huge crowd of Indians with slings and clubs also watched, having already sacked the *corregidor*'s residence and offices. Existing peasant dissatisfaction with conditions in the region found ready outlet in Tupac Amaru II's organization of rebellious forces. His network of friendships among local Spaniards brought him considerable overt or covert support from many of them, including the Bishop of Cuzco.

Tupac Amaru II blended a strong element of millenarianism in his movement, promising his Indian followers that if they fell in battle against the hated Peninsulars, they would be reborn. This aspect of Tupac Amaru II's role has usually been overlooked, yet it constituted an important element in the recruitment of peasants to his cause.

In 1780, Tupac Amaru II and his peasant force surprised 600 royalist soldiers pursuing him at Sangarara and drove them into the local church. The rebels fired the church and massacred those who tried to escape. All but twenty-eight Creoles died, and the myth of the infallibility of Spanish arms in confrontation with Indians perished with them.

The conflict between Viceroy Agustín de Juáregui and Inspector Areche and the sorry state of the Peruvian militia exposed by the Lambayeque Mulattos and Tupac Amaru II's nativistic movement convinced the king that basic reforms had to be attempted in Peru. Although Inspector General José del Valle managed to defeat Tupac Amaru II and have him executed in 1781, he complained vociferously about Peru's unreadiness to face any more serious military threats.

As the result of such events and his inspector's reports, King Charles

III instituted massive reforms in the colonial regime. Through his vigorous attempts to take direct charge of the colonies, Charles III became one of the most effective Spanish kings during the entire colonial
experience. Some historians have ignored the crucial role of Napoleon Bonaparte and attributed the political independence movement
in the Spanish New World to various reforms of Bourbon monarchs.
The first and last Bourbon kings were, to be sure, pusillanimous fellows, and the cowardice of Charles IV before Napoleon's legions furthered political disintegration overseas.

On the other hand, the Peruvian viceroyalty constitutes a test case
for the theories of revolutionary causation advanced by some historians. Most of the Bourbon reforms stemmed from the actions of
Charles III, and Jesuit and other writers have blamed his expulsion of
the Society of Jesus from Spain and its dominions in 1767 for the
colonial revolt. Peru provides the negative case: Charles III expelled
the Jesuits from Peru as from the rest of his empire, yet Peru simply
did not rebel as did other colonial areas.

In 1778 Charles III considerably liberalized Spanish metropolitan
control over colonial commerce. He greatly increased the number of
ports in the colonies authorized to trade with Spain and foreigners. He
opened five South Pacific ports: Callao, Arica, Valparaiso, Concepción,
and Guayaquil. Charles III also liberalized the tax structure affecting
ocean commerce. Whatever beneficial effect his liberalization of trade
had on Buenos Aires and other ports, it materially altered the business
style of the great merchants in the guild (*consulado*) of Lima. His
measures economically benefited the Viceroyalty of the Río de la
Plata, which he created in 1776; Chile, which had long been a semi-
independent captaincy-general; and the territory of the *audiencia* of
Quito, attached to the Viceroyalty of New Granada established in
1739. The king's measures changed Lima and Peru by diminishing the
territory of the viceroyalty and by allowing trade that had been arti-
ficially channeled through Lima by law to travel shorter and cheaper
ocean routes.

In fact, Peru experienced an "extraordinary" increase in overseas
commerce during the rule of Viceroy Teodoro de Croix (1784-90),

following the liberalization of trade. The merchants of Lima who suffered most at the hands of King Charles III according to some historians did not rebel. The evidence indicates that while they may have had to alter their style of doing business, they actually profited from the Bourbon reforms as did merchants in other ports. Indeed, those who remained in Lima when San Martín and Bolívar invaded the Peruvian viceroyalty mostly became royalist refugees. In fact, the liberalization of trade not only increased its volume but also legitimized much of the contraband that previously moved outside legal channels.

The series of Indian uprisings in province after province under disaffected Mestizo and Creole leadership generated at least four major royal reforms. Charles III decreed an end to the hated *repartimiento,* or forced sale of goods to Native Americans. He also ordered the end of the corrupt *corregimiento* system, a change linked to his firing of Viceroy Juáregui after his inept handling of Tupac Amaru II. Charles III promoted Teodoro de Croix from Commandant General of the Frontier Provinces of New Spain to Viceroy of Peru. A French nobleman, Croix arrived in 1784 to divide the viceroyalty into seven Intendancies, not counting two in Chile. These combined some fifty-two provinces under direct royal control to a degree never before seen.

This administrative reform set the pattern of regionalism for the rest of the colonial era and provided the basis for forming political departments after independence. The 1784 Intendancies were those of Trujillo, Tarma, Lima, Huancavelica, Guamanga, Cuzco, and Arequipa. The Intendancy of Puno was transferred from the jurisdiction of the Viceroyalty of the Río de la Plata to that of Peru in 1796, an act later contributing to disputes between Peru and Bolivia.

That transfer followed Charles III's third reform aimed at revamping Peru's colonial structure: the creation of a royal court (*audiencia*) at Cuzco in 1787. Thus, toward the very end of the colonial period, Cuzco regained some of its preconquest prestige, after having decayed into a very provincial town. Finally, the fourth set of reforms that Charles III ordered carried out in Peru in the wake of the 1776-83 protests sought to convert the colonial militia into an effective fighting force.

Thus, the pace of institutional change picked up markedly in late colonial times. Unfortunately for the future of Spain, both Charles III and his successor could not resist involvement in debilitating European power struggles. Spanish international policy led eventually to Napoleon's occupation of the Peninsula, a disaster that contributed mightily to the rapid disintegration of the Spanish empire and political independence for its colonies.

Peasant uprisings and Indian millenarian movements did little in and of themselves to upset the course of colonial exploitation of the Peruvian population and resources. Long after independence, on the other hand, these events took on considerable symbolic and ideological importance as Peruvians cast back in time to identify the precursors of the nation.

Because urban Mestizos almost invariably and necessarily led peasant protests, Peru's historical quest for true domestic heroes has focused on them. In a country whose population is now largely Mestizo, with a substantial Indian minority, identification with the new racial and ethnic amalgam fosters crystallization of a unifying set of national values.

Two such Mestizos of late colonial times are so regarded. Tupac Amaru II, José Gabriel Condorcanqui, has become a symbolic figure of great contemporary importance in Peru. Another Cuzqueño, Mateo García Pumacahua, is perhaps a truer precursor of independence, although scarcely as popular today. Ironically, Brigadier García Pumacahua, hereditary *curaca* and high-ranking officer in the Cuzco Indian noble militia unit, participated in the Spanish defeat and capture of Tupac Amaru II. His revolutionary stature came after a coup d'état installed him as president of the *audiencia* in Cuzco and a leader of an abortive Sierra movement for political independence in 1814. Even as a revolutionary, García Pumacahua symbolizes well Peru's dilemma created by the Napoleonic wars. At the end of the Bourbon period, Peru remained a royalist kingdom. Its leaders won their reputations serving the king, and they typically made their fortunes exploiting the Indian peasants.

Chapter 6 • The Process of Political Independence, 1808-1826

Events in Europe, rather than domestic peasant protests, eventually led to Peru's gaining her political freedom from Spain. In 1808, French dictator Napoleon Bonaparte marched through the passes of the Pyrenees Mountains into Spain. He forced King Charles IV to abdicate in favor of his son Ferdinand VII, then deposed the young king and installed his own brother on the Spanish throne. Napoleon's dethronement of the Spanish king sent social and political shock waves throughout the Spanish overseas possessions. Colonies such as Peru were kingdoms of the ruler rather than integral parts of the Spanish nation. A grave and very real question as to the relationship between the colonies and Peninsular governments existed, therefore, from the moment Charles IV abdicated. Both Peninsular Spaniards and Creoles and migrant Peninsulars overseas were, if nothing else, culturally intensely legalistic and eager to dispute sovereignty under the unprecedented political conditions created by Napoleon.

French intervention triggered efforts to establish alternative governments both on the Peninsula and in the colonies. Many local leaders overseas decided to strike for immediate regional independence, without regard for the ideas of the Peninsular parliament convened at Cádiz in Free Spain. Individualism fostered a plethora of uprisings, but tended to keep these movements localized and relatively ineffectual when opposed by royal authorities. Viceroys, intendants, and other officials employed their professional armed forces very effectively to rout the rag-tag mobs mobilized by charismatic precursors of political independence.

In South America, residents of Chuquisaca (formerly known as La Plata and Charcas and later as Sucre) and La Paz in Upper Peru struck for liberty in mid-1809. The president of the royal *audiencia* of Cuzco marched into Upper Peru, defeated the rebels, and occupied Chuquisaca to terminate that regional movement. Peruvian royal officials returned *de facto* control of Upper Peru to Lima from Buenos Aires, where Argentine rebels achieved success.

A parallel uprising occurred in Quito in 1809. The Peruvian viceroy ordered troops into that area. It also reverted to Peruvian control by 1812, after being under the jurisdiction of the Viceroyalty of New Granada.

In Peru proper, rural Indian peasants in the Huánuco region launched late in 1811 another peasant protest against extortion and mistreatment in the Sierra. Urban Peruvians, who mobilized numerous Indians to overwhelm royal forces in the city early in 1812, planned a widespread revolt. They sent messages to Cajatambo, Conchucos, and Huaylas urging rebellion, and Huamalíes province did rebel. Soon local Indian contingents fell to fighting one another over local issues. Moreover, their attacks on non-Indians frightened initially rebellious Creoles and Mestizos into renewed loyalty to the viceroy. Therein lay one key to the failure of such provincial protests to further independence: a racist colonial heritage paralyzed intercaste cooperation. In 1813, the Tarma Intendant brought up 500 men and four cannon to decisively defeat the outgunned Huánuco protesters, who carried only slings, sticks, or lances.

The most noteworthy local revolt occurred in the former Inca capital in 1814. Imprisoning royal officials, rebels named Brigadier Mateo García Pumacahua head of their forces and president of the *audiencia*. A Mestizo in his sixties, Pumacahua was a hereditary *curaca* and officer in the Cuzco noble militia unit. Marching southeast, one rebel force briefly occupied Puno and La Paz, but abandoned both after being defeated by a royalist regiment. A second rebel column liberated Andahuaylas and Ayacucho before a royalist colonel dispersed it.

Pumacahua himself led a third rebel force to Arequipa. There it recruited, among others, a youthful versifier named Mariano Melgar who romantically extolled Native American virtues. Royal troops engaged this column in 1815 and killed some 1,000 without quarter. They executed the captive García Pumacahua and Melgar, providing Peru with two martyrs but not a single hero of independence. The royalist commander then marched his troops across Upper Peru to confront free Argentine troops. The Peruvian Creole commander of the royalist force overextended his lines, and the Argentines quickly ended his threat to their continued independence.

Argentina still faced the danger that other royal armies might march down out of the high altitudes of Upper Peru. With Chile still firmly under Spanish control, the Argentines also faced the prospect of trans-Andean attack along thousands of kilometers of common mountain frontier. The great Argentine strategist José de San Martín launched, therefore, a strategic offensive aimed at destroying royalist power in Peru. He collected troops in Mendoza and trained them. Then San Martín led his men across the Andes into Chile during the South American summer of 1817 and defeated a large royalist force at Chacabuco.

Peruvian Viceroy Joaquín de la Pezuela dispatched to Chile a new army, which defeated San Martín at the beginning of 1818. San Martín rallied his forces and routed the royalists on the plains of Maipu, thus liberating Chile from Spanish rule. This freed Argentina's long Andean flank from the threat of royalist attack in what some historians consider the most brilliantly led military campaign ever carried out.

Following his strategic plan, San Martín next assaulted royalist power in Peru. The newly independent governments contracted a noble English naval officer to establish and lead a naval task force to facilitate troop movements. This Alfred Lord Cochrane weighed anchor at Valparaiso in January, 1819 to attack Lima and establish rebel naval supremacy in the South Pacific. In September Cochrane's ships landed the first invasion troops at Paracas Bay to carry out'one of the most spectacular campaigns of the war under José Arenales. Capturing several officers who then switched to the rebel side, Arenales prompted the cities of Ica and Huánuco to declare their independence from Spain. He also became the first of several rebel generals to decree the abolishment of Indian tribute.

Peru's culturally distinct northern provinces made, however, the most decisive domestic contribution to freedom. Late in 1820, the Creole Intendant José Bernardo Tagle y Portocarrero, Marqués de Torre Tagle, convened the Trujillo city council and advocated independence, to which it formally swore. Leaders in Lambayeque suborned some royalist troops and organized a mob that forced the remainder of the troops to surrender, whereupon the *cabildo* declared independence. The Piura *cabildo* voted for independence in January, 1821, and the crowd forced Spanish officers to surrender the arms in their barracks. Cajamarca and Chachapoyas followed suit. The independent North began to provide San Martín with both troops and funds, spearheading effective Peruvian efforts to achieve independence. Thus, the North demonstrated a perseverance of the cultural unity dating back at least to Chimú times.

The defection of the North led the royalists to abandon Lima and establish themselves in the central and southern Sierra, from which rebel troops retreated. After San Martín entered Lima, a *cabildo abierto* declared for independence. This San Martín proclaimed on July 28, 1821, providing the new republic with its independence day. The sociopolitical preponderance of Lima meant that San Martín's earlier declaration at the provincial town of Huaura the previous November would not be celebrated, even though Peru declared a national monument the house from whose balcony San Martín issued his original 1820 proclamation.

Having assumed formal military and political command of Free

Peru, San Martín set about achieving effective political mobilization. Recruiting many Black soldiers, San Martín decreed freedom for children of slaves. Faced with a royal base in the Indian Sierra, San Martín abolished Indian tribute. Moving toward social revolution by decree, he soon abolished all forms of personal service associated with the term "Indian"—the *mita de minas* and its other forms, *pongos* or household and hacienda tasks exacted over and above labor exchanged for subsistence plot assignments, *encomiendas,* and *yanaconazgos.* In a series of decrees issued in Spanish and Quechua, San Martín even outlawed the use of the term "Indian" and proclaimed Native Americans to be citizens of Peru. Such measures so alarmed many conservative Spaniards and Creoles that they followed the eighty-year-old Archbishop who chose exile. Actually, Peru's Indians were extremely ill-prepared at the end of three centuries of colonial subordination to compete as citizen-equals with Creoles and Mestizos. The latter still almost completely monopolized political and military offices, business enterprises, and access to formal educational facilities. Therefore political liberty decreed for Native American individuals who remained illiterate, poverty-stricken, and monolingual in Quechua or Aymara remained a paper idea.

In attempting a political mobilization of Peruvian society, San Martín correctly assessed it as conservative and structurally colonial, rather than mercantile like his own Argentina. To motivate his generals, San Martín distributed among them haciendas seized from royalists, much as Pizarro had handed out Inca property. Toward the end of 1821, San Martín obtained agreement by many Lima notables to the principle of monarchy for governing Peru and sent an agent to Europe to seek a prince who could move into the political and social keystone position in the governmental and social structure that the Spanish king and his viceroy and their Sapa Inca predecessors had occupied for half a millennium. San Martín evidently recognized that parliamentary or any other form of democratic governance was a recent European invention not necessarily adaptable to Peru.

Yet San Martín also encouraged a "patriotic society" of forty intellectual leaders, who began voicing during the early months of 1822

vociferous opposition to the monarchical plan. As Hispanic individual-
ists, Peru's urban Creole intellectuals were intoxicated by the heady
democratic idealism imported from France. Their colonial orientation
predisposed them to European ideas just as Peru had been predisposed
to the manufactured goods and political concepts of Europe for 250
years. Moreover, their scholastic education in the University of San
Marcos and San Carlos secondary school had been devoid of the scientific and rational approaches. Consequently, it equipped them with
few critical tools with which to evaluate the political dangers inherent
in importing a system of governance from postrevolutionary France to
a country as different as Peru.

The Creole intellectuals who donned a mantle of liberalism failed
to comprehend their own comparative colonial provincialism and short-
comings as politicians. In comparison, José de San Martín and José
Bernardo de Tagle stood out as cosmopolitan statesmen polished by
travel and European experience. San Martín spent years on the Peninsula and in France observing Spanish society both before and after
the Napoleonic invasion and studying postrevolutionary France under
the Emperor. Tagle lived for several years on the Peninsula during its
postinvasion upheavals. Both possessed, therefore, a perspective from
which to evaluate systems of governance that the Creole intellectual
opponents of the monarchy lacked. Peruvian nationalist historians
have understandably lauded the opposition to the monarchical plan.
Historians and political scientists taking a broader comparative perspective, on the other hand, have pointed out that Peru is one of those
Latin American nations whose national politics have been plagued
ever since independence by a futile quest for a functional substitute
for a king.

José de San Martín realized the fundamental weakness of his position in Peru. If he could not mobilize Peruvians behind a prince to
fight the royalists, he also lacked sufficient foreign manpower to defeat
the viceroy's forces in the Sierra. Under such circumstances, that man
of deeds rather than empty words turned to another strategy for winning the war. He sought to mobilize Free Peru on a democratic revolutionary French model and to recruit a foreign general who did have

the manpower needed to complete the ouster of Spain from South America.

In pursuit of the democratic model, San Martín called in 1822 for general elections to choose members of a parliament. In order to carry out these elections, San Martín converted the seven viceregal intendancies into republican departments, borrowing the French term. A prefect, again following the French model, headed each department. The decree divided departments into provinces that closely followed the forty-six *partidas* in the intendancies. Those derived in turn from the original fifty-two administrative *corregimientos* Viceroy Toledo had defined in both Upper and Lower Peru. As such, they continued ethnic and environmental divisions existing prior to the rise of the Inca empire. Thus, environmental reality imposed constraints upon political innovation.

Conversion of colonial intendancies into French-style departments established a form of internal governance that required immediate selection of prefects to support the Free Peruvian war effort. National leaders usually awarded the powerful post to military commanders who led army units during the separatist conflict. Placed in charge of civil administration in extremely large departments, prefects also commanding large army contingents soon came to vie with each other for political control of the country.

While San Martín had been freeing southern South America of royalists, Simón Bolívar was clearing them from the northwestern parts of the continent. Bolívar recognized the same strategic imperatives. Royalist troops reconquered Venezuela after Bolívar's initial success there, so he perforce linked up with rebels in New Granada to liberate both areas. Military necessity carried him into political action and the presidency of Great Colombia. To disperse royalist forces still in the field in the *audiencia* of Quito, Bolívar marched south. With assistance from one North Peruvian contingent, Bolívar won a decisive engagement at Pichincha on April 23, 1822.

That July, San Martín sailed to Guayaquil to convey to Bolívar the need for massive reinforcement of the separatists in Peru and his personal willingness to retire from that stage and leave it to Bolívar. Back in Peru, San Martín convened the first Peruvian Congress, although only fifty-two deputies of the seventy-nine his decree specified assembled.

The very first "election" of parliamentarians in Peru's independent history set the tone for many to follow. Because royalist forces occupied several departments, emigrants to Lima from those jurisdictions selected such of their representatives as sat in the Congress. At least one such delegate was openly accused of having gained election by personally manipulating the subordinate urban Indian populace. Having convened the Congress, San Martín accepted from it an honorific title, but refused to exercise power and left the country. In farewell, San Martín urged the liberated areas "to take charge of their own destinies."

In the authoritarian style of Spanish culture, the pioneer Congress arrogated to itself total power. According to one eminent Peruvian historian, members intervened in a multitude of matters that should not have distracted their attention. This set an evil example followed in later parliaments, whose members occupied themselves with trivialities while they ignored great national problems that cried out for meditation and study. Left to their own devices, the separatist leaders wasted their opportunity to win prompt independence for the country. Potential heroes of the independence movement became scapegoats instead of liberators as they conducted the war *a la criolla,* reinforcing the scorn with which Peninsular officers leading the largely Indian royalist armies regarded them.

Late in 1822, the sovereign Congress recognized the need for an executive branch to the extent of setting up a three-member governing junta, which it still sought to control. With the military outcome in question in January of 1823, nationalistic congressional leaders naively reembarked the Colombian reinforcements Bolívar had sent them. Senior army officers soon mounted the first of what would become many military coups d'état. Several generals "asked" Congress to name José Riva Aguero president. When it hesitated, they mobilized their troops. Congress made Riva Aguero president. Congress and Creole chief executive alike kept San Martín's decree terminating Indian tribute a dead letter, inasmuch as they depended upon such tribute for the bulk of the fledgling state's revenues. Supplementing tribute with forced loans or exactions from urban merchants, the separatists managed to ship an expeditionary force from Callao to the south coast. Under Andrés Santa Cruz, it campaigned into his native Upper Peru only to be forced back to the coast.

General Antonio Sucre arrived in Lima to open the way for Bolívar to complete the strategic destruction of royalist forces. The viceroy's armies helped Sucre by reoccupying Lima. Retreating to Callao, Congress in a rump session made the fateful decision to plead with Simón Bolívar to rescue the revolution. President Riva Aguero was not yet ready to grant that the nationalist revolutionaries could not succeed without foreign intervention. He moved to Trujillo, the largest city and administrative center of Free Peru in the "solid North," and carried with him a small contingent of congressmen. Consequently, the midyear situation epitomized the problems of the sudden introduction of republican governance in an extremely hierarchical society.

Peru possessed two revolutionary governments, neither one with any very valid claim to legitimate representation. The president selected by the sovereign Congress under military compulsion designated Trujillo as the capital. On the other hand, more congressmen than those who traveled to Trujillo remained in Callao to act in concert with non-Peruvian military leaders. The separatist government of Chile accorded diplomatic recognition to both governments. Riva Aguero denounced as illegal actions taken by the Callao rump parliament and decreed its dissolution. The Callao parliament denounced Riva Aguero, deposed him, and substituted the Marqués de Torre Tagle. Surely content with the confusion he had created, the royalist commander withdrew from Lima long before Bolívar landed at Callao with thousands of Colombian troops.

Bolívar assembled some 11,000 troops and marched out of Lima for the intermontane Callejón de Huaylas to condition the men for highland warfare. That move also placed him in a good geographic position to eliminate Riva Aguero as a rival for Peruvian loyalties. One of

Bolívar's lieutenants, the Peruvian Antonio Gutierrez de la Fuente, marched north to Trujillo, arrested the Free Peruvian president, and sent him into exile. Thus ended Riva Aguero's opportunity to be the national hero of independence. Bolívar sent another column north to Cajamarca to disperse Riva Aguero supporters and consolidate his control over Free Peru before he turned south toward the viceregal redoubt. The rump Congress proclaimed a new constitution and elected the Marqués de Torre Tagle president.

Early in 1824, the separatist movement suffered a series of mutinies. Panicking, the congressmen sitting in the diminished parliament placed all political and military authority in Bolívar's hands. This insured that Bolívar would free Peru from Spain. The royalists contributed to that outcome by again occupying Lima. Torre Tagle took refuge in a convent, fearing that Bolívar had ordered him executed. Thus, his chance to emerge as the Peruvian hero of independence ended. When the royalist commander offered Torre Tagle the governance of the city, the ex-president refused. He died ignominiously of scurvy in royalist-held Callao the following year.

Wielding absolute powers, Bolívar issued a decree that profoundly influenced social and economic relations between the Indians and the dominant groups for decades to come. He declared Indians to be as citizens individual owners of the lands they occupied, so that they could sell or otherwise alienate them. Bolívar's decree revoked Spanish colonial reservation of lands to communities. It called for the distribution of communal lands to Indians without fields and the sale by the state of the remaining "surplus," opening the way to legal looting of communal lands.

In mid-1824, Bolívar began to shift his troops to the offensive. Spanish individualism plagued the royalists as well as the separatists, for the commander of Upper Peru set himself up as an independent leader, compromising the power of the viceroy to counter Bolívar's moves. The opposing forces met on the plains of Junín in early August. Bolívar allowed his reckless cavalry to open a 10-kilometer gap between itself and his infantry. The initial piecemeal separatist charge almost turned into a rout. An Argentine cavalry officer saved the saber battle for the revolutionaries, however, when he charged the royalist flank with two Peruvian squadrons that had time to form.

Bolívar returned to the coast, while Sucre and the viceroy moved toward the final decision. Their armies sighted each other early in December near Huamanga (modern, Ayacucho). Viceroy José de la Serna attacked on December 9th by forming his troops into three columns to attempt to turn both separatist flanks. Sucre's right wing not only held, but swept through the viceregal forces to the rear guard. The captured viceroy had little choice but to sign a formal capitulation.

While decisive, the Battle of Ayacucho did not end the fight for independence. Despite his open defiance of the viceroy's authority, the Spanish commander in Upper Peru remained loyal to Spain. General Antonio Sucre marched his multinational army past Desaguadero, therefore, into Upper Peru. Early in 1825, Sucre convoked an Upper Peruvian assembly at Oruro to decide the future of Upper Peru. The death of the royalist leader and destruction of his forces at Tumusla terminated finally the San Martín-Bolívar strategic campaign to liberate all South America from Spanish sovereignty.

The Peruvian Congress reconvened briefly in Lima early in 1825, still only fifty-six strong even though alternates constituted the majority of assembled deputies. The Free Peruvian representatives praised Bolívar, as the people of Peru accepted the realities of 1825 and celebrated the end of hostilities. Tendering his resignation, Bolívar labeled the dictatorship dangerous as well as incompatible with his office as elected president of Colombia. Yet Bolívar's long-time comrade-in-arms and acting president of Colombia in his absence, Francisco de Paula Santander, later concluded that the adulation of the populace of Upper and Lower Peru transformed the level-headed republican revolutionary of 1822 into a dictatorial tyrant in 1828.

Congress voted Bolívar a million pesos and appropriated another million in veterans' benefits. A committee drew up in two days a policy declaration on territorial limits. In substance, the deputies set no boundaries, although they recognized that Sucre's advance raised the territorial issue. Congress dismissed Upper Peruvian petitions for annexation as royalist maneuvers and resolved to charge the Upper Peruvians the cost of the revolutionary expedition force. After fixing a national gold coinage and passing a few other measures, the Governing Congress finally dissolved itself, leaving all power again in Bolívar's hands.

In Upper Peru, delegates elected from La Paz, Santa Cruz, Potosí, Chuquisaca, and Cochabamba provinces met at Chuquisaca. They voted for independence and asked Bolívar to draw up a constitution, which he did. Thus the two Venezuelans determined, with a bumbling assist from Peru's first parliament, that Bolivia become independent. That set the South American stage for Peru's involvement in international warfare that would keep the country embroiled for a decade and a half and lead to a decisive military defeat and wide-sweeping change.

When Bolívar returned to Lima from Bolivia early in 1826, Peruvian unity remained pathetically weak. At least one Arequipa paper and many pamphlets openly advocated dividing the country, displaying resentment toward Lima's dominance. As head of the Governing Council, Andrés Santa Cruz strengthened the fledgling central government by ending attempts by Arequipa Prefect Antonio Gutierrez de la Fuente to retain funds in the department.

Bolívar found intolerable the appearance of an opposition in the new parliament, convened as a result of his earlier call for the election of ninety-eight delegates and fifty-six alternates. The Governing Council headed by Hipólito Unánue soon found an excuse for expelling deputies from three provinces, indicating the narrowness of Bolívar's commitment to representative government. This set a precedent to plague Peru throughout later parliamentary history. After he promulgated the same constitution he had written for Bolivia, Bolívar obliged the deputies who asked him to dissolve Congress by doing so the very same day.

Bolívar's constitution showed his conservatism and egotism. He defined an electoral branch as well as legislative, executive, and judicial branches, copying the French consular model. With the franchise restricted to men of Peruvian nationality at least twenty-five years of age or married who could read and write and carried on a profession, virtually all Native Americans, Blacks, and many Mestizos remained disenfranchised. Bolívar specifically excluded domestic servants from voting.

The Governing Council ordered departmental prefects to convene the electoral colleges to vote on the new constitution. The small group that convened in Lima approved on condition that Bolívar serve as first life-president. As news reached Bolívar of the threat of civil war in Colombia, however, he decided to return there. While Peru celebrated the anniversary of his arrival with great ceremony, Bolívar went secretly to Callao to set sail for Colombia on September 2, 1826.

The rapid gyrations of leadership during the final Peruvian phase of the revolutionary war between 1821 and 1826 had by then set many precedents. Beginning with San Martín and ending with Bolívar, no less than eight men served as chief executive in five years and two months. Thus, the average term in office had been less than eight months. San Martín and Bolívar spent far too much time on military affairs to govern civil affairs. Half the chief executives came from outside Peru. Bolívar destroyed the potential of two Peruvian noblemen who briefly exercised executive leadership—Riva Aguero and Torre Tagle. A third, Manuel Salazar y Baquíjano, impressed everyone as a useful acting chief, yet not powerful in his own right. Hipólito Unánue was much too old to entertain political ambitions, and as a medical practitioner lacked a military power base. Thus, the period of revolutionary war governments from 1821-26 left Peru less well prepared for self-government and an orderly chief executive succession in 1826 than it had been in 1821. Potential leaders had been destroyed rather than trained, creating a partial power vacuum to be filled by ambitious but relatively unskilled *caudillos*.

Two foreign generals and their troops handed the populace of Peru its political independence against strong royalist opposition so as to insure the peaceful freedom of their own homelands. During the four years of conflict that San Martín initiated in 1820 and Bolívar and Sucre terminated at the end of 1824, non-Peruvian army commanders and the British admiral Cochrane consolidated their places in history as the martial heroes of Peruvian independence. San Martín possessed the greatness of character to allow the Peruvian regional leaders an opportunity to set up a revolutionary government and lead their own war. They frittered it away. Thus, Peruvians became independent without domestic heroes of major stature whom they could emulate.

When the fighting ended, there remained multifarious problems. Successful revolutionists had to fashion national governments whose territories had to be determined. They needed to reconstruct economies disrupted by warfare. They wanted to set limits upon the upward social mobility of colonially oppressed sectors of the population who anticipated improved conditions.

Troops of both sides had marched in and out of Lima and across the provinces, affecting thousands of civilians. Much of the food supply, all the firewood, water, and fodder for the armies necessarily came from the countryside. Residents of towns and villages were, therefore, constantly levied upon but infrequently paid for what soldiers took. Apart from material goods, the social impact of thousands of troops settling into Andean towns and hamlets for stays of up to six months was unprecedented. Bolívar and his Colombian troops who trained in the Province of Huaylas stirred the enthusiastic participation of the populace, who felt privileged to serve the Liberator in every way. So strong was the impression that the city of Caraz adopted the Colombian Virgin of Chiquinquirá as the city's patroness.

The Indian peoples felt more than a little ambivalence in responding to the war. Should they support the king who seemed to be the perpetual ruler, protector, and to whom everything was owed? Or should they cast their lot with Creoles and Mestizos who exploited them just as much as did Spaniards? Local responses varied, but one side or the other usually coerced Indian participation in the conflict. The armies confined the Indian military role to that of infantry, grooms, servants, and laborers—tasks that in essence replicated the work of a *mita*.

San Martín's decrees abolishing tribute, *mitas,* and servitude of all types, recognizing the Quechua language, and offering Indians the same guarantees as other citizens proved to be only the precursors of the empty "Indianist" rhetoric that subsequently reappeared in the halls of Lima. In fact, San Martín's good intentions never became operative. Bolívar's later decrees drastically altered the Indian conditions, although not in the manner he envisioned.

The situation differed for slaves and Black freemen. Given the reward of freedom for serving in the separatist forces, Blacks and Mulattos quickly formed army units. Decrees of 1821 and 1822 also prohibited slaves from being used as a medium of exchange and said that education had to be provided for the children of slaves. The 1823 constitution provided that no person born in Peru could be a slave. These measures roused consternation among coastal plantation owners who depended upon slave labor. Their resistance soon led to sharp modifications in revolutionary policies, particularly with regard to army service. Slavery survived the war of independence, but it was greatly weakened as large numbers of Blacks passed into the ranks of the "free castes" in coastal cities.

On July 4, 1825, Bolívar decreed the fundamental relationship between Native Americans and the Creole elite. He ratified his earlier decree vesting communal property in individual Indians. Bolívar set up rules for distributing communal lands to individuals and prohibited the new landowners from selling their real estate until after 1850. Later a literacy requirement replaced the time limitation. The San Martín-Bolívar decrees, as modified by Peruvian politicians, resulted in a massive Creole-Mestizo assault upon the Native American land base that had survived the centuries of Spanish greed. Employing legal, extralegal, and illegal techniques, dominant group members obtained title to former Indian lands. Creole-Mestizo dominated courts recognized those titles.

The human characteristics of Peru altered markedly during the revolutionary era. In spite of the havoc wrought by battles, the impressment of Peruvians to serve in Colombian units repatriated to Colombia, and the emigration of Spaniards and Peruvian royalists, the total population increased. The number of people in the viceroyalty apparently began to increase about 1800. By 1826, contemporary estimates placed Peru's population 18 percent higher than it had been in 1795. Relatively innocent of knowledge of demographic dynamics, one estimator bemoaned the failure of the population to double between the viceregal census and independence. Taking census results and estimates at face value, the population grew at an average 0.6 percent annually. At Bolívar's departure, independent Peru contained about 1,500,000 individuals.

Estimates of the white population indicate that it increased slightly. Eyewitness accounts of the events that occurred during the 1820-24 fighting make clear that large numbers of Peninsular-born Spaniards and Creole royalists fled the cities. Others died fighting in royalist armies. Quantification of royalist emigration is difficult, but it certainly reduced the white population. The white population of independent Peru should, therefore, have been less in 1826 than it had been in 1795. Yet the 1826 estimate of 148,000 was about 3 percent larger than the 1795 figure.

The difference was evidently made up from two sources. A minor source was overseas immigration. Significant numbers of Englishmen and Irishmen, often veterans of the wars of independence, settled in Peru. Most likely the major source of 1826 "whites" was large-scale "passing" of Mestizos into the social ranks of whites. As many as 36,000 may have passed by 1826.

The viceroyalty had contained nearly a quarter of a million Mestizos by 1795. Their rate of increase leveled off at about one percent per year by the epoch of the wars of independence. Their absolute increase in numbers became progressively greater through time, on the other hand. Thus, this post-Columbian exchange hybrid population increased faster than any other sector of the populace. By 1826, Mestizos numbered about one-third of a million souls, but the social category contained only some 296,000.

Importation of Black slaves into Peru continued at the rate of approximately 1,500 annually until 1810. As a result, the slave population was estimated at approximately 50,000 in 1826, a 25 percent increase since 1795. On the other hand, the free Black and mixed population was thought to have fallen slightly. Some Mulattos surely passed into the Mestizo social category. The wars had also wasted a significant number of Black lives. Many Blacks enlisted under the separatist banners to achieve freedom, but battle casualties and diseases in camp sharply reduced the free Black population.

Whatever the actual size of the population in 1825, national leaders tended to conceive of the new nation as underpopulated. As a matter of fact, Peru stood poised at the end of the Bolívar era for a rapid population growth at rates that have accelerated ever since.

To remedy the situation of underpopulation, republican leaders would consistently foster international immigration to Peru. Conditioned by colonial Spanish values, they would encourage European immigration in pursuit of an elusive goal of a white populace. Paradoxically, even Mestizo leaders who paid at least lip-service to the Inca heritage would join Creole *caudillos* in promoting European immigration. In reality, marriage and consensual unions between members of different ethnic groups were already converting Peru into a Mestizo nation. The human characteristics of Peru would alter significantly year after year, regardless of frequent tempestuous political warfare. Victorious politicians could achieve only marginal impacts upon massive biological and social changes well underway by 1826. Just as Peru's internal dynamics limited the power of Bourbon kings to influence late colonial events, they circumscribed the effect of republican policy-makers.

Chapter 7 • Struggles for the Control of Human Resources, 1827-1865

When the Liberator sailed from Callao in 1826, a new era began in Peru. Simón Bolívar's departure left behind a power vacuum that generated domestic conflict. There was no one powerful enough to impose order or procure domestic tranquility. Numerous military leaders who had more or less cheerfully subordinated to this New World Napoleon found themselves suddenly free to contest the chief executiveship among themselves.

Even uncertainty over Peru's physical boundaries generated conflict, because two leading contenders for the Peruvian presidency, José de la Mar and Andrés Santa Cruz, hailed from Cuenca, Ecuador, and La Paz, Bolivia, respectively. For two decades after independence, Santa Cruz worked for a union of Peru and Bolivia, which he would head. Confederation also appealed to General Agustín Gamarra of Cuzco, but he envisioned himself as leader of a resurrection of the *Tawantin-suyu*. In fact, Peru reverted neither to the long *Pax Hispánica* nor to the Sierra might of *Tawantinsuyu*. Instead, leaders conditioned to warfare by the separatist struggle battled one another for political power.

They behaved like postconquest Pizarro and Almagro factions, which engaged each other in constant civil wars until Pedro de la Gasca pacified the colony. No outsider appeared to pacify independent Peru, however, so Peruvians themselves had to work for over two-thirds of a century to remove violence from their political system.

An immensely complex tangle of interpersonal alliances, hatreds, and ambitions among former revolutionary war officers made impossible the rebirth of earlier Andean grandeur. Petty deals and double deals featured behind-the-scenes intrigues while the nearly private armies of the *caudillos* marched to and fro. This situation obtained from the moment Bolívar left the executive branch in the hands of a governing council headed by the Bolivian Andrés Santa Cruz. Agustín Gamarra then served as prefect of his native Department of Cuzco with an army under his command, and Antonio Gutierrez de la Fuente was prefect of Arequipa with another army. Both veterans aspired to supreme leadership.

Realizing that Bolívar's constitution became meaningless with the Liberator gone, the governing council quickly convened the Lima *cabildo,* which that constitution suppressed, and a popular assembly. These groups agreed to call on Santa Cruz to assume power and to convene a new congress within three months. Santa Cruz indeed called for elections, and a new Constitutional Congress of eighty-three deputies convened on June 4, 1827. Once it decided to call the chief executive "president" and provided for a vice-president, the Congress elected José de la Mar by fifty-eight votes to twenty-seven for Santa Cruz, with Manuel Salazar y Baquíjano as vice-president. The deputies then set to work to compose Peru's third constitution, which they finished the next year.

The competition between the Bolivian Santa Cruz and the Ecuadorian La Mar helped Peruvians to develop a sense of nationality that they lacked in 1827. La Mar headed the government of Guayaquil when elected President of Peru, so he had to journey south to assume office. Guayaquil had declared its independence in 1820 and cooperated with Free Peru until Bolívar annexed it to Colombia. As long as Bolívar headed both Colombia and Peru, territorial problems remained in abeyance, but when he left Peru, they surged to the fore. Incidents began to occur that strained Peruvian relations with Colombia and Bolivia. Peruvian newspapers about-faced from their earlier adulation of Bolívar and began to criticize him and Sucre. The Colombian and Bolivian presses responded in kind.

The first international dispute erupted on the southern front. Santa Cruz promoted dissatisfaction with Sucre's rule of Bolivia, and Cuzco Prefect Gamarra began to mobilize troops on the frontier. Led by two Peruvian sergeants apparently acting for Gamarra, the Chuquisaca garrison mutinied in 1828. Sucre faced the mutineers sword in hand, but they fired on him, breaking his right arm and causing his horse to bolt. Dissident leaders soon invited Gamarra and his waiting army into Bolivia. Evidently he embarked on this venture without orders or approval from either President La Mar or the Peruvian Congress. Gamarra encountered almost no organized resistance and signed with Bolivian representatives a treaty providing for repatriation of all non-Bolivian soldiers in that country. Gamarra finally withdrew his army after Sucre resigned.

En route to Colombia, Sucre sought to mediate the growing dispute between that country and Peru, but the Peruvian Congress declared war on May 17, 1828. The Peruvian fleet bombarded, blockaded, and early in 1829 occupied Guayaquil. President La Mar took command of an army raised in northern Peruvian territory governed by Prefect Luís José Orbegoso, and invaded southern Colombia. Sucre returned to the field where his superior generalship and knowledge of the terrain enabled him to halt the Peruvian advance. After delaying his mobilization, Arequipa Prefect Gutierrez de la Fuente used his troops to depose Vice-President Salazar y Baquíjano in Lima on June 6th. The very next day, Cuzqueño Gamarra rose against the president in Piura and had him placed on a corvette to carry him to Costa Rican exile.

Gamarra signed a quick armistice with Bolívar, and representatives of Peru and Colombia met to work out a treaty of limits. They returned in principle to the border between the Peruvian and New Granadan viceroyalties, but their ignorance of the actual geography of the area left many problems to be resolved by later wars and negotiations.

Gamarra and Gutierrez de la Fuente thus firmly established the pattern of generals leading coups d'état that would prevail as Peru's most decisive technique for transferring political power. After their coup, the powerful southern prefects called for elections to the first bicameral parliament of thirty-five senators and seventy-four deputies. Once convened, the new congress rubber-stamped Gamarra as president and Gutierrez de la Fuente as vice-president. The Cuzco *caudillo* achieved the distinction of serving out a constitutionally prescribed four-year term of office for the first time.

At the end of his term, Gamarra sought to impose his choice of a successor, but the congress elected General Luís José Orbegoso. Gamarra then started a civil war. After two years of struggle, Orbegoso called on Santa Cruz, then president of Bolivia, for assistance. The Bolivian seized his opportunity to unite the countries and formed a confederation between Bolivia and a Peru divided into northern and southern states. Peruvian exiles persuaded Chile to intervene. In 1839, a joint force led by the Chilean General Manuel Bulnes with Gamarra, Gutierrez de la Fuente, and Ramón Castilla in its ranks decisively defeated Santa Cruz's Confederation army in the countryside of beautiful Yungay Province. President again, Gamarra attempted to realize his ambition for Peruvian-Bolivian union in 1841. He invaded Bolivia along the shores of Lake Titicaca. Bolivian troops annihilated the invaders at Ingavi on November 18th and killed Gamarra. This defeat ended further attempts at confederation and defined the southeastern frontier of Peru.

From Bolívar's departure in 1826 until 1865, thirty-four men served as chief executive. They disputed leadership in personalistic terms. Two-thirds were revolutionary war veterans, and four out of five were military officers by occupation. One in five was a landed proprietor, one in ten an attorney. As the young republic teetered between centralism and political federalism, the prefects of the huge departments played key roles in the power struggle. At least two out of five chief executives served as prefect prior to becoming president. Only a fourth gained cabinet experience before assuming the chief executiveship, but nearly a tenth of the presidents had previously held this office before 1827. Only a fifth of the presidents served in the senate prior to heading the executive branch.

An element of musical chairs characterized chief executive succession from 1826 to 1865, although the game was deadly, with unsuccessful contenders on occasion being put before firing squads. During the fierce competition, only one-fifth of the chief executives came to power in coups d'état. Yet those transfers of power, plus unsuccessful attempts that motivated presidents to leave Lima to lead government troops combating rebels personally, increased the number of chief executives and shortened tenures. One out of five chief executives served by appointment, while two in five came to office by constitutional succession other than election. Only 12 percent of these presidents took office after being indirectly elected either by the congress or the electoral college.

Relatively young men played presidential musical chairs from 1826 to 1865. One coup leader gained office in his twenties, and the age on donning the presidential sash averaged lower than during any later period. The birthplaces of chief executives reflected the disproportionate influence of the capital city in national affairs. Over a quarter of these presidents were born in Lima, which at that period contained perhaps 6 percent of the national population. Only four cities outside Lima contributed more than a single chief executive. Arequipa provided three, or almost one in ten, while Cuzco, Piura, and Puno had two presidents each, as did Tarapacá Province, which was later ceded to Chile.

Conditioned in most cases by service with Spaniards prior to independence, the military officers who dominated republican politics preserved the colonial military caste's disdain for both manual labor and commerce. Technical advances in industry and agriculture in Europe in the 1830s created a demand for the centuries-deep accumulation of bird dung on Peru's offshore islands and some arid coastal peninsulas. Although the generals made guano a state monopoly, they did not deign to manage it. The Bolivian-Peruvian Confederation had hardly ended when Ramón Castilla, as Minister of Exchequer under Gamarra, negotiated the first contract with entrepreneurs who would export guano to Europe. In 1840, Castilla and English capitalists launched a program of guano-mining for export that would last several decades while financing Peruvian governmental operations and materially increasing the financial attractions of the presidency. Contractors entrapped peasants from certain Andean regions to excavate cheaply the thick bird-dung deposits. Ammonia fumes released from the guano during excavation and sacking shriveled the skin of laborers and blinded some of them. As always, Native Americans paid the highest price for elite prosperity. The fate of Easter Islanders impressed to dig guano, and of other Polynesians brought to Peru in 1854 and 1857 was even worse. Most died under inhuman working conditions.

When Ramón Castilla became president, he initiated a policy of paying revolutionary war debts. The guano windfall paid for veterans' pensions, property damage settlements to royalists, service back pay, and all other kinds of debts. Castilla estimated that the total would not exceed seven million pesos. Then influential entrepreneurs in the capital city bought up claims, and a national financial fever raged as some pressed legitimate claims and others inflated debt values or forged claims. The internal debt mounted to over twenty-three million pesos as the deadline for recovery approached in 1853 during the administration of José R. Echenique. Accusations that Echenique profited from the consolidation of the internal debt helped to topple him.

Guano income financed the national government for many years, allowing it to postpone dealing with the acute problem of perpetual funding. Had it been dealt with, leaders might have been forced to develop a sound fiscal policy and a program of taxation departing from colonial precedents. Guano yielded over thirty-nine million pesos from 1840 to 1856. Guano contracts yielded to the government over fifteen million pesos in 1857, over sixteen million in 1859 and 1860 before the U.S. Civil War and lessening European requirements cut demand and shipping availability.

The rapid growth of government income from guano contract fees renewed European faith in Peru's ability to pay its debts. Peruvian governments found it all too easy, therefore, to float new loans in England and on the Continent by pledging future guano income as security. Peruvian leaders followed the colonial pattern of farming out concessions and delegated guano mining, shipping, and sale to entrepreneurs more interested in their own profit than in paying the government equitable fees.

Through nearly all the years from 1826 to 1865, Peru lacked banks to provide either public or private credit. Because of Catholic objections to charging interest on loans, Spain had not developed banking. Consequently, newly independent Peru depended on foreign sources of credit. The *caudillos,* conditioned by service with Spanish gentlemen-officers to disdain commerce, failed to consolidate their political independence by promptly building economic independence. Only the overseas demand for guano with its attendant large-scale financial operations forced industrial age capitalism upon the Peruvian primary city.

The guano boom greatly increased the amount of cash in the hands of Peruvian urban entrepreneurs; by the early 1860s some stood ready to venture into commercial banking. No less than three banks opened in 1863, one headed by a Belgian, one British, and one capitalized by domestic investors including Manuel Pardo. Thus, the bank as a fundamental credit institution reached Peru nearly four decades after political independence.

Establishment of a British bank branch in Lima in part stemmed from postindependence entry into Peruvian commerce of many Englishmen who had fought with the separatist forces. They captured a large share of the wholesale and even retail trade in the larger cities. In the ten to fifteen years after 1824, English veterans and other immigrants numbered fully one-quarter of the merchants operating on the main public square of departmental capitals such as Huaráz.

While the *caudillos* squabbled over chief executive succession, much real power seeped away from them to merchants. Martial activities demanded financing, so the *caudillos* sought funds from merchants whose commercial activities they scorned. Merchants who financed coups d'état exacted concessions in return to augment their power. The entry into commerce of British, often Irish, revolutionary war veterans accelerated this process of sharing real power.

Despite the fact that the *caudillos* still vied with one another for the presidency, by 1850 Peru had begun to establish sufficient stability to attract some investment. Soon after independence, English capitalists had acquired rich mines to which they introduced steam engines and other examples of European technology. The rapid and careless development of guano deposits offered speculators a chance for quick and large profits. Coastal Peruvian cotton and sugar plantations attracted not only foreign capital, but also brought representatives of overseas capital interests to Lima. The U.S. Civil War in particular opened to cotton exporters new European markets, especially in England. Merchants experienced a period of growth full of potential for the risk-taker.

Although the national government passed from clique to clique, businessmen found that they could prosper because people sought employment on the one hand and consumer goods on the other. Entrepreneurs found it relatively easy to make deals with politicians, lawyers, generals, and landowners all ready to share in business expansion for both patriotic and personal moitves. *Laissez faire* seldom had more active champions than the men who led and governed Peru during this period.

While foreign bankers could meet Peruvian credit needs for nearly forty years, political independence forced Peruvians to build other new institutions rather sooner than banks. Secularization decreed by the anticlerical Bolívar received continued support from later leaders although it posed new problems. The religious orders had founded and staffed many urban hospitals as well as the handful of schools. Secularization lifted the "dead hand" of the church from much property with which such institutions had been endowed during the centuries of colonial rule. This left the government as new owner to manage a large number of urban and rural properties in nearly every province.

A Bolivarian decree in 1825 created a *Junta de Beneficencia* in Lima, headed by an attorney of the new Supreme Court created a year earlier. The *Junta* was to administer hospitals and welfare programs.

In 1826, the government established a Bureau of *Beneficencia* with paid employees to replace the unpaid members of religious orders who had previously tended the sick. The Bureau assigned profits from the lottery started in 1783 to the hospitals, and bullring rents were used to feed the poor. The organization gained a poor reputation, however, and closed some hospitals. By 1832 the Bureau operated only three Lima hospitals, and President Gamarra decreed that their operation be auctioned off. In less than a year, the government returned the hospitals to the Bureau. In other words, the new republic continued to seek a viable mechanism for providing hospital care on a par with that available in colonial times.

In the midst of his many tribulations as president, Luís José Orbegoso provided a solution. In 1834, Orbegoso decreed the establishment of the *Sociedad de Beneficencia Pública de Lima*. This new, semipublic corporate organization became the owner of hospitals with their endowments, responsible for applying income from endowments and other sources to hospital operation and welfare. Orbegoso's genius lay in creating a board of forty prestigious citizens to set policy. They served without pay and met at least quarterly to review *Beneficencia* affairs. The government retained some supervision through the ministry charged with fostering a healthy citizenry. Board members were, on the other hand, independent of the government and normally self-perpetuating. In other words, members nominated their own successors unless the government intervened, which it seldom did.

A measure of the extent to which the *Beneficencia* replaced the church as a major property owner may be seen in the fact that by 1839, the Lima *Beneficencia* already owned 358 houses, or over a tenth of the private houses in the city at that time, in addition to extensive rural estates. By that time, Santa Cruz had decreed that such societies should be created in the capital of every department.

Membership in the various societies that evolved became a signal honor for members of the urban elite, both metropolitan and provincial. This solid social position of society membership appears, for example, in the careers of three late nineteenth-century leaders who headed societies prior to the presidency. Prestige and political advancement were not, however, the only rewards to be gained from society membership. The directors did, after all, manage many large and valuable urban and rural properties. While legislation eventually prohibited members of the boards from leasing properties from the societies they governed, it stopped short of outlawing favoritism to family and ritual kin. Board members often leased choice urban buildings to siblings, nephews, and other kinsmen to conduct lucrative family businesses in the cities. Most of the society endowment lay in rural areas, however, so members most often leased rural estates to their relatives or godsibs.

In some cases, the lessee promptly subleased the rural estate to one or more persons interested in cultivating or grazing it. Naturally, the prime lessee charged a sum sufficient to provide him with a handsome profit. Sublessees in turn tended to extract as much profit from the estate as they could. No lessee had any long-term interest in maintaining permanent pastures or soil fertility; all tended to fully mine estates, causing each successive year's productivity to decline.

The rural estates held by societies often lay hundreds of kilometers away from the board room. Consequently, board members could not exercise effective supervision of isolated properties until communications greatly improved late in the nineteenth century. Some land-greedy provincial landlords carved away significant portions of society-owned estates. At their crudest, such provincial entrepreneurs simply moved their employees and/or livestock into society-owned areas and occupied them. At their most sophisticated, such provincial *gamonales*, as they are known in Peru, obtained court-granted titles via law suits. The lessees conspiring with them deliberately litigated so badly as to lose, without the distant society's board being able to intervene effectively.

The greatest paradox of the republican *beneficencia* system of funding urban hospitals and charity remained the fact that many rural estates included not only land, but also Indian workers attached thereto. When would-be lessees bid at the legally required public auction for the right to exploit such an estate for a stated period of time, they bid more at times for the captive labor supply than for the land itself. On the one hand, the *beneficencia* provided hospital care of the highest quality and prestige to the urban elite. On the other hand, it partly paid for these amenities and ameliorations by the most ruthless exploitation of rural Native American labor tied to society-owned lands. The rural and urban elites manipulated the institutions of government to legalize *de facto* forms of human bondage that parliaments repeatedly made illegal.

The extralegal aggression of land-greedy provincials against the lands and laborers of the urban *beneficencias* constituted merely one of the numerous forms land acquisition by Creoles and Mestizos took after 1825. There was no longer a king to decree measures designed to protect Indians and their property from rapacious non-Indians. The Creoles and Mestizos contesting for political supremacy in independent Peru also disputed economic spoils such as lucrative offices, import or export permits, but mainly farm and ranch land titles for their relatives and ritual kinsmen. Colonial Spanish culture conditioned Peru's new republicans to regard land as the best possible investment and ultimate value. Thus, many socially and economically ambitious Mestizos plunged energetically into a vicious struggle to control land. The favorite target remained the same as it had been throughout colonial times: the Indian. San Martín's decree making Native Americans citizens, and Bolívar's abolition of communal property-holding opened the way for unscrupulous literate Mestizos to obtain Indian lands by fraud and coercion.

The 1828 Constitutional Congress enacted basic Indian policy with high-sounding declarations of purpose. Justice demanded, it said, that both Indians and Mestizos be elevated to the class of landowners. The four policies established by the law that congress passed amounted to a massive attack on Indian property in general, and specifically upon that of indigenous communities. The key provision recognized Indians and Mestizos as owners of the lands they occupied. This proviso attacked the age-old practice of communal leaders assigning fields on the basis of family size each year or so—a usufruct system. The law authorized owners freely to sell or otherwise dispose of their land if they could read and write. While this policy appeared to leave land in the hands of the illiterate Indian masses untouched, it in fact provided little protection for nonliterate owners against a literate dominant group willing and ready to forge bills of sale, mortgages, and other documents that could transfer land titles.

The law provided that landless Indians and Mestizos should receive fields from boards set up in the departments. This led to another assault on Indian communal lands because "surplus" holdings could be found only at the cost of the indigenous communities.

Unscrupulous men building large haciendas and small farms could purchase lands from Indians, despite all safeguards. Although San Martín and Bolívar decreed an end to Indian tribute, as had an 1811 colonial decree, Free Peru did not abandon that major revenue source until the end of the nineteenth century. Even before Bolívar left Peru his Minister of Government reestablished, in July, 1826, Indian tribute and tribute-registration to provide basic national government financing.

Post-Bolivarian governments gave tribute a different name. Indians paid a head-tax euphemistically called a *contribución*. Even though Mestizos and whites were also legally subject to pay a *contribución*, the legislation was so selectively enforced that Indians became its principal and remained almost its only victims. Native Americans therefore required cash to pay the head-tax and stay out of jail. Men building up estates could easily find Indians in need of cash to whom to lend money, taking in return mortgages on their land. Indians who needed a loan were likely not to be able to retire a mortgage, so that moneylenders could amass considerable estates over a period of time.

Independent Peruvians selectively obeyed or avoided republican decrees and parliamentary enactments, just as they had obeyed convenient portions of viceregal or royal decrees and disregarded inconvenient provisions. Respect for law became even less than it had been in colonial times, however, inasmuch as presidents and members of parliament lacked the royal mystique that had lent an aura of authority to the king's decrees. Land-greedy Creoles and Mestizos found it convenient to obey San Martín's decree making Indians citizens, but to ignore sections of the very same decree outlawing personal involuntary servitude. This discriminatory style of law enforcement facilitated rapid accumulation of land resources in the hands of new dominant classes. Provincial estate-builders sometimes simply invaded and seized Indians lands. Usually they found legal pretexts for gaining title to the small plots of freeholders, but the most tempting large tracts of indigenous communities required force. Their special legal status under the crown ended, indigenous communities fought back as best they could but suffered serious handicaps. Bolívar's decree of individual land tenure meant in practice that indigenous communities lost their former legal status as corporate bodies. Bolívar legally destroyed their leadership by the stroke of his pen. Consequently, community leaders bore a heavy burden of having to represent their community members extralegally, outside the law. Thus, land-greedy outsiders could bring the weight of the courts and other institutions to bear upon community leaders and destroy their positions. If every member of the threatened community did not rally around its leadership, land-grabbers could destroy it by dividing members into factions and then buying out those willing to sell.

Estate-builders destroyed many indigenous colonial communities during the century following San Martín's landing on the coast of Peru. Yet a large number managed to survive. As a matter of fact, the social, political, and economic pressures brought to bear by land-grabbers had the effect of socially unifying some communities. They became "closed corporate" communities. They closed their ranks against outsiders and became secretive about community affairs as a necessary condition for maintaining existence.

The pressures bearing on indigenous communities did encourage them to distribute lands to individuals as Bolívar's decree had intended. When communal leaders could not act legally for all community members, communal land seemed safer with legal title in the names of individuals who adhered to a rule of not selling to nonmembers. Many did succumb to temptation or were forced or hoodwinked into selling, so that the community land base materially diminished after 1826. Spanish-style laws of inheritance required equal apportionment of estates among heirs. Peru applied such laws to Indians once they became citizens, which subdivided production units through the years until some became too small to be productive. At the same time, the population of indigenous communities grew, so that members were divided over issues of land assignment and control at the same time that they tried to maintain a united front against outside *gamonales*.

Only in 1854, while elected President José R. Echenique struggled with rebel former President Ramón Castilla for control, did the Creole elite decisively improve the legal condition of the two most oppressed ethnic groups, again reduced to slavery and tribute-payment by the 1839 Constitutional Congress. Scrambling for support while still only a self-declared president, Castilla abolished Indian tribute on July 5, 1854. Income from guano concessions annually placed millions of pesos in the exchequer and seemed to diminish the need to tax Indians. Toward the end of the year, Echenique went Castilla one better when he decreed freedom for Black slaves serving two years in the army. The congress meeting at Huancayo in support of Castilla's rebellion confirmed his abolishment of tribute, and in December, Castilla decreed the complete freedom of slaves. In 1855, Castilla's government budgeted a million guano fee pesos to pay owners for freed slaves.

Peru's shift from freeing slaves during the war of independence to reestablishing slavery and the slave trade to abolition constitutes one example of the wild gyrations in some major policies produced by unending contests for the presidency. Yet the bureaucracy eventually stabilized itself. National ministries and local government divisions not only continued to function but actually expanded. The republican government assumed more and more tasks that the colonial regime had either controlled or ignored. The growth in the national bureaucracy began in earnest as government operations expanded to include educational facilities, foreign affairs, finance and budget operations in addition to military matters. Opportunities for white-collar employment, which the Spaniards had tried to monopolize under the colonial regime, opened up for literate Creoles and Mestizos, enhancing the demand for education as a means of upward socioeconomic mobility.

Peruvians imported the U.S.-French revolutionary idea of a literate, informed electorate, but required well over a century to build a national public school network. At the secondary level, numerous new *colegios* opened their doors between 1827 and 1865. Ayacucho and Huaráz acquired such schools in 1828, followed by Chiclayo in 1832. In 1840, politician-educator Domingo Elías joined in founding the *colegio* of Our Lady of Guadalupe in Lima. Nationalized a few years later, this became and long remained perhaps the most prestigious secondary school in Peru. Guadalupe classmates occupied key posts in government, commerce, and letters. Trujillo gained a *colegio* in 1854. Such provincial secondary schools assumed particular importance in reducing the need for educational migration to Lima and Cuzco.

The second Castilla regime initiated in 1855 a major overhaul of San Marcos University. It incorporated five independent faculties into the old school to try to convert it into a truly multidisciplinary university along recognizably modern lines. The faculty argued colonial privilege against government intervention in order to resist and to weaken reform. The hitherto independent medical school became a key addition to San Marcos in 1856.

The republican Peruvians also founded a number of specialized teaching institutions as the country struggled to import new technologies developed elsewhere. The Free Peruvian government tried early with little apparent success to transfer the Spanish military school model. In 1847, the first Castilla regime founded a military *colegio* and a naval school. During Bolívar's last year in Peru, a midwifery school had opened its doors in Lima, and in 1854 a nursing school began instruction there. Despite such innovations, general sanitation and health conditions remained so bad that the death rate in Lima was not lowered below 35 to 40 per 1,000 until nearly the end of the century.

Spanish colonial rule left Peru a grim public health legacy. Only the royal diffusion of smallpox vaccination early in the nineteenth century improved life expectancy. Many Old World diseases characteristic of lowland areas, particularly malaria and yellow fever, made death-traps across the coastal valleys. The situation improved only slowly and haltingly, as political leaders accepted technological innovations originating in Europe and North America.

As in most developing countries, Peru suffered from very high infant mortality, caused largely by the many diarrhetic disease agents
common in the environment. The street system prescribed by colonial
law fostered the spread of water-borne disease agents, given the habits
of urban Peruvians. Cobblestoned streets sloped from the houses toward the center, where water ran through a ditch. That open ditch
provided domestic water, but also operated as a sewer. Housewives
and servants dumped garbage in the street to be consumed by pigs
and poultry or cats and dogs, which then added their feces to the semi-
liquified residue that gradually coated the ditches. Human excrement
joined the same nitrogen- and germ-rich mixture abounding in intes-
tinal parasites. Canons of modesty led most men to urinate against
building walls rather than directly into the street, but this custom contributed a rank sulphurous odor to narrow downtown streets.

Improvement of potable water supplies in Peru's cities began to
appear first in those areas where foreigners called most often and demanded water that at least looked clean and did not quickly become
undrinkable in ships' tanks. The increase in shipping that stemmed
from guano exploitation beginning in 1840 led to Callao's acquiring a
potable water system in 1846 and Islay in 1847. By 1856, both Lima
and Callao boasted potable water distribution and sewage disposal systems, which the government then turned over to a private company.
These improvements in environmental sanitation failed in and of
themselves to lower urban death rates markedly, but they set a trend.

Private enterprise contributed to that trend in some ways. A glass
bottle and demijohn factory opened in Lima in 1838, for example.
Several water-borne diseases could still be transmitted on reused, un-
washed bottles, of course, and reused these scarce containers certainly
were. Once doctors and nurses began to teach the value of washing,
on the other hand, bottles provided a better utensil for sterilization
than handmade ceramic containers or *chicha*-drinking gourds.

In 1863, a German brewer founded in Callao a brewery that expanded to become a major purveyor of a nutritious, sanitary substitute for home-brewed *chicha*. Municipalities tended to outlaw *chicha*
production, ostensibly on sanitary grounds, although often really as an

ethnically discriminatory measure, inasmuch as *chicha* was denigrated as an "Indian" beverage.

The generally healthy rural population grew steadily and provided migrants to augment urban populations despite high city mortality. Periodic estimates of the national population and summations of available tax register lists make clear that the population increased at a rather steady rate from the end of Bolivarian rule to the midcentury war with Spain.

The government's official newspaper estimated Peru's population in 1826 at 1,325,000 persons: 320,000 on the coast and a million in the Sierra and the rain forest. The government considered that 51 percent of the population was Indian, 22 percent Mestizos to 11 percent whites, and only 3 percent free colored persons with another 4 percent slaves.

During the brief union of Peru with Bolivia, Santa Cruz ordered a population count based on head-tax registration that indicated 1,373,736 persons. During Castilla's first administration, in 1850, the government again undertook to count the people. Tax records for Indians and rural and urban property owners provided the basic data—inaccurate because tax-dodging has always been a major activity. The count rose nonetheless to 2,011, 203. Inasmuch as the errors in 1850 probably were of much the same magnitude as those of 1826, the two counts suggest a definite increase. The population apparently increased by 45.7 percent during the 14-year interval, an annual average rate of over 3 percent. The improbability of such a high rate of increase suggests that tax-collection techniques improved enough to achieve a fuller 1850 count than was possible in 1836.

In 1861, parliament ordered a civil register set up for voters as well as a national population census. The 1862 count for political ends came from commissioners appointed by prefects, and probably yielded a result that undercounted the true population. It counted 2,487,916 persons, which indicated a 24 percent increase over a dozen years, or an annual two percent rate of increase.

Despite such evidence of a rapidly growing population, Creole and Mestizo leaders shared the misconception that Peru was chronically underpopulated and short of labor. To some extent the impressive figure for Peru's total area bewitched the leadership into ignoring the visible reality of a limited arable land base. Moreover, profit-seeking plantation owners wanted more cheap field labor in the coastal valleys than they found or could entice there. The hostile disease environments of the coastal oases discouraged Sierra Indian migration. The Black populace declined after slave imports stopped because of the acute shortage of Black women and miscegenation, as well as disease mortality.

Guano profits began around 1840 to foster capital expansion and technification of oasis export agriculture. Increasingly powerful landowners sought cheap labor abroad to cultivate and harvest new cash crops such as cotton. The racially prejudiced Peruvian elite preferred European immigrants, but the republic failed to compete successfully with the United States and Argentina for European migrant farmers.

Europeans avoided migrating to rural Peru for several reasons. The country lacked a police system to keep its rural areas and roads even as peaceful and secure as the U.S. Indian frontier. At the time Charles Darwin visited Peru, in 1839, bandits attacked and robbed the British consul on the road between Lima and Callao, which was the most well-traveled route in the nation! Black and Mestizo bands of highwaymen constantly threatened traffic on the roads. Thus, installation of the "English train" between Callao and Lima during Castilla's first government in 1851 marked a dramatic step in Lima's urban growth. It helped put an end to banditry along that route, speeded communications with the port, and helped to establish a sense of progress. Still, the railroad that reinforced Lima's primacy attracted European migrants there, not to the coastal valleys linked by roads still infested with highwaymen and consisting mostly of sand.

In plain economic terms, Peru's land-greedy elite also failed to find areas of arable land to open to immigrants at prices competitive with those offered in Argentina or the U.S. Cultivators had long since settled on the arable lands, and plow and windmill technology could not subjugate millions of acres of prairie grasslands. The high cost of passage to Peru compared to the Atlantic nations, and Peru's image of political instability did not prevent British and other European migrants from settling in Lima and other Peruvian cities. Thus, the failure of Peru to offer potentially profitable farming opportunities in safe rural regions must be considered the basic reason for its failure to attract Europeans to its rural areas.

When plantation owners failed to obtain European labor, they turned to Asia. Grape and cotton grower Domingo Elías, one of Peru's wealthiest politicians, together with a partner imported seventy-five Chinese at Callao in 1849. This act opened modern Chinese migration to Peru. Presented with a *fait accompli,* the parliament passed a general immigration law, which encouraged European immigration. The main object of this "Chinese Law" was, however, to authorize after the fact the importation of Chinese coolies.

José R. Echenique shared the elite vision of Peru as underpopulated when he became president early in 1851. On the other hand, he objected to importing "people of such bad race and so inappropriate, which has yielded such bad results." Echenique suspended the 1849 "Chinese Law," and in 1853 asked parliament to pass new immigration laws. Struggling against Castilla to stay in office, however, Echenique lacked the power to terminate coolie importation.

Cosmopolitan Lima had included Chinese residents since at least 1613 and had successful Chinese businessmen in the nineteenth century. Runaway laborers, or those who finished out their contracts, made for Lima and Trujillo. They eventually created small Chinatowns in both cities, with Chinese restaurants and other specialized ethnic businesses. Many Chinese immigrants acquired Peruvian wives, typically Mestizos.

A variety of other changes further concentrated the good parts of Peruvian life in Lima. Technological innovations improved Lima's urban ambience before they could act upon other parts of the country simply because Lima was already the decision-making site of government. In 1847, Melchor Charón demonstrated a gas lighting system to President Castilla. Four years later, the regime contracted with Charón's company for 500 gas lamps in central Lima. Castilla returned to the Pizarro Palace in time ceremonially to light the first gas lamp in 1855. Within two years, the system served 2,200 street lights and over 5,000 lamps in offices, stores, and private homes. Although poor families continued to light their homes at night with oil lamps and candles, gas lighting achieved the first fundamental change in the nighttime appearance of the city since Amat's time and facilitated movement at night until the advent of electricity over thirty years later.

Other shifts in the relative importance of Lima and the provinces occurred because colonial customs continued. The Spanish king had chartered the cities and defined the boundaries of the provinces. Republican leaders in parliament or the presidency found it difficult to refuse to do the same in response to demands from provincial officers to share the political power and social glory of Lima. A process of creating new departments began in 1828. By 1865 the number had doubled to fourteen, and provinces proliferated in like proportion. This made more provincial towns departmental or provincial capitals so that they too acquired government offices and guano peso payrolls for their staffs. Such settlements indeed gained social prestige relative to the more provincial ones. Yet this process weakened each departmental capital relative to Lima, because the area in which each prefect could now mobilize opposition to national policy diminished.

Lima gained still other advantages over the provincial cities through social innovation. Throughout colonial times genetic kinsmen plus godsibs, and religious sodalities and orders augmented by royal honorary orders sufficed to embed people in society, save for a handful of formally educated men who formed close ties to classmates. To the extent that internal migrants to cities organized to pursue social or economic goals, they did so on the basis of common territorial origin. With independence and its increased uncertainties, many people felt a need to create alternative groups in whose membership they could repose some confidence. Common service in the revolutionary army proved too weak a bond on which to rely, inasmuch as personal ambition often dissolved it and later service in republican military units generated new loyalties. Many officers joined secret Masonic lodges, which at least promised to create strong alliances with other members.

New Peruvians such as British tradesmen brought with them a cultural propensity to form voluntary associations for both commercial and social purposes. They and other civilians holding economic power formed private clubs. The most important of these came to be the *Club Nacional* founded in 1855. A century later, people would remark that Peru's really important decisions were made, not on the *Plaza de la Inquisición* where the parliament building stands, but on the *Plaza San Martín*. The latter had the *Club Nacional* edifice on one side, the Military Casino on a second, and offices of a powerful corporation on a third. Other influential citizens formed the similar *Club de la Unión* in 1866. Its members have played more of a role in Lima urban affairs, perhaps, than in the national affairs of prime interest to members of the *Club Nacional*. These two clubs in and of themselves long comprised major influences upon public affairs. Their members stood more or less at the peak of society. At the same time, they drew emulation both from parallel clubs formed in provincial cities and the more specialized clubs founded later in Lima, such as the Country Club and the Military Casino.

Government and business provided an occupational and professional base for a nascent urban middle class. Wearing the European-style clothes of the moment, the men of Lima between 1827 and 1865 might have been indistinguishable from those of any other similar national capital city. The women, too, were style conscious, but retained a manner of behavior and dress still reminiscent of the previous colonial century. The famous *tapada,* or semiveiled dress derived from Moorish custom, characterized female public etiquette in Lima as well as in other former Spanish colonial cities.

Republican Lima society still luxuriated in the services of servants and slaves. The status of Blacks constantly fluctuated in the minds of uncertain leaders of the congress and the executive. That of Indian and Mestizo servants remained as subordinate as it had always been. The lower-class population of Lima and other cities constituted the vast numerical majority. Lower-class living conditions had not changed materially since colonial times, although certain routes of social mobility that previously had not existed began to open. Political independence brought more freedom of geographic movement, especially for those with rudimentary literacy and some technical skill. Newly created educational facilities in Lima, Arequipa, and Trujillo increasingly attracted the sons and later the daughters of the small-town elites seeking to expand their provincial horizons.

Rural Indians remained, however, mired in the socioeconomic swampland of serfdom, debt peonage, and isolation. While they formed the cornerstone of the nation's agricultural economy and its greatest human resource, they remained socially and politically marginal, at best. The urban upper and middle class could talk with paternal eloquence about "our Indians" and the "noble heritage" on occasion, but in all other ways they regarded the Indians as childlike and destined to remain so forever.

Peru continued to develop its own distinctive cultural character despite the continued rigidity of the social structure. Biological mixing of peoples produced a parallel cultural fusion. The Lima urban area in particular showed the effects of the process. In the postindependence generation, this emergent culture increasingly came to be identified with that which was "Peruvian." Creole food, music, and popular dances, which owed much to the Blacks and Mulattos, became representative of coastal culture. The earthquake-inspired holy days and celebrations were incorporated into this Creole culture. The popular festival called *Amancaes,* begun in Lima in the seventeenth century to celebrate the feast day of St. John on June 24th, featured the mass participation of thousands of Limeños. Picnics, guitar-playing, dancing, horsemanship, and games made this a popular annual expression of solidarity in which people from many social classes participated.

Despite all its deficiencies—easily seen in retrospect—Lima represented the model other provincial cities emulated. Lima's primacy not only remained undisputed, but in fact Lima increased its lead over Arequipa in population, institutional complexity, and innovations. In part because of political rivalries, which had clear regional bases in Arequipa, Cuzco, and Trujillo, these provincial cities carefully maintained their own uniqueness and asserted their political and cultural importance.

Chapter 8 • From One Master to Many, 1865-1895

Peru arrived at a political, economic, and social turning point in 1865. Late that year, a rebellious prefect deposed the last revolutionary war veteran to serve as president, bringing a new political generation to national command. Aging and death also contributed, of course, to the disappearance of such revolutionary war leaders. Yet the supply of veterans did not run out for some years more—one such general, for example, became Minister of War in 1872. The political revolution of 1865 stemmed rather from the failure of men reared in colonial agrarian culture to change their country at the same pace as industrializing nations were then doing.

The long competition for the presidential sash between veterans of the wars of independence had delayed technological and social innovation in Peru. The growing numbers of wealthy merchants and plantation owners—the sort of men who founded the new social clubs—held postcolonial values. They placed railroad building and other forms of industrial development ahead of the agrarian traditions. Consequently, the new generation of political leaders that emerged in 1865 sought to make up for the time spent disputing relatively fixed goods

instead of creating a new transportation industry and other innovations. Despite their enthusiasm for rapid industrial development, most
post-1865 politicians demonstrated little more sophistication than their
caudillo predecessors in financing large-scale public investments. Thus,
they resisted only indifferently the multiple foreign demands for varying degrees of control over Peruvian policies and resources.

The first foreign demands came from Spain, but they stemmed less
from some specific legacy of the revolutionary war than from the cal-
lousness that years of tyranny over Native Americans had bred in the
caudillos. One of the domestic policies of the generation of *caudillos,*
with their late colonial, agrarian views and racial prejudices set, was to
Europeanize the population by fostering European immigration. In
1859, therefore, Castilla's government authorized the entry of 1,000
Spanish colonists. Under this program a Basque recruited 175 fellow-
Basque immigrants to grow cotton on shares on Hacienda Talambo, a
north coast estate with a history of labor difficulties. The owner,
Manuel Salcedo, evidently treated the immigrants almost as arbitrarily
as he had become accustomed to treating domestic laborers. One immigrant complained to Salcedo in August, 1863. A foreman took
armed employees to expel the immigrant, and Basque group leaders
resisted. A shootout left at least one dead and several wounded.

After he collected depositions about the incident, the Chepén justice of the peace ordered the Basques imprisoned by the very hacienda
employees who had just assaulted them. On the third appeal, the Supreme Court affirmed a lower appellate order to imprison two Basques
for four months and overruled a higher appellate court order to try the
gamonal Salcedo. The matter did not end there, however, because this
agricultural labor protest differed from those that occurred frequently
in rural Peru in that the protesters were Spanish citizens. They could
not only test their rights in Peru's courts, but also had a foreign government to look after their welfare, which Native American peasants
and tenants did not. What were rather typical court proceedings in
Peru thus led to a formal protest from the Spanish consul. Peru told
its consul in Spain to insist that the government was not responsible

for the Talambo incident. What was customary and usual in landlord-tenant relations in Peru proved to be internationally unacceptable.

Spain reacted forcefully. A Spanish naval division conducting a scientific expedition had called at Callao on July 10, 1863. The Talambo incident occurred after the division had sailed, on July 17th, but prompted the division to return in mid-December. A Spanish council of war decided the fleet should occupy the guano-rich Chincha Islands. After a special Spanish emissary treated unsatisfactorily with Peruvian authorities, the ships disembarked their scientists. Cleared for action, the fleet in April, 1864, overpowered the 160-man garrison and 1,000 guano-diggers on the Chincha Islands. It also captured a merchant ship in Callao and notified the Peruvians that their country had not negotiated formal peace with Spain, only a truce. Now that Peru had adopted a hostile course, Spain argued, she, in turn, was seizing the guano islands. She announced that she would service Peru's foreign debt obligations but garner the guano profits as recompense. The wealth of the guano islands, then, reinforced Spanish concern with her emigrant citizens in Peru.

Diplomatic negotiations and maneuvers continued through 1864. Spain reinforced her Pacific fleet with three frigates and a new 7,000-ton armored battleship. Her Minister of Marine, General José Manuel Pareja, a native of Lima, took command. President Juan A. Pezet, who had succeeded to the office as vice-president after the death of fellow war of independence veteran Miguel San Román, appointed ex-president Manuel I. de Vivanco minister plenipotentiary to treat with Pareja.

At the end of January, 1865, Pareja delivered an ultimatum giving Peru twenty-four hours to agree to the Spanish position. Vivanco signed the treaty of peace and amity on board the Spanish *Villa de Madrid* on January 27th. Early in February, Pareja landed at Callao to visit Prefect General José Miguel Medina. Some 154 Spanish sailors landed; 90 went to Lima and 64 spread through the port of Callao. Altercations took place and a crowd killed a Spanish sailor. The mob then began to sack the homes of resident Spaniards and to damage the

Lima-Callao railroad trains. Pareja threatened to bombard Callao if the government did not control the mobs. Other incidents followed.

When news of these events reached Arequipa, its prefect, Mariano I. Prado, started on February 28th the revolutionary "Restoration of National Honor." Numerous political leaders disowned Vivanco's treaty signature, joined the revolt, and called for Vice-President Pedro Diez Canseco to assume the presidency. Southern cities rapidly joined Prado's movement. Col. José Balta rebelled at Chiclayo in April and gained control of the north in May. On November 6th gatekeepers opened a gate in Lima's protective colonial wall to a revolutionary column. The Lima garrison, led by Francisco Diez Canseco, the vice-president's brother and prefect of Lima, lost four-fifths of its numbers defending the capital for Pezet during a six-hour struggle. Once the Restoration forces took control, acting president Pedro Diez Canseco disbanded the army loyal to Pezet and ordered the deposed president and members of his cabinet, Canseco's brother Francisco included, brought to trial. Such were the divisions of loyalties the crisis produced.

Don Pedro called for congressional and presidential elections. Refusing to assume dictatorial power, he sought to transfer constitutional power to the new congress. Impatient revolutionary leaders would not wait, however, and on November 26th, some 500 persons convened on the Lima Plaza de Armas and proclaimed Col. Mariano I. Prado Dictator. Prado's government declared war on Spain and formed an alliance with Chile, which was already fighting Spain. Ecuador joined the alliance on January 30, 1866, followed by Bolivia.

The Spanish fleet moved from Chile to Callao late in April. Its commander issued an ultimatum, hoping, it would now appear, to bring about the fall of Prado. The population of the metropolitan area feverishly prepared for combat. Women, children, and older men evacuated Callao, but a multitude of patriots mobilized there. Many worked on new fortifications, and even schoolboys formed special fire companies. The Spanish admiral opened fire at 12:15 P.M. on May 1, 1866. Under the direct command of Secretary of War José Gálvez, Callao's defense batteries, constituting perhaps forty-five cannon in all, held their fire until the Spanish flagship delivered two broadsides.

Then Gálvez ordered one fort to open fire, shouting, "Spaniards, here we return to you the January 27th treaty!"

Within twenty minutes, a Peruvian shot put the *Villa de Madrid* out of action. Shortly thereafter, however, a Spanish shell exploded near the powderbags for the guns in the fort, killing Gálvez and several other senior officers and men. Thus, Peru gained a prototypical republican hero: one who died in his moment of greatness.

Soon after 2 P.M., the heavily listing *Berenguela* withdrew from the Spanish firing line, followed by the *Resolución* and then the *Almansa*. At 4:40 P.M., the Spanish flagship ordered a much-reduced fleet to withdraw. Both Spain and Peru celebrated victory. Having exhausted its munitions, however, the Spanish fleet weighed anchor on May 10th to cross the Pacific and refit in the Philippine Islands. In effect, that ended the war. Peruvians could celebrate a national unity unparalleled since the war of independence.

The brief war with Spain brought Peru to the very brink of economic disaster by accelerating the pace at which the nation turned itself over to overseas creditors, a practice initiated during the guano boom. Attempting to solve wartime problems, Peruvian regimes borrowed so heavily from abroad that they mortgaged major national assets for over a century. Nothing in the agrarian-mercantilistic colonial period or even in the early republican years had prepared political leaders to protect effectively the national interest from sophisticated financiers in industrial nations.

A fleet of warships purchased abroad constituted a major expense. During the first forty years after Bolívar's departure, his successors did little to found a shipbuilding industry. Consequently, Peru became more dependent upon foreign shipbuilders, whose products outclassed domestic ones, than it had been even in colonial times, when the isolation of west coast South America protected Chile, Peru, and Ecuador from European power politics. By midnineteenth century, the rapid increase in the size and speed of ships using steel hulls, steam engines, and propellers instead of sails significantly reduced the dangers of traversing the Straits of Magellan. While Peru's need for modern ships increased, the politicians had preserved their agrarian value framework.

The Pezet government resorted to the same measures that revolutionary war leaders had employed nearly forty years earlier. Peruvian agents scoured the shipyards of Europe to locate warships to purchase. In France, naval officers found in 1864 two wooden corvettes originally laid down for the U.S.—the *Unión* and *América*. Each displayed 1,600 tons propelled by a 500 HP engine and carried fourteen Voruz cannon. Peru obtained from English shipyards a 2,000-ton armored frigate, the *Independencia,* and a 1,100-ton monitor, the *Huascar.*

Peru also depended upon foreign suppliers of arms and munitions. Imported Blakely cannon were perhaps the most effective guns in the Callao batteries during the battle of May 2, 1866; the 300-caliber Armstrong cannon that helped to repulse the Spanish fleet's attack also came from abroad. Rifles and cartridges had to be purchased overseas in great numbers in order to arm Peruvian soldiers with up-to-date weapons.

Successive administrations therefore financed the purchase of defensive weapons and the brief actual conflict by the same means previous ones had employed to pay the cost of the national bureaucracy. They let contracts to guano distributors in return for loans advanced against guano sales profits. Just before the war, the German concessionaire obtained an extension of its contract in November, 1862, for a four-year period, advancing a sum equal to future receipts. That set a pattern for wartime financing. From February, 1864, through October, 1865, Peru obtained a dozen loans ranging from 200,000 to 4,000,000 pesos from German, Belgian, French, Dutch, Italian, Peruvian, Spanish, Portuguese, and U.S. concessionaires and extended their contracts anywhere from four to six years.

Peru's truly grandiose debt resulted from an April, 1864, authorization by the Permanent Committee of Congress to negotiate a loan of 50,000,000 pesos. Peru's minister in London, Federico L. Barreda, obtained the loan in February, 1865. Part of this sum was raised by public subscription, while the guano concession for Great Britain guaranteed interest and amortization. The effort eventually yielded Peru 9,655,632 of the new *soles* defined as the basic monetary unit when Peru adopted the metric system. The payment of previous advances required 2,306,571 of those and 875,000 went for commissions. The S/. 6,474,041 realized went to purchase the *Huascar* and *Independencia* and to pay Spain three million soles. Some of the French concessionaire's mid-1865 loan paid for the *Unión* and *América*.

By the time the Prado dictatorship took power at the end of 1865, the new Secretary of the Exchequer, Manuel Pardo, reported that Peru owed its guano concessionaires 20,430,000 pesos in advances and loans. While enjoying the guano windfall, no Peruvian regime had developed a sound internal financing system. Consequently, income from other sources amounted to only 3,000,000 pesos annually, while even the peacetime budget ordinarily ran about 12,000,000 pesos. Dictator Mariano I. Prado would have liked to repudiate all the contracts executed under the Pezet and Diez Canseco governments, but did not quite dare to do so while Peru needed credit.

After Spain's ships left Peruvian waters, Peru continued to borrow abroad. As minister in the U.S., Federico Barreda joined with a Chilean representative to negotiate a ten-million-peso loan. By 1868 Peru's foreign debt had mounted to over forty-two million soles. The Secretary of Exchequer necessarily dealt very largely with guano concessionaires. Unable to break existing contracts, Secretary Manuel Pardo sought to ameliorate them.

The government also borrowed within Peru. The Pezet regime sought a million pesos at six percent interest. It obtained 492,000 pesos, increased in value by one-quarter as a consequence of the change in monetary unit from the peso to the sol. The rebels financed their Restoration by promissory notes, which the dictatorial government recognized once it gained power. Thus, internal debt added up to 7,000,000 soles by 1865. When Pardo took up his responsibilities as Secretary of the Exchequer, he faced a situation in which Peru owed guano concessionaires almost ten million soles from 1866 guano sales. Pardo then undertook what no Minister of Exchequer had done previously. He formulated the first republican annual budget relating expenditures to income, called for increased taxes, and reduced expenditure.

Pardo's taxes were not especially original. A 3 percent export tax affected silver, gold, nitrates, wool, cotton, sugar, rice, and tobacco. Pardo imposed the same 3 percent on cane alcohol and documentary stamp sales. He assessed rural and urban property owners 4 percent of the estimated yield of their holdings. He set the head-tax on Native Americans at the equivalent of twelve days' wages—the latter differed in various provinces. Each of Pardo's taxes aroused opposition from those they affected.

Domestic credit institutions increased while Peru mortgaged its resources overseas. Pardo founded a National Mortgage Bank in 1866 while Minister of Exchequer. Two years later, Pardo presided as director of Lima's *Beneficencia* when it founded a savings bank called the *Caja de Ahorros*. The *Caja* invested in government securities and mortgages and paid its depositors 6 percent interest, but limited their accounts to S/. 1,000. The *Caja de Ahorros* still functions.

The Bank of Lima organized in 1869 with a capital of S/. 3,200,000 opened early in 1870 in Lima and Callao. The Dreyfus commercial house quickly organized the *Banco Nacional del Peru* in Lima with a capital of twelve million soles distributed in 12,000 shares of S/. 1,000 each, of which Dreyfus held 4,000. A Bank of Trujillo opened in 1871; the Banks of Tacna, Piura, Arequipa, and the Bank of Junín in Cerro de Pasco opened in 1872, and a bank appeared even in Ascope in 1873. By 1872, however, Lima dominated banking as it already did other economic activities, with six banks compared to two in La Libertad Department, a pair in Arequipa, one each in Piura, Cerro de Pasco, and Tacna, and branches in Cuzco and Puno.

Lima gained steadily improving administrative control over its national hinterland because the Prado and later regimes fostered interurban telegraphic communication. Only Lima and Callao possessed a telegraph connection when a ten-year contract granted in 1857 expired. Prado nationalized that service, but turned it over to Carlos Paz Soldán after authorizing him to build a line from Lima to Lambayeque. As telegraph lines reduced the time messages required to travel between major cities from days to hours and minutes, a new degree of economic and political integration became possible.

At this same period, the Yankee entrepreneur Henry Meiggs and local capitalists began to change the physical nature of colonial Lima. They obtained government permission to tear down the massive defensive wall. The first strike by workers in Peru had occurred in 1685 during the erection of that wall, and the first workers' strike in slowly industrializing Peru came in 1872 among laborers tearing it down. Meiggs and his associates planned to create new urban blocks in the space gained. Their plan failed, but removing the wall opened up an area where later regimes built new sections of the city on a French model, with wide avenues, sidewalks, and numerous round multiple-street intersections with circular parks in the middle.

The nationalistic Prado government undertook other reforms Peruvians considered so liberal as to arouse opposition to the Restoration. The dictatorial government abolished some of the separate tribunals and legal codes inherited from colonial times, the special courts of commerce and exchequer, the Ancash and Junín departmental courts, among others. It reduced the number of judges in other courts and cut judicial vacations, although it raised judges' salaries. It created a new "Central Court" to try cases involving public officials. These actions brought the executive into conflict with the Supreme Court, whose justices were required to swear allegiance to the revolutionary regime. Prestigious judges refused and left the court, only to be reinstated by a conservative Constitutional Congress in 1867.

Prado's Minister of Justice and Education, José Simeón Tejeda, labored to impose a uniform curriculum in secondary schools. He sought to reorient them toward vocational training rather than traditional college preparatory courses. The regime moved away from the traditional agrarian concept of sex roles: an 1866 decree proposed public instruction of females and provided that women would be allowed to teach primary school classes. The Constitutional Congress in 1867 called for a secondary school for each sex in every provincial capital. These laws remained like many other idealistic central government actions, a dead letter for the moment.

Minister Tejeda instituted university reform. He abolished the colonial *Colegio de San Marcos* as an independent unit in San Marcos University. He created faculties in the university of Jurisprudence,

Sciences, and Letters and, in spite of objections from Lima's Archbishop José Sebastian de Goyeneche, a Theology faculty. The liberal
revolutionaries of 1865 labored, like Bolívar, to diminish the strength
of Peru's conservative church establishment. Peru still exercised the
state *patronato* derived from Spain—the right of national approval of
church actions. The archbishop insisted upon publishing a papal bull
and letters without remitting them to the Ministry of Foreign Relations and Ecclesiastical Affairs or obtaining parliamentary approval.
Minister Tejeda thereupon cut off the government subsidy to the archdiocese.

The dictatorial government also reformed the fiscal administration
of numerous sodalities that carried out public devotions. These voluntary religious associations founded under colonial rule operated under
ecclesiastical authority with regard to their ceremonial behavior. The
civil authority regulated their administration of funds collected to
finance their activities. In 1853 President Echenique had established
a *Junta* to supervise these sodalities, and in 1865 the Prado regime decreed that the Lima *Beneficencia* should administer the sodalities.
Archbishop Goyeneche objected in vain.

Prado's Ministry of Government in 1866 issued new municipal regulations concerning architecture, public health, the market, water supplies, artisans, servants, funerals, bell-ringing, and other aspects of
urban life. These regulations attempted to end the practice continued
since colonial times of carrying the Viaticum from churches to the
homes of dying persons in great processions accompanied by tolling
church bells. The new laws provided that the Viaticum be conducted
privately. Needless to say, clerics resolutely opposed the liberal legislation, and the regime tossed a number of defiant priests into jail.
Prado freed them, nonetheless, when the Archbishop donned his
elegant vestments and called upon the chief executive to ask for their
freedom.

The dictatorship issued also in 1866 an Organic Regulation for the
municipalities, which had, prior to that, received checkered treatment.
The Bolivarian regime had formally abolished municipal governments
in 1826. They resumed operations in 1828. Echenique formally re-

established them in 1853. Now the dictatorship even allowed foreign citizens to serve as members of municipal councils, but it organized accounts, budgets, and resources.

The dictatorship thus instituted a series of measures that affected the everyday behavior and pocketbooks of much of the population. As a result, it grew unpopular as the patriotic euphoria and unity of May 2, 1866, dissipated. Prado called for elections for the presidency and a Constitutional Congress. This seventh Constitutional Congress since independence convened February 16, 1867, and produced a new constitution. Prado immediately dropped his dictatorial powers and reported to the body on his fourteen-month tenure. Seizing the bit in its teeth, the congress assumed full powers and established a mixed conservative record. It guaranteed freedom of the press, but rejected a bill to expropriate temporal properties of the church. It established Roman Catholicism as the state religion by a wide margin, and prohibited public worship by any other denomination by a close vote. It outlawed any new guano contracts with concessionaires and ordered guano destined for each importing power to be auctioned off to the highest bidder. It forced Prado's cabinet ministers to appear in parliament to answer questions, yet kept Prado as provisional president and certified his election as constitutional president.

Rural-urban migrants and bacteriological scourges continued to write biological history, particularly in coastal cities, quite without regard for political events. In 1867, yellow fever raged in Lima and Callao. Lima *Beneficencia* Director Manuel Pardo reported that 4,445 of the 8,478 burials in the cemeteries the society operated were yellow fever victims. If Lima's reported 1862 population of 89,434 had increased to about 93,250 in 1867, yellow fever mortality alone reached some 48 per 1,000 in addition to a 40 per 1,000 death rate from other causes.

Like germs, new social ideals entered Peru from abroad and generated clashes between their advocates and entrenched vested interests. Following the formation of powerful private clubs not long before the war with Spain, at least two other important kinds of voluntary associations emerged in embryonic form. One was the Indian defense organization; the other was the political party.

The rigorous collection of the Indian head-tax levied by the dictatorship caused Indians of Huancané in Puno Department to rebel early in 1866. They rose up against the local officials who mistreated them and the provincial elite who garnered the profits from the cattle and wool trade, the mining of minerals, and Indian labor. Their particular target was *pongaje*—the requirement that they provide unremunerated compulsory personal service, a practice that was declared illegal in San Martín's 1822 decree. This Indian protest movement differed from many that occurred earlier and many that followed in that it found a champion of national stature. This was Juan Bustamante, a successful wool dealer in Cabanillas and Puno. He had served as a deputy in the 1856 convention, and had fought as a colonel in the May 2, 1866, defense of Callao. In 1867 Bustamante acted as the representative of the Huancané Indian protestors. In mid-1866 Bustamante asked congress to pass basic Indian legislation. He circularized generals who had served as prefects in Cuzco and Puno to inquire about the conditions of the Indians. Consequently, a new voluntary association called *La Sociedad Amiga de los Indios* was organized to stimulate public, primarily urban, interest in Native Americans among persons not directly competing with them for scarce rural resources. This began serious efforts to improve Indian status.

An early result of the Huancané revolt and Bustamante's initiative seems to have been a stirring of the consciences of members of parliament over ever-fierce provincial exploitation of Indians. Early in 1867, congress repealed the head-tax, largely at the urging of Cuzco Deputy Mariano Herencia Zevallos.

Conservative Arequipa rejected the new 1867 constitution. Other cities joined the revolt and forced Prado to resign. Anti-Prado forces stoned Bustamante to death on January 3, 1868, after defeating his Native American supporters. A full army division "pacified" the region.

Cuzco's Senator Pío Benigno Mesa introduced a bill in the conservative 1868 parliament to abolish compulsory service by the Indian authorities Toledo put in office, known variously as the *alcaldes, regidores, fiscales,* and other colloquial terms. The bill prohibited Indians from being forced to sponsor festivals. The anti-Indian elite sent this bill to committee to die. Yet the executive removed a Cuzco prefect who launched a sophisticated campaign to deprive Indians of their land titles.

The other important type of voluntary association that appeared during the presidential election campaign in 1868 took the form of "Civic Clubs" supporting the candidacy of a civilian. They anticipated the *Sociedad Independencia Electoral* formed in 1871, which became the nucleus of the *Civilistas,* Peru's first recognizable political party. By 1872, politicians opposed to military dominance were able to elect Manuel Pardo to the presidency. Something of the reformist nature of the great statesman's regime is indicated by the fact that it carried out the first direct enumeration of the population since independence. The 1876 census enumerated 2,699,106 persons of whom 57 percent were Native Americans and 35 percent white and Mestizo.

The *Civilistas* aroused the fears of the clerics because of their anticlerical bent and emphasis upon modern scientific teaching and concerns. A strong current of anticlerical feeling had long been present in Peru, even in colonial times, despite the pompous *Te Deums* celebrated some six to eight times a year in the great Lima cathedral in the formal presence of the ministers of government and the head of state. Anticlericalism grew during republican times and many members of the elite joined the Free Masons. "Free thinkers" abounded among the middle class and intelligentsia and the growing urban labor force. Disillusion with the clergy was less openly expressed in the provinces. Instead, Mestizo male leaders developed a rich store of anticlerical humor and did not attend church for long periods save on official feast days.

Not surprisingly, in view of the depth of the conflicts between the powerful groups, the Restoration revolt presaged another thirty years of unstable chief executive succession in spite of the *Civilistas.* Several of the eighteen men who acted as chief executive served full constitutional terms, but coups d'état placed 44 percent of the eighteen in power, twice the pre-1865 rate. A fifth of them were elected and as many succeeded constitutionally.

Two-thirds of these presidents were army officers compared to four-fifths prior to 1865. Two wars greatly reinforced the influence of the army, resulting in what a leading Peruvian historian has labeled "the second militarism." Two-fifths of the post-1865 chief executives helped to defend Callao on May 2, 1866. The small decline in the proportion of officer-presidents represented real civilian headway. Although a veteran of the Restoration revolt, Manuel Pardo won election in 1872 as a civilian. He served a full term and conveyed office to an elected successor in 1876, thus setting a vital precedent. The *Civilistas* created a small alternative to *caudillismo*.

With an average age of fifty-one years on first taking office, the 1865-95 chief executives were perceptibly older than those from independence to 1865. Half were in their fifties. Lima's preponderance fell slightly to a fifth of these chief executives, while Arequipa supplied the same proportion, and Cuzco half as many. A fifth of them belonged to the landed aristocracy. Half of the presidents had served as cabinet ministers, twice the pre-1865 proportion. Not quite two-fifths had been prefects, so cabinet experience became more important than prefectural position after 1865. Over four-fifths, a slightly higher proportion than before 1865, came to the presidency with important previous executive experience.

Post-1865 political leaders broke abruptly with previous executive indifference to industrialization. Enchanted by visions of a socially and economically integrated Peru, they committed government resources to railroad construction. Army officer-presidents failed to generate concurrent industrialization projects of other kinds, however, so overseas creditors who financed Peru's railroads continually accumulated claims against the national patrimony.

Transportation costs prior to 1865 had produced some grotesque consequences that post-1865 presidents hoped to alter by large-scale movement of cargo by rail. The Andean highlands in Junín Department, for example, produced wool sold on the export market in quantities large enough to provide a structure for Peru's new colonial relationship to industrialized countries. A wealthy landowner might sell wool for twelve pesos per quintal to European buyers. Freight charges from Jauja to Lima ran from seventy to eighty pesos per ton. Pressing and wrapping the bales added one peso twelve reales per quintal. Sea freight from Callao to England ran six to seven pounds per ton plus 18 to 20 percent for insurance, customs commissions, and other related costs. In England, the purchaser often resold the wool to a washer, who added some shillings more for his operation and resold it at a profit to a textile factory. The same importer who brought the raw wool into England often exported finished cloth back to Peru. Woven cloth added the freight cost by sea to Callao, a 30 percent import duty, shipment from Callao to Lima, customs commissions, and once again freight charges of eighty pesos from Lima to Jauja. Thus the people sitting on Peru's throne of gold beggared themselves.

Once income from guano appeared secure after the war with Spain, national executives plunged feverishly into railroad construction. Colonel Prado's Restoration regime awarded a contract for a Pacasmayo-Lambayeque railroad and another for an Eten-Chiclayo-Lambayeque-Ferreñafe road in 1867.

When General Pedro Diez Canseco ousted Prado, he moved quickly to initiate construction of a longer railroad from the coast to his native Arequipa. He had let a contract for this route during his first administration, only to have the contractor back out. Diez Canseco called in U.S. railroad entrepreneur Henry Meiggs and accepted his 1868 bid for S/. 12,000,000.

The next president, Col. José Balta, set a course of railroad construction that physically and psychologically altered the nation. He contracted for eight major lines:

Arequipa-Puno	S/. 32,000,000	completed 1876
Callao-La Oroya	27,600,000	reached Chilca 1878
Juliaca-Cuzco	25,000,000	completed 1909
Chimbote-Recuay	24,000,000	reached Huallanca 1922
Ilo-Moquegua	6,700,000	completed 1876
Pacasmayo-Cajamarca	5,850,000	reached Guadalupe 1874
Salaverry-Trujillo	3,234,756	completed 1876
Paita-Piura	1,945,600	completed 1875

Presidents Diez Canseco and Balta together launched railroad projects costing over 140 million soles. The planned line from Chimbote's great harbor through the Callejón de Huaylas would never reach Recuay, and completion of some other lines required decades. Construction began promptly, however, on the southern and central roads. Meiggs submitted plans for a central railroad in 1868, signed a contract at the end of 1869, and laid the first stone for Lima's Montserrat station on New Year's Day in 1870.

While Meiggs plunged energetically into building track, he enjoyed profits. He worked out agreements with the Balta regime in 1869 that affected national finance and sovereignty for over a century. Instead of selling bonds to the public to raise construction money, the regime turned bonds over to Meiggs as he paid for materials and labor. Inasmuch as these bonds had no established market value, the contractor inflated his charges to avoid losing money. On the last day of 1869, the Minister of Exchequer confirmed Meiggs's great powers to issue bonds amounting to 11,920,000 pounds sterling.

By 1869, Peruvian leaders became conscious that inflation had greatly increased prices during the previous decade and a half. Balta brought in a young newspaperman, Nicolás de Piérola, as a reform Minister of Exchequer. Thus, Piérola dealt with Meiggs on behalf of the government in 1870, after severely criticizing the 1869 relinquishment of government control over its foreign debt to the Yankee. Piérola began to pay Meiggs cash. Although he reasserted government management of its credit, Piérola pursued the familiar policy of large-scale borrowing abroad. In 1870 Peru obtained a loan from Dreyfus, the dominant guano trader, for S/. 59.6 million. That huge sum and its prompt expenditure for railroad construction not only reinforced the inflationary trend, but also fostered a boom psychology. Balta's regime embarked upon an even larger loan scheme in 1871, seeking 15 million pounds sterling, equivalent to 75 million soles, and later raised its goal to 36,800,000 pounds. The issue failed when the bonds went on sale in 1872. Dreyfus, who had already agreed to converting remaining 1865 bonds and some other minor conversions, purchased 4,000,000 pounds' worth. The net result to Peru, however, was the loss of all guano sales revenue. Peru received S/. 700,000 monthly from Dreyfus under their 1869 contract for two million tons of guano. The 1870 loan consumed three-sevenths of that sum for debt service, and the remaining four-sevenths went to service the 1872 loan. By that time, internal debt stood at less than 13 million soles, an amount insignificant in comparison to overseas obligations.

Railroad construction also brought about new conditions in terms of the evolution of track-laying gangs and the importation of additional Chinese laborers, some of them from the U.S. The long-range importance of railroads lay in the introduction of rapid and economical mechanical transportation. Railroads linked numerous isolated oases into new socioeconomic regions and fostered massive internal migration, which enhanced the population growth of the Lima-Callao metropolitan area.

Railroad service promptly brought high freight costs tumbling to a fraction of their pack-train level and provided rapid passenger movement between cities. The economic and social consequences reached great magnitudes. By 1870 Meiggs had laid enough track to put 78 kilometers of the central railroad from Callao through Lima to Cocacharca in service, expanding the zone of immediate dominance of the primary city in a new way.

In 1871 regular service began over the railroad uniting Ferreñafe with Lambayeque, Chiclayo and Monsefú down the valley and Pueblo Eten and the Port of Eten on the coast. That railroad provides a fine example of the sociocultural consequences of uniting population centers with mechanical transport. Despite the Inca and Spanish conquests, the Indians of Pueblo Eten continued to speak the Yunga language of the ancient Chimú kingdom. That linguistic continuity stemmed in large part from the geographic isolation of Eten, separated by fields and sand from other settlements. Favorably located close to marine food resources in a fertile and well-irrigated valley, the Eten Indians could survive while minimizing their social and economic interaction with outsiders. The railroad allowed shopkeepers to invade Eten with irresistible consumer goods. It proved to be an overpowering attraction to Eten Indians, especially the younger ones, who began to ride the cars to see the sights elsewhere in the valley. The Eten Yunga-speakers had to learn Spanish in order to communicate with shop-keepers, conductors, and such, and they learned to be ashamed of their own tongue. Within a relatively short time after 1871, this last pocket of prehistoric Yunga language vanished. The people of Eten had, moreover, to enter into the full-blown cash economy in order to in-dulge their propensity for riding the railroad and buying new goods. They had to produce surpluses for sale on a scale never previously achieved in their largely self-sufficient settlement-centric economy.

The same economic problem faced the nation. From the time civil-ian Manuel Pardo became president in 1872, he labored mightily to balance the budget and institute a fiscal policy that would diminish dependence on foreign lenders. With the state's guano income com-pletely obligated to service debt, Pardo faced a nearly impossible task. The failure of the 1872 bond issue signaled, morever, the end of the long free ride on unearned guano income that had financed national governments for a generation. The internal economy faltered as its import-export businesses suffered from imbalances and exchange diffi-culties heightened by the world depression of 1873. Customs receipts, the largest single source of income left, dropped steadily from 8,253,034 soles in 1873 to 5,541,664 soles in 1875 before picking up again to S/. 6,885,214 in 1877. By 1876, however, Peru was firmly gripped by economic depression.

In 1877, Mariano I. Prado's second regime approved a contract with "The Peruvian Guano Company" to distribute this fertilizer in all world markets outside the U.S., China, Japan, and the Antilles. Prob-lems continued, nonetheless, with Dreyfus, and new ones arose. Be-cause of market conditions, the Peruvian Guano Company failed to deposit funds in the Bank of England on January 1, 1879, to service Peru's foreign debt. Peru went bankrupt on the eve of war.

Peru soon plunged into a war for which it was totally unprepared militarily, economically, and most of all culturally. Veterans of the Spanish war attempting to establish the principle of transfer of power via elections found themselves spending large sums to suppress repeated coups d'état attempted by ex-cabinet minister Nicolás de Piérola. Internal and external debts mounted while rapid technological changes overseas left Peru's expensive guano-financed armaments outmoded. Peru's most distinguished republican historian summed up the cultural characteristics of national governance at the time as "amateurish." By that he meant that the state was "inauthentic, fragile, corroded by impurities and anomalies." It suffered from unstable chief executive succession, sometimes faked elections, an inefficient parliament of uncertain origins and false democracy. It lacked well-organized armed forces, competent commanders, trained officers, modern equipment, or efficient administration. It also failed to mobilize any significant support for the elite Creole regimes among the Native American masses of the Sierra. Peru lost the War of the Pacific, therefore, long before the conflict began. That international conflagration stemmed in one sense from lax diplomacy during the war of independence.

Chile and Bolivia still shared what had been the colonial boundary between the Captaincy General of Chile and the *audiencia* of Charcas. Vague frontiers mattered little until industrial development elsewhere created a demand for and lent value to mineral deposits in the Atacama Desert. When guano became valuable, Chile began to push its frontier northward, while Bolivian leaders largely ignored the remote, extremely arid Pacific littoral. Able Chilean diplomats negotiated in 1866 a treaty with a Bolivian *caudillo* that enabled Chile to share profits with Bolivia from the zone between 23° and 25° South latitude. In 1866 and 1868, Chileans discovered vast nitrate of soda and borax deposits and obtained a Bolivian concession that led to the building up of the port of Antofagasta and a road inland. Moreover, another Chilean discovered in 1870 rich silver ore just south of parallel 23° S. A powerful mining enterprise and large-scale commerce dominated by Chileans and Britons arose.

In 1876, a Bolivian *caudillo* levied a tax that the powerful concessionaires refused to pay. Bolivia revoked the concession. Within a week, Chile presented an ultimatum demanding international arbitration; Peru sought to mediate. Bolivia blocked the Peruvian effort, and

Chile landed troops at Antofagasta on February 14, 1879. Bolivia declared war on March 14th, and Chile formally went to war with Bolivia and Peru three weeks later.

While its population was smaller than that of the northern allies,
Chile was ethnically and culturally more unified. It had 'forged ahead
under stable government regimes: six presidents had succeeded one
another constitutionally during the forty-eight years after independence, compared to Peru's twenty regimes, of which thirteen had seized
power by violence. Chilean leaders achieved naval superiority in 1874
by purchasing two armored ships. They armed all army units with
standard Comblain rifles and acquired scores of modern Krupp cannon.

The well-mobilized Chileans promptly occupied the Bolivian littoral
and moved to Peru's frontier. Admiral Miguel Grau miraculously kept
a vastly superior Chilean fleet on the defensive for four months with
his obsolescent monitor dating from the war with Spain. During a
naval battle off Angamos, a Chilean shell exploded on Grau's bridge
and Peru gained another hero-martyr.

As soon as Chile controlled the Pacific, it landed troops at Ilo to trap
Peruvian and Bolivian forces at Tacna and Arica. The Krupp cannon
turned the tide at both cities. The Chileans carried Arica's fortifications on June 7, 1880, giving Peru a new crop of hero-martyrs headed
by Francisco Bolognesi and Alfonso Ugarte.

The Chilean fleet began to bombard Callao early in September, and
devastated the north coast ports and plantations. Landing over 22,000
men, Chile commenced its conquest of Lima in mid-January, 1881.
Peru lost several thousand men, a high proportion from elite families
fighting bravely but "amateurishly" as badly armed and undertrained
militia against over seventy modern artillery pieces and numerically
superior professional troops. Chorillos and Miraflores fell quickly.
French Admiral Abel Bergasse Du Petit Thouars, with English and
Italian naval support, arranged a peaceful change of control of Lima
proper.

Cut off from its hinterland, Lima suffered acute and continuing
poverty. Family wealth was lost, food often was scarce, unemployment

ran high, and the money situation turned desperate. The paper money first issued prior to the war became badly inflated. An estimated 80,000 persons remained in Lima when peace came, but its population declined by emigration as well as a mortality rate of 43 per 1,000. Natives of provinces all over Peru abandoned occupied Lima for their *terruños*. Having migrated to Lima for upward social mobility to begin with, such refugees sought to avoid returning to farming and animal husbandry at home. Many opened schools, therefore, regardless of their specific occupational training. In numerous areas competition between such private schools became fierce; the new schoolmasters charged parents comparatively low tuitions, bringing an elementary education within reach of thousands of rural families who could not afford to educate their children at the small number of expensive prewar institutions.

As an indirect consequence of the war, the formally educated sector of the population rapidly increased. The success of refugee teachers in creating a profession in the provinces firmly established teaching as an avenue of upward social mobility. This made teaching and professions requiring formal instruction major social goals of peasant families, greatly reinforcing the existing prestige of formal education. The hundreds of new provincial schools trained, moreover, a new wave of rural-to-urban migrants.

Chile quickly occupied major coastal cities after taking Lima. It briefly tolerated a provisional president named by 150 Lima-area notables, but shipped him to Chile under arrest when he proved stubbornly nationalistic. This provisional president, Francisco García Calderón, constituted only one fraction of Peru's leadership. Nicolás de Piérola seized power when constitutional president Prado left for Europe to seek support. After his Lima defense proved pitifully inadequate, Piérola fled to the interior. When he resigned, Lizardo Montero led the resistance movement as García Calderón's vice-president. Yet, Col. Miguel Iglesias had to organize a Free North government with an elected regional parliament to negotiate peace. Starting his personal moral crusade to reestablish peace on April 1, 1882, Iglesias signed a peace treaty in 1883. Peru ceded Tarapacá Province and agreed to a plebiscite to be held in Arica and Tacna to determine ultimate citizenship of the inhabitants.

Gen. Andrés A. Cáceres harassed Chilean occupation forces from one end of Peru to the other, strengthening Iglesias's hand in negotiations. His bravery gave Cáceres an undeniable claim to postwar presidency, but saddled Peru with another era of *caudillo* governance.

The Chileans gave Peruvians little quarter until Admiral Petit Thouars reminded them of European standards of civilized warfare. Even after Chile occupied coastal cities, it maintained only fleeting occupation of some parts of the mountain interior. Peruvian guerrilla forces gave Chileans even less quarter than Chile accorded coastal Peruvians and Bolivians during the early stage of the war. The rural phase of the conflict produced, therefore, enduring rancor between Chileans and Peruvians.

Wherever Chilean occupation forces marched, they made entrepreneurs and institutions pay huge indemnities. These materially reduced the cost of the war to Chile, while greatly increasing that of Peru. Apparently the Chileans spared clerics from their exactions. In any event, opportunistic parish priests in various provinces persuaded Native American authorities in charge of surviving indigenous communities to make over title to their lands to the clerics to "protect" Indian assets from the Chileans. After the war, the Indians found themselves converted into peons on haciendas the priests now had their relatives manage or had already sold at handsome profits. Such events underlined the extent to which Peru then continued to be a colonial concatenation of competing, land-greedy classes and ethnic groups quite incapable of coalescing into a unified nation.

Peruvians in every quarter tasted the bitter socioeconomic aftermath of defeat. Chile removed much of Peru's prized national library and many of its historic documents. That was a great scholarly and symbolic loss to the intelligentsia. Ricardo Palma, a politician-scholar, received the task of retrieving what he could as new library director. His efforts not only renewed the library, but also resulted in publication of perhaps the most famous Peruvian literary work during the first century of the republic, *Tradiciones Peruanas*. Serialized in the periodicals of the day, this work gained great popularity, recounting the serious and comical events of Peruvian life and history.

In the financial sector, two government mortgage banks and five commercial banks in Lima failed, as did banks in Piura, Trujillo, and Arequipa. Only two commercial banks and the *Caja de Ahorros* of the Lima *Beneficencia* survived the holocaust. These were the only banks not heavily involved in guano and nitrate finances. Despite these reductions in credit capacity, European lenders demanded their due, and internal needs became more pressing than ever as the population continued to grow.

As usual in Peruvian economic crises, one policy was to tax the public, especially the Indians. The government directed prefects to collect the infamous head-tax on Native Americans, which had repeatedly provoked violent protests, and to charge an added tax on salt. The latter funds were destined for the patriotic purpose of regaining Arica and Tacna from Chile. This goal, however, was little appreciated by the Indian populace, whose interest in politics was marginal at best, but who did have to purchase salt.

In Ancash Department, the prefect also insisted that the Indians perform more free work than was customary in the reconstruction of churches, roads, and other public facilities. Early in 1885 a Native American leader, Pedro Pablo Atusparia, and thirteen other village mayors, protested to the prefect over the abuses of taxation and courvée labor. Atusparia was not only an *alcalde pedaneo* or mayor of his village, but also the head of a *varayoc* network in hamlets surrounding the departmental capital of Huaráz. As in most highland areas, the traditional colonial system of indirect rule established by Viceroy Toledo operated virtually unchanged. Atusparia, like his counterparts elsewhere, carried his silver-adorned staff of office, wore a ceremonial cape, and kept his hair in a single long braid as evidence of his manhood. The prefect in colonial style sent the protesters to the district governor, who jailed them and humiliated them by having their braids cut off. When word of this action spread, the peasantry overran Huaráz. The Indians freed the fourteen mayors, drove out the garrison and the officials, and sacked the houses of wealthy landlords and merchants—especially the Chinese with whom they often traded and whom they apparently intensely disliked. After capturing the capital, the rebels gathered strength and swept down the Callejón de Huaylas. Led by Atusparia and others, they captured several other provincial towns.

The central government dispatched an army battalion to reconquer the Callejón. Moving upvalley, the troops attacked and recaptured Huaráz while the Indians were celebrating the major annual festival of the Invention of the Holy Cross on May 3d. After winning a bloody battle a week later, the government had some leaders of the revolt executed, but most retired to their villages as the "duly constituted authorities" returned to their posts. This uprising produced no immediate material benefits for the Indians, inasmuch as the Callejón de Huaylas continued under the hacienda tenure system and landlord domination. Atusparia visited Lima, however, and became recognized as a folk hero, eulogized by the growing number of Lima intellectual Indianists such as Manuel Gonzalez Prada. Although other Indians reportedly poisoned Atusparia after his return to the Sierra, his name subsequently acquired a romantic aura in Ancash. Peasants widely identify with it and with the goals Atusparia sought, so he contributed an important psychological component to later changes.

Postwar governments could not postpone a day of reckoning with foreign creditors as easily as they could that with Andean Indians. Interest continued to accrue on outstanding external debts, particularly the large loans of 1869, 1870, and 1872, and the economic state of the nation could hardly have been worse. In 1886 British bondholders dispatched the son of W. R. Grace, an Irish entrepreneur with large Peruvian holdings, to arrange measures to recompense them. A rump parliament in 1889 approved a much-discussed contract between Peru and the bondholders. The latter agreed to cancel the government's responsibility for earlier debts in return for sixty-six years of control of the major railroads, exemption from import duties on materials brought in for railroad use, free access to major port piers, a government subsidy of 80,000 pounds sterling for thirty-three years, and two million tons of guano over a period of time. The bondholders formed the "Peruvian Corporation" in 1890 to manage these enterprises and raised another 1,500,000 pounds to finance railroad reconstruction and extension. This mortgaging to foreigners of both the country's most valued resources and greatest technological accomplishment struck a very serious blow at national pride.

Because of government bankruptcy, Peru only slowly resumed railroad construction after the disastrous War of the Pacific, during which Chilean forces had destroyed 500 kilometers of track. Work began only in 1891 on the Juliaca-Sicuani road that opened two years later, when work began on tracks north from Lima to Huacho. In 1895 construction crews completed the Cuzco-Puno branch line of the Southern Railway. By 1895, then, the Southern was essentially completed as the longest line in Peru with 932 kilometers of track. Its Puno terminus connected with Bolivian roads by steamer across Lake Titicaca. Bolivian traffic would account for a fourth of its total freight, which gave this road the highest ton-kilometer ratio in Peru.

The Southern Railway magnified the importance of Mollendo as a seaport, despite the difficulty of disembarking cargo in its surf. The railroad maintained the importance of Arequipa. Because of the size of international trade with Bolivia, both legal and contraband, the railway insured the steady growth of Puno on Lake Titicaca. An almost solely railroad town called Juliaca sprang up at the junction of the Arequipa-Puno and Puno-Cuzco lines. Today Juliaca is the most important commercial center of the lake region.

The Central Railway topped out during this period and reached La Oroya. That achievement brought a significant new hinterland directly into Lima's orbit, providing the capital city with visitors, migrants, fresh milk, garden produce, and slaughter animals.

Other railways completed by 1895 were coastal valley lines quickening and unifying the oasis economies and linking their plantations even more firmly into the world commodity market by reducing freightage costs from field to seaport and waiting steamships. Eight major coastal valley rail networks that connected important oasis cities with ocean ports also fostered increased steamer travel to and from the capital. Thus an important consequence of transportation improvements was a sharp increase in Lima's rate of population growth. Between 1876 and 1891, the city apparently grew only 4 percent, a rate much less than one percent per year. Between 1891 and 1898, on the other hand, Lima increased by over 9 percent, an annual rate well over one percent. Improvements in urban sanitation helped to make this difference by reducing the death rate, but migration from provincial cities generated the greatest part of the increase.

As Peru slowly recovered from the war with Chile, the introduction of electricity accelerated the pace of urban technological and social change. The Peruvian Electric Construction and Supply Company inaugurated its first system in Lima in 1886. Nearly a decade later, the first electric plant was set up to generate electric power for industrial uses. An Italian immigrant founded a small wool-weaving plant in 1886. Mariano Ignacio Prado Ugarteche and Juan Manuel Peña provided capital to expand it in 1890 as the *Sociedad Industrial Santa Catalina,* a durable enterprise. These capitalists turned to electric power to operate the machinery and formed an electric company in mid-1895.

Potable water service to the main areas of Lima and some suburbs was resumed by 1884. Citizens voluntarily restored the zoo and exposition hall. Literary circles began to redevelop, with such leaders as the critic and iconoclast Manuel Gonzalez Prada. The first labor organizations appeared.

Foreign colonies added much human diversity and many new skills to Lima during the latter part of the nineteenth century. Italians formed a highly entrepreneurial group ready to cast its lot in the new national climate. One of the first to arrive in 1850 was a geographer, Antonio Raimondi, self-exiled from Italy's civil wars. He traveled extensively throughout Peru, studying and recording his findings and correcting maps. Of particular importance were his ample descriptions of the mineral wealth and the Sierra regions, which he especially loved. The congress had his works published upon his death in 1890, and he at once became a much-eulogized personage.

Raimondi's countrymen busily followed other occupations. To provide aid and welfare for their fellows, they started in 1862 an Italian Beneficent Society. In 1866, the Italian colony founded the first Lima fire-fighting company. In 1872, it began to publish a newspaper in Italian, and in 1880 organized a social club. Individually, Italians invested in textiles, banking, agriculture, commerce, food processing, and petroleum.

English residents occupied many powerful commercial and managerial positions reflected in high social prestige. They organized their own Anglican church, cemetery association, social and athletic clubs. The Lima Cricket and Lawn Tennis Club was organized no later than 1865. It acquired a playing field, and as soccer gained popularity in Great Britain, the group became the Lima Cricket and Football Club. It slowly admitted Peruvian members and by 1892 a Lima team played a Callao team on its field. *Futbol* thereafter diffused rapidly to the remote corners of Peru.

By 1895, Peru stood precariously on the brink of sweeping change. Poor fiscal management by amateurish political leaders had prostrated the country after guano sales provided it with unearned prosperity vitiated by rampant inflation. The huge wealth of the maritime zone, which poured out of the country, failed to pay for even the railroads, which basically altered the socioeconomic structure after 1895. Consequently, British creditors held a three-quarter century mortgage on the major lines. Maritime wealth did found a small coterie of very rich Peruvians who adopted a life-style characterized by conspicuous consumption, emulation of European customs, and elitist domestic politics. Members of this Lima elite founded their own Union Cricket Club in 1893 and added soccer in 1894.

Chile had by force of arms defined Peru's southern boundary and subjected its people to humiliating defeat, costly in terms of casualties, money, and greater destruction of capital plant than that wrought by any earthquake. By 1895, however, the War of the Pacific lay far enough in the past for Peruvians to have recouped some of their losses. Still, the exchequer relied on an Indian head-tax, which engendered bloody revolts in 1866, 1885, and 1892, for some of the national and most of the departmental government income. This practice raised the question whether Peru was preparing to enter the twentieth century—a century dominated by mechanical technology developed in Europe and North America during the nineteenth century—or continuing to look back toward its agrarian past.

Chapter 9 • Realignment of Forces Within the Nation, 1895-1930

In 1895 yet another revolution, one fueled by considerable popular participation, convulsed the governing elite. José Nicolás de Piérola led this revolt against President Andrés A. Cáceres. The revolution itself may seem paradoxical, in that Cáceres was a professional military man and a hero of the War of the Pacific, while Piérola was a civilian antihero of that war. In addition, Piérola had seized the presidency once before by a coup d'état but then had failed to keep the Chilean invaders out of Lima. The long history of violent pursuit of the presidency characteristic of Peru's style of political succession is thus brought up to the watershed year 1895. Piérola was by then a man of middle age with long involvement in national elite power politics.

Yet the true paradox in the event lies less in the past than in the future. Amazingly, Piérola behaved during his second term as president in ways that no one might have predicted on the basis of his previous career. Inaugurated on September 8, 1895, Piérola executed in effect a 180° turn away from many of his earlier beliefs and policies. He acted energetically to alter many dimensions of Peruvian life.

The Piérola regime became a turning point because this once arche-typically "amateurish" president channeled thought and government policy in more quantitative, technical, and secular terms than anyone else had ever before. He moved deliberately to foster national develop-ment, for example, when he created a new Development Ministry in 1896.

Quantitative ways of thought became intertwined with seculariza-tion and increased democracy. One devout prime minister resigned be-cause Piérola promulgated a law allowing civil marriage for non-Catholics. Priests opposed that law not only on doctrinal grounds, but also because they received fees for marrying people. Inasmuch as priests also received fees for performing and recording in their parish registers baptisms and burials, they again resisted when Piérola de-cided to collect vital statistics. Establishing civil registration of births and deaths fell to district mayors, who after 1896 were directly elected by local residents. Many districts began their civil registers only after a decade or more of struggle. Even then, clerical opposition and bu-reaucratic inefficiency caused such haphazard recording that Peru to this day has not achieved an accurate national registration of vital statistics.

Piérola governed as head of a National Coalition formed by the elitist Civil and Democratic parties to depose Cáceres. In contrast to the pattern of his whole career, Piérola abstained from the demagoguery that had earlier served him well. His refusal to feed many of his fol-lowers at the public trough earned him the sobriquet of "ingrate." Thus setting an example of civilian government, Piérola served out his term despite constant and determined parliamentary opposition.

Very important for the future, Piérola refused to follow the Mexi-can example of Porfirio Díaz. At the end of his term, Piérola would not arrange to remain in power, or support his brother or his vice-president to succeed him. Consequently, the Civil Democratic alliance settled on a former Development Minister. Party leaders felt that if Peru were to achieve a new political climate, it would benefit from four years under a provincial gentleman-engineer not closely associated with past *caudillismo*.

To prepare for the crucial 1899 transfer of power, Piérola insured that he would be the last chief executive indirectly elected by the electoral college. In 1895 he submitted a bill providing for direct election, which parliament approved late in 1896. The new law created a *Junta Electoral Nacional* to supervise elections and to set up and maintain electoral registers. It limited the franchise to literate individuals and established provincial boards to form the civil registers. By 1899, 108,597 literate citizens had registered to vote, and official returns showed that 58,285 did vote. Inasmuch as the national population exceeded 4,500,000, the franchise remained very tightly restricted. Nevertheless, voters in the first popular presidential election numbered 13½ times those who had put Piérola into office. In the postcoup 1895 election, 4,310 qualified members of the electoral college cast 4,150 votes for him.

Beginning with Piérola, only eight men served as chief executive until late August, 1930. José Pardo B. served nearly eight years and Augusto B. Leguía served a record fifteen years, so tenure averaged 4.4 years despite four brief terms. No post-1895 chief executive had previously served as a departmental prefect, while half had been cabinet ministers and half had served in parliament. All gained significant earlier government experience before assuming the presidency, including the officer who led a 1913 coup d'état.

The nineteenth-century importance of departmental prefects in national politics clearly ended with the 1895 reforms that centralized economic power. Piérola's most important policy break with the past terminated the Indian head-tax late in 1895. Piérola's first Minister of Exchequer asked parliament to abolish it. Recognizing that this supposedly general levy had degenerated into an Indian tax, the Minister labeled it "odiously unjust and the necessary cause of abuses and violence, especially against the indigenous class which is almost the only one which pays it." A Chamber of Deputies committee found that this tax provided the bulk of revenues spent by the departments, especially those in the Sierra with large Indian populations. Parliament further centralized taxing power in 1896 by shifting income from property sales taxes to the national treasury from the departments.

All eight chief executives save one were civilians. This is the only period in Peruvian history when civilians enjoyed such dominance. Three of them were attorneys, two engineers, one a businessman, and one a journalist-politician. The eight chief executives averaged 51.6 years of age on taking office, hardly older than their pre-1895 counterparts. Lima supplied a fourth of them, as did Arequipa, and coastal natives achieved a seven-to-one advantage over Serranos. While three-fourths of the presidents of 1895-1930 were more or less duly elected to an initial term, over a third of them actually gained office once via coups d'état. Once the French military mission contracted by Piérola professionalized Peru's army officers, no coup d'état could be carried out without the approval of the military high command. This situation has not ended coups d'état. Col. Oscar Benavides deposed an elected civilian president in 1913 in the precedent-setting army "institutional" coup of the twentieth century. Others would follow in 1930, 1933, 1948, 1962, and 1968. Thus, Piérola's military reforms bear analysis.

The officer cadre held little affection for "The Caliph," as Piérola was nicknamed. Not only had Piérola lost Lima to Chile after seizing the presidency, but his guerrillas had also defeated the regular army in 1895. His victory with rag-tag forces convinced "The Caliph" that Peru lacked a capable army, which he believed it required. An officer cadre top-heavy with decorative leaders without technical training relied on impressment to recruit soldiers. Colonial Spanish martial law, only slightly modified, still governed military behavior. Repeated attempts to establish a military academy failed to achieve continuity of training, much less permanence. Technological changes in armaments and communications outside Peru made the nineteenth-century "amateurish" officers obsolete.

Piérola undertook, therefore, a fundamental army reorganization. He contracted a French military mission that arrived in 1896 and began work on a practical military school at Chorrillos in early 1898. The future course of power politics radically altered. Whatever discontinuities later regimes displayed, Piérola introduced a permanent and fundamental change in the armed forces. French training led to professionalization and technification; it fostered a strong institutional loyalty that replaced the rampant individualism of 1821-95 and came to rival ecclesiastical loyalty to the church.

"The Caliph's" regime also reformed the antiquated military code, drawing upon the 1878 and 1890 Spanish codes. The updated military law tended to expand military jurisdiction by subjecting citizens to military courts for many types of actions. It made robbers, arsonists, kidnappers, those who cut telegraph lines, moved or obstructed railroad rails, destroyed bridges, or attacked trains subject to military justice. This 1898 code remained in effect until President Oscar Benavides replaced it in 1939 with a revision that retained many of its features. Parliament voted compulsory military service in 1898, so conscription brought lower-class draftees to serve under white-Mestizo officers.

Peru created a general staff school in 1904, with important consequences: army officers became professionals who pursued studies beyond the bachelor's degree level. President José Pardo, Manuel's son, furthered military improvement during his first term, although he did continue to purchase naval vessels abroad. His administration diffused military skills among civilians. It began to sponsor shooting matches in 1905, and accorded recognition to shooting clubs that met its standards in 1907. This regime began a central quartermaster service in 1904, which improved supply acquisition through standardized purchasing and by increasing military manufacture of clothing and other supplies. Pardo expanded the French military mission, and outstanding graduates of the war school spent periods with the French army. The General Staff set up a topographic service, and hired engineers and an inspector general to begin building up service institutions and competent service personnel who in time paralleled those in the civilian government.

Officers gradually created a very strong semiautonomous institutional society within the nation. Each service acquired its own hospital in Lima staffed with some of Peru's best medical personnel. Until the 1962 coup d'état, retirement benefits of full pay kept retired officers in the life-style to which they had become accustomed. Special military-operated schools educated officers' children. Military consumers' co-operatives enabled officers to purchase goods at prices well under civilian cost. Moreover, the military enjoyed the privilege of importing certain highly desired consumer goods duty free.

Many civilian recreational establishments charged uniformed customers the same price as children, rather than adults. The armed forces also developed their own recreation facilities, including the influential military casino in Lima and special ocean beaches. Thus, the armed forces gained socioeconomic power and pride fostered by the visible benefits of institutional socialism supported by the public.

The armed forces also operated a major educational system for conscripts, including the best vocational schools in the nation. Officers took particular pride in the ability of the army to stop conscripts from chewing coca, a major symbol of the Indian abhorred by cigarette-smoking middle-class urbanites. The urban middle classes contributed a constantly increasing proportion of the officer cadres as the twentieth century advanced. Sons of aristocratic families found ample opportunities in multiple civilian careers open to them, but the armed forces became a principal avenue of upward financial and political mobility for ambitious middle-class boys. The refrain of a popular Creole waltz —"How I love those military men"—had more than trivial meaning for the public.

For lower-class men, service as conscripts lasted only a couple of years and brought only sharply limited upward mobility in rural settlements. Migration from farms and rural towns to major cities became a far more important route to economic improvement and social betterment for lower-class citizens. By 1895, rural-to-urban migration began to assume massive proportions that would be greater yet in the twentieth century. Growing rural population densities on a relatively fixed land base, continued landlord domination, and officials who imposed courvée labor and other negative features of rural life combined to "push" people off haciendas and out of indigenous communities. At the same time, coastal plantations and cities exerted a strong "pull."

The fundamental dynamic of dissatisfaction in rural Peru was increasing population density. Unless Piérola possessed some extraordinary sense, he could not have known that his regime witnessed a fundamental transition in Peru's demographic situation. No Peruvian could then have perceived accurately what occurred because Peru took no national census between 1876 and 1940. Even partial censuses of cities were few. It seems clear only in retrospect that the late 1890s witnessed the beginning of a rapid population increase in accord with other modern Latin American patterns.

Peru probably contained 4,500,000 persons when "The Caliph" seized power. The Mestizos, who constituted the fastest growing sector of the population since conquest, still multiplied most rapidly, but Indians remained in the majority. Indians made up the bulk of the harshly exploited rural peasantry and constituted the labor force upon which the domestic economy largely depended.

The growth in population after independence made no impression on either government officials or the public at that time, although it should have: the total number more than tripled by 1895. Such an increase produced fundamental socioeconomic changes, particularly in rural areas. As the numbers rose rapidly, the sudden and extensive increase created a human demand on the nearly fixed agrarian base unknown since shortly after conquest. A threefold population increase in republican times required Peru to grow or import three times as much food by 1895 as it had in 1821, or else consume less per person. The tripling of population between independence and 1895 increased rural human densities in proportion, inasmuch as most Peruvians still lived in the countryside. That in itself constituted a force impelling emigration to a city, because economic opportunity perceptibly diminished in both the indigenous community and on the hacienda.

Hacienda populations grew faster than owners could expand them. Landlords had, therefore, to allow tenants smaller subsistence plots from which to feed themselves, or to allot more area to such plots. The latter process reduced the land available for commercial farming while the former impoverished the laborers. Population dynamics thus fostered a shift from extensive to intensive land use. Because most landlords failed to improve their production technology, they became dissatisfied with estate profits and left for a city. Because most tenants failed to adopt improved farm practices, they became progressively more impoverished and resentful of the system.

Surviving indigenous communities fared even worse. On the one hand, they lost land to white and Mestizo entrepreneurs forming haciendas, so their land base shrank. On the other hand, community population steadily increased. By 1895, the land base had been almost entirely allocated to individuals. So mature family heads held all the land, leaving sons the galling choice of dependence on their fathers or emigration in search of alternative opportunities for making a living and founding a family.

Numerous improvements in the urban environment attracted migrants to Lima and other coastal cities. By 1895, Lima offered a complete educational system, scores of churches, theaters, fire companies, police protection, running water, sewage disposal, many lighted and paved streets, trolleys, and a range of employment unknown in rural areas. About 1895, the cumulative impact of technical changes such as a potable water system, sewage disposal, medical care in *Beneficencia* hospitals using discoveries of Lister, Pasteur, and others overseas, plus preventive medical measures, brought the urban death rate below the birth rate for the first time in Lima's history. Modern medical and transport technology finally penetrated Lima sufficiently to change it from an endemic and epidemic disease pest-hole, where high death rates decimated the ranks of Sierra migrants, into the healthiest settlement in the country.

At least one public health measure of the Piérola regime significantly improved the city's communicable disease environment. In 1896 Peru made vaccination compulsory throughout the republic. As late as 1891, Lima had suffered 889 smallpox deaths, and smallpox would not be eradicated from the countryside for many decades. Yet the 1896 law quickly lowered the death rate in cities where it could be immediately enforced, making them yet more attractive to the surplus rural population.

While rural migrants could have been no more conscious than Piérola of the gross population trends, they could and did hear about the many improvements that had been made in Lima. Trolley cars, paved streets, and clear water supplies attracted migrants who may not have been aware of quarantine stations, mosquito abatement programs, and other public health efforts. The result was accelerated internal migration from 1895 on, with Lima steadily gaining in absolute numbers and proportionately to the rest of the country.

The Central Railway in 1895 reached La Oroya at the margin of the rich and heavily populated Mantaro Valley, thus enlarging Lima's migration hinterland sufficiently to account for part of the later population increase. The Juliaca-Cuzco Railroad also opened to traffic in 1895, considerably facilitating migration from the heavily populated Cuzco Department to Arequipa, and to Lima by railroad and coastal steamship. By 1903 Lima contained an estimated 130,000 persons, adding another 10,000 during the next five years. The city apparently grew through immigration and natural increase at a rate of 5,000 annually to 180,000 in 1916.

Meanwhile, improvements in urban transportation created by trolley electrification, the introduction of bicycles and automobiles, and further developments in rail systems linked Lima and its port of Callao and beach resorts into a single metropolitan area. In 1908 that larger Lima contained almost 173,000 inhabitants compared to 141,000 in the city proper. The primate city area held about 224,000 persons by 1920 on the eve of an extensive urban beautification and reconstruction program sponsored by President Leguía. Migration to Lima accelerated during his administration, so that the metropolitan area held some 384,000 persons by 1931, a gain of 160,000 inhabitants or 71.5 percent.

As the pace of internal migration accelerated, another important expansion of voluntary associations occurred, most notably in the primate city. At least as early as Piérola's regime, migrants to Lima began to form regional clubs. Natives of Arequipa Department formed the Arequipa Department Club in Lima, met from time to time, sponsored social dances, and numerous other functions. Migrants from other departments did likewise. Migrants from Lucanas Province founded a provincial club in Lima and lobbied government offices for material aid for their home province, as did people from other provinces. Natives of Huaylas District organized a district club in Lima for the same multiple purposes. Migrants from almost every hamlet in the country banded together in even smaller sport and social clubs. By New Year's Day of 1901 the regional associations had reached such numbers that their need for meeting places led them to found the *Asamblea de las Sociedades Unidas.*

For many years this organization provided rooms for regional club members to meet in an expansive old colonial-style building with a large interior patio and multiple rooms. Regional associations multiplied to number several thousand by midcentury. In a society in which few meetings convened promptly, regional association meetings had to begin when the *Asamblea* or similar meeting halls scheduled them, and end on time to free a room for the next meeting. Thus many provincial migrants to Lima learned the difference between the indefinite *"hora peruana"* and the exact *"hora britanica"* or "British time."

Many regional associations went on to grander meeting places. The large departmental clubs, especially, collected funds to purchase or build their own clubhouses. These provide pleasant places for dances, dinners, facilities for large-scale entertaining, and family recreation. The regional clubs played a significant social integration role. Migrants with political ambitions built patronage relationships with those from the same *terruño,* providing economic and social favors in return for political allegiance.

Because club membership stems from common territorial origin, these associations encouraged urban integration along regional lines. The clubs performed a key function of marriage information exchange. The young migrant to the city without kinsmen and ritual kinsmen always risked marrying a scoundrel or adventuress, especially when he or she came from an area where parental choice of spouses for offspring still occurred. Regional clubs helped to prevent such unions by functioning as a surrogate community—a colony of *paisanos*—providing a setting in which proper mates could be found. The clubs thus encouraged regional endogamy: marriage to other natives of the region of known antecedents, i.e., "people of confidence."

Directing a migrant to persons he could trust was a most important club function. By migrating, a person exposed himself to great anxiety because everyday affairs became distressingly unpredictable. This hap-

pened when the migrant removed himself from a usually large extended family and an even larger network of his own and his kinsmen's ritual relatives. If the migrant were educated to some degree, his
move also separated him from his classmates. The regional associations
thus served to restore these groups of confidence to an extent. Even
when feuds and rivalries of the native region carried over to the city,
migrants preferred to deal with known enemies rather than the unknown social world from beyond the *terruño*. Distrust of strangers runs
very high in the city.

Regional associations helped migrants with other social and economic adjustments. Earlier migrants helped later ones by advising
them about urban attire. The poncho widely worn in the Sierra even
today is not thought acceptable in Lima. Earlier migrants who had
found economic niches in the city also introduced newer ones to pro-
spective employers, partners, and associates. Thus, a majority of the
men who migrated to Lima from one mountain village became dressers
and vendors of poultry, and many another occupational niche is filled
by migrants from one or a few places.

Although regional associations fostered the integration of migrants
into the capital city's life and economy, they created their own social
recreation activity during the workers' few free weekend hours. This
originally took the form of dances and *terruño*-style meals, but as the
metropolitan area expanded, increasingly of athletic contests. Regional
clubs formed and sponsored soccer teams that competed on weekends
in leagues playing on open spaces wherever they could find them. As
teams proliferated, scheduling became very difficult, inasmuch as the
thousands of lower-class migrants carried on their recreational programs virtually "behind the backs" of the urban elite, which never
built stadia adequate for the hundreds of teams playing on weekends.
Wives, sisters, and other female relatives of players prepared regional
dishes to sell during the games along with beer to raise money for club
and *terruño*.

The Piérola regime witnessed the consolidation of the beginnings
of *futbol,* as it did of many other twentieth-century phenomena. Soccer, cricket, high jump, 100-meter run, and tug-of-war competitions

inaugurated the opening of the first Peruvian stadium in mid-1897. Soccer rapidly outclassed all other sports. It spread to all classes from its Lima high society beginnings. By 1912 the largest coastal cities acquired professional teams grouped in leagues playing a regular schedule. Aside from this commercial spectator sport aspect, soccer became the most popular athletic activity throughout Peru. It reached settlements in the remotest portions of the Sierra. Even in the indigenous communities, half of those recognized by the central government in 1962 had constructed soccer fields by their own efforts, no matter how difficult the terrain on steep slopes where the villages nestled. Thus, the national sport became not bullfighting or any of the Basque ballgames, or any U.S. sport, but English *futbol*.

Breaks with colonial traditions in other sectors were as slow in coming because they were often tied to the traditional norms of privilege or bound up in legal codes of long standing. Military law was not the only area of Peruvian law still derived from colonial practice in 1895. In 1896 the parliament finally authorized the executive branch to revise the most antiquated code of all: that governing mining, which still followed the Mining Ordinances of 1785. The new code took effect in 1900. By then, copper ores running as high as 30 percent metal had been discovered near Cerro de Pasco and only awaited completion of the Central Railway to be fully exploited.

U.S. technicians explored the Cerro de Pasco region in 1900, and U.S. capitalists formed the Cerro de Pasco Mining Company. In 1902 it purchased many mines in the region and began to ship over the La Oroya Railroad. It began to smelt ore in 1906 and by 1914 had built a hydroelectric complex to power its mines and mills. In 1922 the company installed in a canyon near La Oroya a smelter that created serious air pollution. Workers in La Oroya began to die from lethal accumulations of arsenic, lead, zinc, and antimony carried in smelter fumes. Potatoes, barley, and cultivated and natural grasses began to die in the area where particles precipitated, and the fumes and minerals taken up by forage plants killed sheep, horses, and cattle. Within two years, pollution ruined 700,000 hectares of Peru's most productive range lands. The government required the corporation to install a filtering system in 1925, but it was not completed until 1942. Meanwhile, the Cerro de Pasco Mining Corp. purchased hundreds of thousands of hectares of farm and range land. It hired animal geneticists to develop its own high-quality breed of sheep and it improved the once-ruined pastures.

This episode enabled the company to become the largest single sheep breeder in Peru and to supply meat at subsidized prices to its company stores. That eased the financial burden of its paternalistic commissary operations, especially when union negotiators demanded cheap meat, bread, and other commodities rather than augmented wages. The episode also created a large pool of dispossessed farmers desperate for jobs near their homes. It scarcely required the Byzantine reasoning of Lima politicians for most to conclude, rightly or wrongly, that the corporation deliberately built its smelter to pollute the area in order to achieve such goals. Subsequent behavior by U.S. corporate managers has not dissuaded Peruvians from that belief. That the Cerro de Pasco Corp. had cheated them was one of the few points on which both landlords and indigenous community peasants of the central highlands could agree!

Overseas demand for copper to make wire for expanding electrical networks enabled the Cerro de Pasco Corp. to earn huge profits for decades. It hired not only miners and mill-hands, but also upper-class attorneys and engineers, and it subsidized politicians. Moreover, the type of U.S. diplomatic representation sent to Peru created a tradition whereby the resident manager of Cerro de Pasco Corp. called the ambassador to his office for what amounted to instructions. After World War II, when U.S. military and economic aid catapulted the Peruvian ambassadorship into a position of great power, the embassy became known as "The House of the Viceroy." Peruvians resented both corporation and the neocolonial "viceroy."

Peru's end-of-century commercial law was less antiquated than its mining code, having been updated in 1853. In 1898 a committee began to study the 1885 Spanish commercial code and recommended modifications for Peruvian usage, so new laws were approved in 1901. Meanwhile, the age of capital-intensive enterprise that profoundly af-

fected North Atlantic countries in the eighteenth century reached
Peru at the end of the nineteenth. Between 1896 and 1899, corporations appeared that were capitalized at 25 million soles. Three insurance companies capitalized at S/. 6,500,000 headed the list. By way
of a comparison, customs income was six million soles during the same
four-year period.

New credit institutions replaced those that had failed during the
War of the Pacific. Peruvian entrepreneurs founded the Bank of Lon-
don and Peru, the International and the Popular banks capitalized at
S/. 3,500,000 between them. The Italian Bank founded in 1889 by
capital from the 300-strong Italian immigrant business community in
Lima augmented its capital by half a million soles. Not until World
War II made a change of name advisable did it become in 1941 the
Banco de Crédito, Peru's largest commercial bank.

Technological changes that had earlier transformed northwestern
Europe came to Peru at the century's end. Woolen textile companies
augmented their capital during the Piérola regime, and new ones entered the field. In 1895, as owners began to electrify these plants, the
regime freed electrical equipment from import duties and encouraged
electrification in Arequipa, Cerro de Pasco, Tarma, Jauja, and Huancayo as well as Lima. There an electric company replaced gas lights
with electric bulbs. In 1902 it finished a reservoir supplying water to
operate two 450-kilowatt generators, running a third with fossil fuel to
serve 1,800 public light posts and 8,500 private lights in Lima and its
beach suburbs. This company steadily expanded its hydroelectric generating capacity through construction and merger with the electric
enterprise supplying the textile mills, Callao's electric company, and
three trolley lines. In 1910 the merged enterprises took the name
Empresas Electricas Asociadas. By 1920 this new unit produced
47,400,000 KWH and two years later began to bury its cables. It
expanded production to 79,100,000 KWH by 1929, but could hardly
keep pace with population growth.

Other technical corporations to form between 1896 and 1899 included a match company, shoe factory, ceramics company, dock op-
erator, gas company, milk pasteurizer, brick maker, public bath enter-

prise, and provincial-urban potable water companies. Incorporation of coastal plantations sharply separated these capital-intensive enterprises from traditional Sierra haciendas. The Cartavio sugar mill was incorporated along with Paramonga, San Nicolás, Guadalupito, and a Cañete oil factory. Sugar exports tripled from 1891 to 1898.

Even the government created a large corporation to collect taxes. Parliament at the end of 1895 abolished the old Spanish system of farming tax collection out to individuals who bid for this privilege. It authorized the government to establish a corporation to replace them. This corporation raised a million soles in capital by selling 10,000 shares at S/. 100 each. It paid the treasury half what it took in after charging 15 percent of gross taxes for overhead. Inasmuch as this constituted a reform, one can but infer that treasury receipts from tax-farmers must have been low indeed. In 1897 parliament increased the treasury's share to three-fourths after collecting fixed costs. Soon after 1900, Minister of Exchequer Mariano Belaunde refused to renew the company's contract. In 1902 the government contracted with a new *Sociedad Nacional de Recaudación* set up by the Banco Popular. It charged only a 6 percent fee.

In 1905 four commercial banks formed a *Caja de Depósitos y Consignaciones* to take custody of valuables in litigation and monies generated by government offices. By 1914 a Minister of Exchequer complained that shareholders were no longer the small investors Piérola had envisioned, but capitalists on a grand scale. The corporation collected taxes not only for the central government, but also municipalities, departments, and the educational system. This arrangement endured until 1963. President Fernando Belaunde Terry, *Don* Mariano's grandson, then expropriated the corporation and converted it into the National Bank.

Another Piérola fiscal innovation stemmed directly from the War of the Pacific. Peru would have to pay Chile ten million soles if the inhabitants of two occupied provinces voted to return to Peru. The impoverished treasury needed funds for this goal, so in 1896 the government nationalized salt deposits and works and made its sale a government monopoly. This revenue measure affected every family and roused great opposition to Piérola, but salt remained a government commodity.

Increased exports integrated Peru into the world market sufficiently to persuade "The Caliph" to follow the European trend toward placing money on a gold standard. Piérola acted decisively and quickly to end a reliance on silver that dated from the discovery of the Potosí silver mines. With the sol down to twenty-two British pennies, Piérola closed the mint in 1897. A year later the mint began to strike gold pieces, and by mid-1899 it had placed over 56,000 pounds in circulation. Ten-*sol* notes became known as "pounds" in 1897 when Piérola made customs duties payable in sterling at ten soles per pound.

Piérola nearly doubled government expenditures. Income in 1894 had been S/. 6,794,528. In 1896, Piérola's budget reached almost eight-and-a-half million, and two years later it exceeded ten million. The deficit totaled nearly three million soles during Piérola's term, not counting over two million for unanticipated military operations and special sessions of parliament. Piérola's solution was not new: he borrowed needed funds. Nevertheless, Piérola ended federalism, greatly centralized fiscal and political power, and began building a large bureaucracy to intervene in increasingly numerous spheres of economic activity and social relationships.

The proliferation of corporations under Piérola reflected Peru's belated recognition of the utility of this specific form of voluntary association discovered in England centuries earlier. Once men of ability with money formed corporations active in plantation agriculture, mining, and maunfacturing, they soon formed common interest groups to acquire sectoral influence. In 1896, Piérola decreed that members of an existing Agricultural and Mining Society might split into three more specialized organizations.

The National Agricultural Society split off to represent the interests of great plantation owners. Its early power showed in the government's founding a National Agricultural School in Lima in 1902. Other corporations organized the National Mining Society in 1896. Its collaboration with government agencies later gave it virtually official status, and its power became great. Representatives of at least some of Lima's small industrial community decided to found the National Industrial Society in 1896. Weak at first compared with the agricultural and mining societies, it gradually gained strength.

The richly rewarded capitalists of 1896-99 did not have things entirely their own way, because industrial strikes began. Toward the end of August, 1896, some 500 textile workers in an English-owned Vitarte factory struck for higher wages than 30 centavos, improved food, and a reduction from sixteen working hours. Printers struck to have wages restored to the 1869 level. Pastry cooks also struck before the year ended and achieved their objectives.

Technological changes overseas continued to stimulate socioeconomic adjustments. Parliament voted to exonerate typewriters from import duties in 1902, but the president vetoed the measure as favoring only well-to-do purchasers. Parliament passed the law again in 1903, however, on grounds that it would create a new occupation for poor people—one of its most accurate predictions. All too often, politicians announced ambitious development programs with high-sounding phraseology that promised much. Then, they borrowed heavily abroad to pay for programs that served in the end to enrich only a few favored families and to disillusion a peasantry whose needs for real agrarian reform and access to education were not met.

Curiously, the automobile aroused less opposition than had typewriters. A bill to exempt autos from import duties became law in 1903. The first automobiles imported were quite literally "horseless carriages" suitable only for urban travel. Before long, however, as motor vehicles increased in power and durability, professional drivers emerged as a new occupational specialty and national integration progressed rapidly.

Engineers and intellectuals began to urge the central government to launch a highway construction program as early as 1903. Yet Augusto B. Leguía claimed that no true automotive roads existed when he came to power the second time in 1919. In 1921 Leguía decreed a Road Conscription Law aimed at rapidly building a basic road network with courvée labor. It directly revived the *mita* system: it required able-bodied males between 21 and 50 years of age to work twelve days each year constructing roadway. It called on males 18 to 20 and 51 to 60 to work six days annually on roads. The law required municipal governments to provide food and drink for workers in areas where this was existing custom for public works crews called out by municipal authorities. It also stated that municipal governments would pay workers the standard daily wage of the region. Abuses of the legal power the law vested in municipal authorities to force men to work on public projects led to great resentment and its immediate repeal when Commandant Luís Sánchez Cerro led a coup d'état that deposed Leguía in 1930. The Leguía regime claimed to have built 18,169 kilometers of automotive highways in use by mid-1929.

Nicolás de Piérola made the organization of mass-participation political parties inevitable when he instituted direct elections. Peruvian parties have tended to follow a European splinter model and to retain a high degree of Hispanic individualism. Thus, the story of the founding of truly influential movements can be told largely in terms of key intellectual-organizational innovators.

The first organizational current that significantly influenced twentieth-century events began at the end of the nineteenth century under the leadership of Manuel Gonzalez Prada. Ranging widely in his written and spoken criticism of the society in which he lived, Gonzalez broke ground for later political theorists. He also organized a sort of party apparatus and intiated programs of public education that actually motivated upper-class, well-educated youths to go out into the streets to teach in "popular universities." Among the aspects of society that incensed Gonzalez Prada was the traditional economic exploitation of the Indian population. Other eloquent people had indicted the nation for its treatment of Indians, usually with little effect on policy. Gonzalez Prada finally organized the continuing movement known as *"Indigenismo"* or championing the Indian.

The *Indigenistas* wrote and spoke persuasively enough to change the tenor of governance. After Leguía seized the presidency in 1919, the parliament acted as a constitutional congress. *Indigenismo* gained an important victory in the new constitution put into force early in 1920. This document recognized the legal existence of the Indigenous

Community after a century of legal suppression. Luís E. Valcárcel had emerged from Cuzco as a fiery apostle and foremost writer of *Indigenismo*. During Leguía's dictatorship, Valcárcel and his associates prodded the regime into establishing a small section of Indian Affairs in an existing ministry. It began to extend official recognition to surviving communities. Beginning in 1926, the Leguía regime recognized 321 Indigenous Communities by 1930.

In 1930 Peru began to suffer economically from the developing worldwide depression. Inasmuch as President Leguía had financed many of his grandiose projects with foreign loans, the economic crisis of credit quickly converted the aged strongman into another victim of overseas borrowing. A relatively low-ranking officer who had several times failed to launch a serious revolt against Leguía easily obtained armed-forces backing that ended the era of civilian rule interrupted by only one military intervention.

Chapter 10 • Political Party–Armed Forces Contest, 1930-1968

P eruvian history from 1895 to 1969 seems to the outside observer to have followed a fairly unified course. Events in the twentieth century followed necessarily from policy decisions at the end of the nineteenth. Peruvians who lived through these years, on the other hand, share a strong perception that life since 1930 differs from life before 1930. The period 1930-33 constitutes a significant watershed in the Peruvian psyche. Major Peruvian historical synthesizers, for example, stop at 1933, evidently too personally involved in later events to analyze them dispassionately.

The world-wide economic depression of the 1930s created great hardship in Peru, especially in its cities, so it contributed to the psychological separation of the eras. Yet a more pervasive and enduring change occurred in the mechanisms for setting national policy. In 1931 Peru finally entered an era of mass political mobilization.

During the thirty-eight years following the fall of Leguía, mass-participation party administrations alternated with armed-forces institutional governments. Fifteen chief executives served an average 2.5

years each, because several times men headed the government briefly
during transitions. Three presidents—a civilian engineer-investor and
two generals—served over two-thirds of the thirty-eight years. The alter-
nation of civilian and military leaders brought eight officers and seven
civilians to Pizarro's palace, in contrast to civilian preponderance during the previous thirty-five years. Ten, or two-thirds, arrived at the
palace following a coup d'état, while only three first became president
by election. These chief executives averaged some fifty-four years of
age on taking office, the highest figure since independence. Only one-
fifth had previously acted as cabinet ministers. Five of these presidents
were born in Lima, the highest proportion since 1821, while two came
from Arequipa. Natives of coastal cities outnumbered Serranos three-
to-one.

Indeed, a striking feature of mass-participation parties and the
political process after 1930 has been the concentration of political
mobilization efforts in coastal cities. Peru became increasingly urban
at a rapid rate during these years. When the government finally managed to conduct another national census in 1940, the Lima-Callao
metropolitan area contained over half a million residents. That represented a nine-year gain since 1931 of almost 180,000 persons, a 46.6
percent increase in a decade when U.S. cities typically lost residents.
Peru then held roughly 7,000,000 persons, so the primate city housed
8 percent of the total, compared to 3.8 percent in 1876.

Industrialization and a flourishing export economy based on copper,
cotton, and fish meal made from Pacific anchovies at Callao and other
ports, attracted a million migrants to the Lima-Callao area during a
twenty-year period. When Peru enumerated its population again in
1961, 1,632,370 persons resided in the primate city. With this increase,
the metropolis held 15.7 percent of the nation's populace, leaving no
doubt as to its overwhelming dominance.

Other coastal cities also grew rapidly as their urban environments
improved. During World War II, U.S. aircraft sprayed the newly discovered insecticide DDT on coastal and mountain valleys to eliminate
mosquitos. Because extremely arid desert or barren mountain slopes
separated oases, this spraying permanently eliminated insects transmit-

ting disease. Human life expectancy dramatically increased in coastal oases, further encouraging migration to Arequipa, Trujillo, Chiclayo, Piura, and Tacna. Only Huancayo among Sierra towns expanded as rapidly.

Government planning and development in conjunction with an unanticipated boom in anchovy and tuna processing at the great bay of Chimbote stimulated the most spectacular urban growth outside Lima. The central government set up a development corporation for the Santa River. It constructed a hydroelectric generating dam upstream from Huallanca and installed large electrical generators during the 1950s. Cheap electric power allowed the government to build a steel-making plant at Chimbote that utilized coal from deposits served by the Chimbote-Huallanca Railroad and iron ore shipped from Marcona. That major industrial installation needed a large number of workers and began to attract migrants.

The quiet peasant fishing port of Chimbote was a favorite honey-moon spot with less than 5,000 inhabitants in 1940. With the same small farming hinterland and a stinking, polluted bay, Chimbote in 1961 contained some 60,000 inhabitants, living largely in squatters' settlements. By 1972, Chimbote held 159,000 people and was the fifth largest city after Lima-Callao, Arequipa, Trujillo, and Chiclayo.

Electrification also allowed the spectacular growth of the metropolis. The *Empresas Electricas Asociadas,* struggling to satisfy increasing customer demands, scrambled to find financing as the economic depression worsened and Peru passed through political convulsions in 1930-33. Using operational income, it set out to achieve an even daily flow in the Santa Eulalia River using sixteen headwaters lakes. It added large generators in 1951, 1952, 1955, 1958, 1960, and 1961. In 1957, it began its most ambitious project, the diversion of glacial waters flowing to the Amazon onto the Pacific slope. Cutting a 10-kilometer tunnel through the Andean summit took nearly five years, but Peru's most powerful 60,000-kilowatt generator, using this diverted flow, entered service in 1964, followed by a second in 1965. Thus, private enterprise kept pace with explosive population growth in the metropolitan area and furnished power to run Peru's largest concentration of industry. The area consumed over 70 percent of the elecrticity used nationwide. The utility's service made its shares the favorite investment for the general public among the small number traded actively on the Lima stock market, paying an 8 percent annual return.

One reason the outsider perceives more continuity in Peru's twentieth-century history than Peruvians do, perhaps, is that the political parties that strove for and achieved a significant measure of mass participation were founded during Lequía's long regime. They simply began to contest elections in 1931, and the contest between one strong regional party and the armed-forces leadership characterized national policy-making thereafter.

The American Popular Revolutionary Alliance, usually referred to as APRA, sprang from the fertile brain of a young man from Trujillo. Víctor Raúl Haya de la Torre emerged as a leader in the university reform movement while student body president at San Marcos. He helped to organize textile and sugar workers' unions and to protest some of Leguía's more flagrant dictatorial measures. Haya led a mass street protest against dedicating Peru to the Sacred Heart of Jesus, a trivial but highly symbolic issue. Haya demonstrated student political strength by stopping the plan, and Leguía responded by exiling him.

Haya de la Torre spent some time in Mexico analyzing the ideology and organization of the 1910 social revolution. He then founded APRA. Haya consistently maintained that APRA is a native American party, radical but not Communist. He coined the concept "Indo-America" to express the racial unity of those countries such as Mexico and Peru with large Indian and Mestizo populations. Haya also emphasized initially *Indigenista* goals for Peru, but building party strength among plantation workers meant speaking to the coastal proletariat rather than to Andean peasants.

Despite its Americanism, APRA does possess similarities to Old World radical parties. The cell structure resembles the Communist model. Cell organization served APRA well by keeping it alive during periods when it was illegal in Peru and persecuted by the police. APRA resembles other major leftist parties in being international. Closely related parties gained power in Venezuela and Costa Rica, but

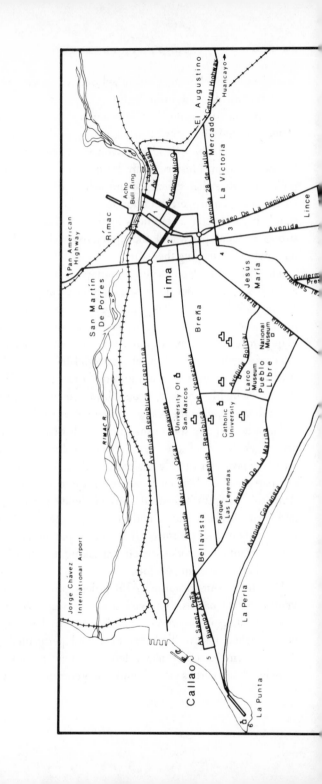

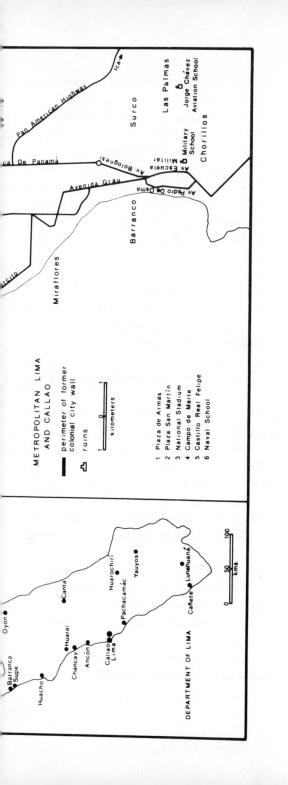

METROPOLITAN LIMA
AND CALLAO

■ perimeter of former
colonial city wall

⌂ ruins

|———————|
0   1
kilometers

1 Plaza de Armas
2 Plaza San Martín
3 National Stadium
4 Campo de Marte
5 Castillo Real Felipe
6 Naval School

Pan American Highway

Ica →

Surco

Las Palmas

Jorge Chávez
Aviation School

Military
School

Av. Escuela Militar

Chorillos

Av Bolognesi

cal De Panamá

Avenida Grau

Av Pedro De Osma

Barranco

Miraflores

rcito

DEPARTMENT OF LIMA

Oyon ●

Barranca
● Supe

Huacho ●

Canta ●

Chancay ●
● Huaral

Ancón ●

Callao ●
● Lima

● Pachacamác

Huarochiri ●

Yauyos ●

Cañete ●
● Lunahuaná

|——|——|——|
0   50   100
kms.

this internationalism hurt APRA's chances for success in Peru. Beginning in the mid-1930s, the Peruvian APRA, or "People's Party" as it has preferred to be called, tried to shed its international image and strengthen its credentials as a purely Peruvian entity.

Haya de la Torre was one of a trio of Leguía-period rebels to found parties that endured. All three were intellectuals as well as organizers. Haya has produced during a long life an endless stream of books, pamphlets, newspaper articles, and speeches, some of them hours long. Hildebrando Castro Pozo proved to be less prolific, while José Carlos Mariátegui, who wrote rapidly as well as eloquently, died at a comparatively early age. Like Haya, Castro Pozo came from the north coast, in the frontier department of Piura. He published at great length on the "socialist" heritage of the Incas and Andean indigenous communities, as one might expect the founder of a socialist party to do. Castro Pozo wrote not only as an urban theorist, however, but also as a more-or-less systematic field researcher. He actually went out to study at first hand the surviving phenomenon of the indigenous community, which many *Indigenistas* and Mariátegui rather idealized.

Peru's Socialist Party never achieved a large and lasting electoral following, but has significantly influenced the intellectuals in all parties. As a pragmatist unfettered by party discipline wielded from another country, Castro Pozo could work effectively toward reform of the system. Socialists could take jobs in the ministry responsible for conducting Indian affairs and introduce technological innovations to the indigenous communities so that they would become better able to compete with the increasingly technical operations of the landed elite.

The third party organizer, José Carlos Mariátegui, was a more urbane descendant of a family prominent in elitist politics since independence. He came under the influence of Communist thought in France, where he received part of his education. In 1928 Mariátegui published seven essays about the reality of Peru. Immediately profoundly influential, these essays have been republished so often as to become the best-selling single work by a Peruvian author. With such wide distribution, they also became fundamental points of departure for political thought thereafter.

Mariátegui extended his influence by taking a major role in organizing a Peruvian Communist Party. Although this party never achieved a large membership, it gained influence greater disproportionately than its voting power. This was because of the relatively high proportion of intellectuals it attracted who were influential in education, the letters, and politics generally. Its power has stemmed from its ideas and the excellence of their expression by Marxist intellectuals. Moreover, the strong resemblance of Peruvian capitalism to the sort Karl Marx described and condemned has lent Marxist socioeconomic analyses peculiar and continuing applicability.

This party maintained some semblance of discipline and unity for many years, yet it was weakened by splinter movements like those that plagued leftist parties elsewhere. Reflecting the Stalin-Trotsky split in the U.S.S.R., Peru early acquired a Trotskyite Worker's Party. The break between the Chinese and Russians produced a parallel split into "Moscow Communist" and "Peking Communist" groups. When Chairman Mao Tse Tung launched the "Great Leap Forward" in China, the Peruvian *Pekineses* further split into radical and conservative factions. Consequently, the party and its successor splinters never acquired sufficient electoral following to contest seriously even one parliamentary seat.

After three mass-participation-style political parties appeared in reaction to the sociopolitical structure of Peru under Leguía, the size of the electorate rose rapidly, twice through extensions of the franchise. In 1931 the national electoral commission removed the property qualification for voting and instituted the secret ballot. Votes cast then rose to some 300,000, and by 1945 to approximately 450,000. The vote increased almost eightfold in the forty-six years after the first direct presidential election.

APRA emerged as the major party after the coup d'état that toppled Leguía. Haya ran for the presidency against Commandant Luís Sánchez Cerro, leader of the coup and head of an ephemeral Fascist-style party. Haya and his followers expected to win despite Peru's long history of domination by postcoup military leaders. Inasmuch as the professional military establishment ran the interim government and election in the depths of a world depression, a Sánchez Cerro victory might have been predicted. The electoral result became an immediate matter of dispute and remains such. No one will ever be certain whether Sánchez Cerro or Haya had the most votes, but the interim regime announced that Sánchez Cerro won.

Outraged by what they regarded as military theft of the election, APRA partisans resorted to force. Overestimating their own power and popular support, they attacked the army. APRA partisanship reached its apogee, and its direct action achieved greatest success in the culturally distinct north. The party seized control of Trujillo and a number of other northern cities at a high cost in army casualties.

The 1931 revolt proved that no coup d'état can succeed without army high command approval. The armed forces reacted strongly to the APRA challenge and turned savage after APRA partisans "executed" in APRA terms, or "massacred" in army terms, approximately 5,000 officers and men of the Trujillo garrison who had surrendered. That incident made permanent and bitter the already awakened armed-forces opposition to Haya de la Torre and his party.

The armed forces regained control of the entire republic relatively quickly, sending those APRA activists not executed into exile abroad, to prison, or into hiding. Sánchez Cerro took office only to be assassinated in 1933, an act widely attributed to APRA. Consequently, Marshal-President Oscar Benavides kept APRA outside the legal pale. Only when Manuel Prado Ugarteche supervised a reasonably open election in 1945 was APRA able to muster its strength behind a coalition headed by José Bustamante y Rivero. Coming into the Bustamante cabinet, APRA ministers proved to be unable to control postwar inflation and scarcity of food and other consumer commodities, so that the military coup d'état in 1948 gained much popular support.

Coup leader Gen. Manuel A. Odría again outlawed APRA, dispersed its leadership, and closed its newspaper. At the end of his term, Odría enacted a constitutional amendment enfranchising women. With this action, Odría more than doubled the size of the electorate.

Consequently, 1,249,000 or so votes were cast in 1956, a 177 percent increase over 1945. Many jokes circulated about women voting for the young, handsome architect Fernando Belaunde Terry, but the grey, conservative engineer-businessman Manuel Prado y Ugarteche won. Women tended to vote on pocketbook issues, as might have been expected from the massive female support for Guillermo Billinghurst's 1912 populist candidacy using the slogan "a bigger loaf of bread." Women influenced Billinghurst's election even though they could not vote, in the first real threat to the male aristocracy. That women voted their purses in 1956 and later appears in Odría's strength in the 1962 and 1963 elections. After violent incidents early in the 1962 campaign, Odría's wife campaigned mostly in his place. Her appearances reminded other women to whom they owed the right to vote and the stabilization of food prices and household necessities. Odría received nearly one-third of the votes cast in both elections with three major candidates. In 1962 Odría carried three departments, notably Lima with the greatest concentration of female electors in Peru, especially in the lower socioeconomic classes.

In 1956 the age of genuine mass political participation finally dawned but APRA had to join in the electoral process unofficially and illegally. Reportedly it formed an alliance with candidate Prado to throw APRA voting strength to him in return for legalization of the party after his inauguration. Prado did legalize APRA so Haya de la Torre could run again in 1962. About 330,000 more citizens exercised the franchise in 1962 than in 1956, reflecting swiftly increasing literacy and political mobilization. Thinking itself the majority party, APRA once again overestimated its popularity in an election that pitted Haya against Odría with a personal party and Belaunde Terry with his new, energetic Popular Action Party comprised largely of middle-class adherents. The geographic distribution of votes showed APRA to be a regional party dominant only in the old Chimú territory of northern Peru and the plantation agriculture area of Ica Department. In an exceedingly close three-way election, unofficial tabulations left in doubt whether Haya received even the one-third plus one vote constitutionally required for election. Belaunde immediately cried "fraud" and openly requested military intervention to keep Haya from taking office on the basis of the still "unofficial" tally. The military high command did then accuse the national election board of complicity in fraudulent APRA voting. Conscious of continuing military opposition to him because of the events of 1931 as well as a widespread belief that he was homosexual, Haya met with his old enemy Odría. They reportedly worked out a compromise under which Haya would throw to Odría APRA votes in parliament, which would settle the uncertain election outcome. That would give Odría a large parliamentary majority and the presidency.

The military carried out a coup anyhow, purged voter registration roles, and certified Belaunde's victory in new elections in 1963. That year 115,000 more voters cast ballots, a total of some 1,796,000 out of just over two million registered voters. The Odría Union and APRA deputies and senators elected that year formed an opposition majority coalition in parliament known as the "marriage of convenience." The Haya-Odría pact and marriage of convenience completely alienated from Haya personally and APRA as a party many of their more idealistic and once most enthusiastic supporters. Some of the most radical APRA partisans turned to small leftist parties or violence.

The sheer numbers of voters after 1956 created for the first time political conditions comparable to those in democratic nations with longer histories of political mobilization. The increase in the number of literate persons greatly augmented the circulation of newspapers and their political impact, while the newly available radio diffused much political information and propaganda.

Another phenomenon greatly politicized Peru from 1962 to 1966. Peruvians experienced no less than five intensive nationwide electoral campaigns employing the mass media to an extent never before possible. First came a presidential-parliamentary election in 1962 with extensive personal campaigning by candidates of three major and four minor parties. After the army annulled the 1962 balloting with a coup d'état, it called for new elections the next year. The three major candidates, plus one new minor presidential hopeful, again campaigned across the country and galvanized the mass media. Numerous provincial splinter parties contested parliamentary seats on local issues.

Once in office, President Fernando Belaunde Terry called the first municipal elections since 1919. Major parties and regional political groups contested offices energetically to capture power in the municipalities that would reinforce their national positions. Parliamentary elections followed again in 1965, and municipal elections came again in 1966. Consequently, by 1966 the populace had been thoroughly politicized. Voters who watched television, listened to the radio, or read newspapers were kept very aware of correlations between party programs and strengths and the policy decisions made in parliament and by the executive branch of government.

Like the small Socialist and Communist parties, both APRA and Popular Action advocated agrarian reform and greater control of foreign capital by measures ranging from stricter enforcement of laws already on the books to nationalization. Thus, parliament and the chief executive had to agree on some reforms. A succession of members of rapidly changing cabinets carried out on a small scale a mild agrarian reform act. The executive branch paid greatly augmented salaries to teams of technocrats with ready-made solutions to difficult socioeconomic problems. It inexplicably failed to crack down on foreign corporations, particularly the International Petroleum Company. That subsidiary of Standard Oil of New Jersey actually managed to gain greater concessions from negotiations initiated to reduce its independence. That created a politically explosive situation in a country where many citizens questioned the very legality of its title to the oil it pumped from the La Brea and Pariñas fields near Talara on the far north coast.

Political dissatisfaction with the Belaunde regime also arose from the great sense of disillusionment that followed the very high expectations Belaunde raised when he took office. The prolonged political campaigns of 1962 and 1963 with their drumfire of promises filled people with a sense of euphoric anticipation that the new regime would quickly change the old state of things for the better. The unprecedented political mobilization of the electorate posed a danger that elitist politicians making extravagant campaign promises failed to foresee: political innocents expected promises to be kept once the military inaugurated Belaunde on July 28th and returned to their barracks.

Two days after inauguration, metropolitan newspapers trumpeted startling news about political mobilization of a nonpartisan type never previously achieved. Residents of the Indigenous Community of San Pedro de Cajas in Junín Department had overnight occupied hundreds of hectares of range land along the Central Highway ostensibly owned by the Cerro de Pasco Corporation. The people of Cajas maintained that the land was either in litigation between their community and the corporation or had been illegally acquired by the latter. Their "recuperation" force demonstrated a side-effect of a compulsory military service law that brought Indian conscripts into the army for two years of training.

Former conscripts from San Pedro de Cajas who had reached the rank of corporal or sergeant while in national service led the "recuperation" operation. They mobilized the community's cooperative bus service vehicles, taxis, horses, and organized infantry units to occupy various sectors of the disputed land on a tight schedule with national banners whipping in the altiplano breeze. Caught up, perhaps, in the rhetoric of his own campaign, which had ended only a few weeks before, Belaunde's Minister of Government did not order the Republican Guard shock battalions, which had repressed numerous peasant "uprisings" during the Prado regime, to evict the San Pedro de Cajas forces from the occupied area.

Peasant community leaders throughout Peru listened to radio reports or read newspaper accounts of the San Pedro de Cajas "recuperation" of communal land rights. They, too, had served as conscripts, become literate, and now shared the nationwide euphoria as to the immediate future. Within days scores of peasants, many of them army veterans, mobilized community task forces to invade areas on their boundaries that were in dispute with elite landowners or foreign corporations. Between July, 1963, and June, 1964, the metropolitan press reported well over 200 separate estate takeovers. Peruvian peasants displayed a degree of spontaneous nonpartisan, though highly political, mobilization not witnessed since 1572.

The mobilized peasantry reversed for the first time the historic Indian loss of land. The provincial upper class had supported Belaunde as an authentic member of the traditional political elite born into the powerful Arequipa "clan." Now it pressed for protection of its vested interests. Toward the end of 1963, Belaunde appointed his minister of Government as Ambassador to France and replaced him with a new cabinet member who did dispatch the Republican Guard battalions to stop peasant land recuperations. While most peasants retreated under the threat of police repression and promises of future land reform, some succeeded in holding onto their gains.

The Belaunde regime turned to the parliamentary struggle with the majority APRA-UNO coalition over precise provisions of a land reform law that would initiate legal agrarian reform. The 1962-63 military leaders had decreed the "bases for governmental agrarian reform." Undoubtedly the military institution intended the next civilian regime to begin serious land reform. Members of parliament wrangled interminably in the view of radical urban political activists caught up in great expectations of prompt basic socioeconomic changes. So they resorted to direct action.

Hugo Blanco, a Quechua-speaking student leader from Cuzco, ventured into remote La Convención Valley to organize serfs and peasants. The valley landlords and plantation administrators were well known for their oppressive treatment of Indians. Trotskyite Blanco quickly advanced from union organizer to guerrilla leader. Severely exploited peasants rallied behind this charismatic urbanite who came to them with sincere advocacy of social justice.

Other urban radicals belonging to or closely aligned with international leftist parties soon mounted a well-armed guerrilla movement. Trained abroad, they robbed banks to obtain funds and then dispersed themselves to various spots in the highlands of Peru to mobilize the peasants. Their goals and motives were transparently partisan rather than broadly populist and their command of Quechua was as seriously deficient as their knowledge of peasants. The would-be Ché Guevaras consequently failed to mobilize many peasant fighters or find much support.

Belaunde sent the army to put down the guerrillas. Senior generals commanded detachments in a wide field of operations. The modern army sealed off great sectors of southern Peru for months at a time, and exterminated the guerrillas. It packed Blanco off to a comfortable jail cell where he wrote short stories and received a stream of admirers.

The army high command resolved, however, during this campaign that it would never again allow itself to be placed in the position of killing certain citizens to protect the property interests of others. The guerrilla campaigns destroyed whatever hope had been kindled that basic change for the better was on its way, a hope widely held by key army officers who led the most unified large institution in the country.

When hundreds of communities demonstrated how well mobilized they had become by recuperating their lost lands, APRA suddenly rediscovered its long-neglected *Indigenismo*. The party diverted major resources from its conventional coastal proletariat organizational programs to a crash effort aimed at organizing indigenous communities. APRA had already set up a National Peasant Federation prior to the 1962 elections. Yet it failed to achieve much progress in affiliating indigenous communities outside the areas of existing APRA strength.

A high proportion of the peasant communities already belonged to a mosaic of regional federations. Socialist and Communist politicians had organized some regional federations, yet their national success differed little from that of APRA. Peasant community leagues displayed real strength where they joined together in pursuit of regional goals.

The Puno situation illustrates how strong peasant organizations arose independent of major parties from specific local conditions. The large Quechua- and Aymara-speaking population in Puno lived in constant contact, through contraband trade, radio broadcasts, and personal travel, with the heady rhetoric of social revolution in neighboring Bolivia after 1952. The Puno Indians suffered a devastating drought in 1955-56, which resulted in extensive emigration and unrest. In the aftermath of the drought, a trio of Mestizo brothers who held strong personal ambitions succeeded in mobilizing thousands of Puno peasants into "leagues." With that support, these Cáceres brothers controlled departmental politics. They represented the department in parliament, where they promoted regional interests throughout the 1960s.

Apparently, the strong influence of centuries-old environmental and cultural factors kept peasant leagues regional in nature. Thus no single political group or person could pretend to speak for peasant interests on a national scale. While often discussed, appealed to, and used by ambitious politicians or parties, Sierra peasants wielded little influence in the selection or direction of national policy.

APRA's Sierra mobilization effort gained new strength for it in the Huancayo region. That led to the founding early in the 1960s of an APRA-influenced provincial university in Huancayo. Students attending the new *Universidad Communal del Centro* often came from indigenous communities in the Mantaro Valley and identified strongly with these communities. They achieved a direct link-up between the university as an intellectual center of innovation and the indigenous communities of peasants receptive toward changes in agricultural technology, marketing structures such as cooperatives, and other innovations.

Organization of this institution constituted only one phase of an expansion of higher educational facilities early in the 1960s. Student demand for higher education forced the government to establish eight new state universities and supported seven new private ones. The increase of the literate population set in motion by refugees during the War of the Pacific accelerated markedly during the twentieth century. The first regime of Manuel Prado y Ugarteche crucially stimulated primary and secondary education. Prado emulated Mexico by sending "cultural brigades" out into isolated monolingual Indian areas to offer the peasants training in simple technical and agricultural techniques and basic reading and writing skills. A new basic education law promised to any settlement whose inhabitants built their own schoolhouses that the government would assign teachers. Hundreds of peasant communities put up school buildings. The national Ministry of Education indeed assigned them teachers, thus greatly expanding the primary educational plant and teacher corps at minimal costs. Later, Peru also adopted from UNESCO and Mexico the strategy of establishing nuclear peasant schools. These provided central schools with staff educational specialists who visited smaller satellite schools.

As the primary school expansion produced increasing thousands of graduates, the Ministry of Education built and staffed secondary schools in departmental and then provincial capital cities. A very large, frustrated pool of secondary school graduates seeking higher education built up by the end of Prado's second regime in 1962. Existing universities numbered seven: liberal arts schools at Cuzco, Trujillo, and Arequipa, with the ancient San Marcos, the National Engineering and National Agricultural Schools, and the Pontifical Catholic University in Lima. These universities could not provide enough classrooms and professors for those who wished to enter. Late in the 1950s, therefore, Prado's administration reestablished the former University of Huamanga in Ayacucho, in the central Sierra.

Prado's first regime had made formal elementary and secondary education more widely available, leading to a demand for new universities and his second regime provided a model for answering this demand. Nongovernmental forces mobilized to expand the number of schools along with those created by the government. APRA opened a branch of its Huancayo university in coastal Huacho. It moved some instructors to Lima and set up what became the *Universidad Federico Villareal*. The church opened a second Catholic University in conservative Arequipa and another branch in Ayacucho.

The greatest concentration of new institutions of higher learning appeared in the primate city. The first new private school came into being toward the end of Prado's administration when parliament voted to allow a high level of student participation in faculty-student cogovernment at San Marcos. The high-quality but conservative medical faculty resigned en masse and set up a private medical school. A former minister of labor became rector of the small but good-quality Lima University specializing in business administration. The private *Universidad del Pacífico* and *San Martín de Porres* opened in Lima, as did the church-sponsored Sacred Heart university for women. A technical college appeared. With U.S. government funding, the Stanford Research Institute helped to establish a graduate school of business, a pioneer institution in type and level.

Provincial cities pressured the Ministry of Education for new public universities. In response, it established agricultural schools at Tingo María on the eastern Andean slope and Lambayeque on the north coast. The latter merged with a liberal arts faculty founded in nearby Chiclayo. Piura gained a business-technical university, Puno the Altiplano Technical University, and Iquitos an Amazonian university. Coastal Ica, Cajamarca in the northern Sierra, Cerro de Pasco in the central Sierra, and Huánuco on the edge of the upper rain forest obtained regional universities.

Thus, numerous interests participated in expanding higher education facilities fourfold within a single half-decade and in doubling enrollment between 1961 and 1965. University students and recent graduates responded to their increased access to some of the good aspects of life with ever-increasing expectations. Consequently, they also shared fully in the disillusion that spread through the country with the civilian Belaunde regime elected in 1963. Like every other sector of the population, students desired more rapid gratification than Belaunde and his parliamentary opposition provided by 1968.

Numerous as students were in Peru in 1968, they lacked the power to change a national regime in a complex nation with a large national police force and strong armed forces. The latter did possess the requisite power. World War II had brought with it a strong United States effort to supplant German and French military missions in Latin America with American ones, especially after the fall of France and U.S. entry into the conflict. The U.S. effort succeeded in Peru. Peruvian officers began to attend U.S. military and naval academies and specialized schools and participated in Panamá Canal Zone maneuvers of the U.S. Southern Defense Command. The United States either sold its weapons, aircraft, vessels, and vehicles to the Peruvian armed forces or gave obsolescent equipment as military "aid." U.S. military advisers encouraged "civic action" programs, especially Amazonic penetration road construction. This process endowed the army with equipment and financial budget that in time exceeded those of the Ministry of Development, reinforcing a growing military superiority complex vis à vis civilian government institutions and its record of accomplishment.

In 1950, the armed forces created a Center of Higher Military Studies (CAEM). Within a very short time, it profoundly influenced the thinking of senior officers. Pursuing a goal of preparing the high command to defend Peru, CAEM employed a largely civilian faculty. While instructors represented a wide range of political views, they stressed reformist or revolutionary analyses, solutions, and programs. Officers attending CAEM classes concentrated on studying problems and future prospects. For a decade they learned to be dissatisfied with the current state of their country and its civilian socioeconomic structure. CAEM proved to be tremendously influential in heightening concern among senior officers with national socioeconomic issues. Just what role the armed forces should play in defending vested interests against citizen demands for economic equality and social justice became a key military concern. At the same time, CAEM's short-course format militated against full presentions of the complexity of issues and may well have tended to make solutions appear to officer-students sheltered by their institution easier than in fact they were. In its first decade of existence, in any event, CAEM stimulated officers to solve long-festering social problems.

CAEM, its instructors and officer-students, participated in a fully urban way of life, along with millions of other Peruvians. That city pattern differed from rural patterns not only for demographic but also cultural reasons. While residents of rural towns listened on transistorized radios to broadcasts of urban theories about political solutions to national problems, they took personal action to solve those that loomed largest in their eyes. Many rural peasants, freeholders, and even townsmen still shared the Indian work ethic rather than the elite Spanish disdain for labor. Consequently, even after the Leguía regime's road law was repealed, peasants continued to open farm-market access roads for their towns. A typical case occurred in the District of Huaylas, where work parties continued building by hand its 17-

kilometer access route to the highway until they finished it in 1942. So in 1944, Peru claimed 9,238 kilometers of automotive highway along the coast and its lateral primary penetration routes, supplemented by 21,986 kilometers of secondary access roads. By 1962, half of the officially recognized indigenous communities had opened truck trails to main highways.

The building of new access roads goes on. In 1964, for example, residents of the western slope indigenous community of Mayobamba started work on the final 11 kilometers of access roadway separating their village from the road at the hot springs resort of Chiuchín at the base of their mountain. They had already worked on every section of the penetration road from the Panamerican Highway to Sayán, from Sayán to Churín, another hot springs resort, and from that road to Chiuchín. Finally, they were able to initiate their ultimate road project to link their own home town by truck and bus directly to urban Peru.

While thousands of rural people worked on modifications of the old Road Law scheme of six or twelve days' labor on an access road per month or year, the elite national administrations devoted some resources to main highway projects. When the depression of the 1930s threw thousands of men out of work in the Lima-Callao metropolitan area, the government turned the Central Highway into its equivalent of U.S. work-relief programs. The depression labor force, which cost the government relatively little, carried the highway over the Andean summit alongside the railroad at an elevation of 4,843 meters, linking the agriculturally rich Mantaro Valley mixed farming communities with the urban food market. Specialized truck farming expanded in that zone beyond the ribbon of fields accessible to the Central Railroad.

Completing and paving the coastal Panamerican Highway became a top-priority World War II project. This road united the coastal oases for the first time into a single socioeconomic and cultural area. Several bus lines provided economical and rapid transportation from city to city. Automobiles with reinforced springs provided even faster intercity transport for higher fares. Thus, Piura or Arequipa lay only ten

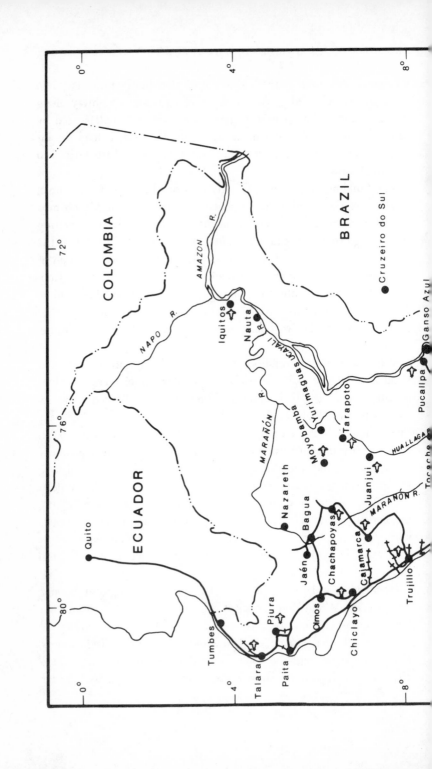

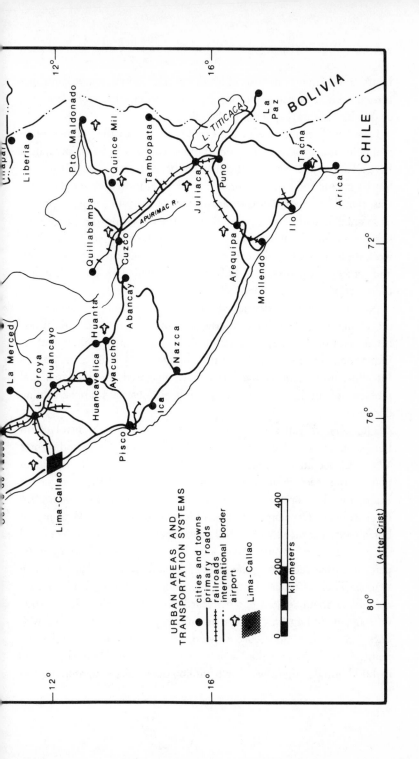

URBAN AREAS AND
TRANSPORTATION SYSTEMS

● cities and towns
━━ primary roads
┼┼┼┼┼ railroads
─··─ international border
⇧ airport
▨ Lima-Callao

0   200   400
kilometers

(After Crist)

hours' travel from Lima instead of several days. Then, national regimes turned their attention to cutting east-west penetration roads from the coastal base across the Andes to the rain forest.

President Fernando Belaunde Terry tried to turn the nation's attention eastward to the vast Amazonic wilderness, which, he claimed, held Peru's future. He was not the first politician to embrace this notion, but he committed more resources to it than any predecessor. His idea was to build a "marginal road" at the edge of the rain forest to connect Colombia, Ecuador, Peru, and Bolivia, thus opening the jungle's resources for human use. Belaunde reinforced the army corps already at work there, increasing the expensive modern road-building equipment, and letting out contracts to U.S. concerns, which failed to complete their sections before Belaunde's fall from power.

New colonies were developed with government encouragement, as the regime sought to attract Sierra peasants to a new life. Belaunde lifted taxes on businesses operating in the Amazon region as further inducement to investors. While the population of some areas around Pucallpa, Iquitos, and Tingo María have increased, the developmental problems of the jungle region pose enormous obstacles for the coming decades.

The United States government became increasingly involved in Peru's financial and developmental affairs during the second World War. "Cooperative" services in health, agriculture, and education planted the seeds of involvement that blossomed into the work of the International Cooperation Administration and then the Agency for International Development. Technical experts and Washington bureaucrats packaged U.S. assistance. They supervised and directed the use of loans totaling about $100,000,000 from 1960 to 1970, 60 percent authorized during the early and middle years of the Belaunde regime. Then U.S. aid dropped from a total, including loans and direct aid, of about $90,000,000 per year in 1963 to less than $25,000,000 in 1969, including $3.5 million for military aid. Deciding how well U.S. aid programs succeeded depends on one's nationality and viewpoint: $21.8 million of the loans went largely to hire U.S. contractors to build jungle highways; $30.6 million for projects reinforcing the predominance of Lima; and $31.1 million on various agricultural projects, mostly coastal irrigation works. The World Bank also loaned large sums for expanding north coast irrigated areas. In general, these were high overhead investments directly benefiting U.S. companies or Peruvian capitalists. Proponents promised the ordinary citizens far more than they finally delivered to them, because rewards failed to "trickle down" according to theory. Dependence on U.S. loans for financing national development continued to put Peru at the mercy of external capital, rankling nationalistic Peruvians.

The Inter-American Development Bank loaned Peru funds in the mid-1960s to initiate an expanded Indian integration program in seven Sierra regions. By 1968 the program had carried out a number of classified studies and had led to the hiring of many highly paid employees but accomplished little. *Indigenismo,* which remained a movement rather than becoming a political party, was on its way out. The 1933 constitution kept the 1919 provisions legalizing Indigenous Communities. By 1940 Peru joined other American states in forming the Interamerican Indian Institute. Peru set up a domestic counterpart. When Carlos Monge Medrano, former medical school dean, became director of the Peruvian Indian Institute, he found ways to alter the situation of selected Indians through pilot programs. Monge contracted with Cornell University in 1951 to conduct an experiment in scientifically guided change at a Sierra hacienda in Vicos, Ancash. He agreed to have the International Labour Organization conduct in the Lake Titicaca area another improvement program that stressed vocational training. These programs enabled Monge to obtain appropriations for the Institute to mount limited similar programs of its own and through contract with Cuzco University in Kuyo Chico, Cuzco. Although the efforts at Vicos and Kuyo Chico were symbolically important and achieved modest success in their areas, they were but lonely reminders that the "Indian Problem" still remained at the bottom of national priorities.

During three presidential campaigns, Fernando Belaunde Terry developed a personal variant of *Indigenismo* out of his contact with outstandingly industrious communities. In office, he attempted to mobilize volunteer labor to construct roads, schools, and other facilities. He established an interministerial organization to promote this bootstrap approach. It set up "central" provincial offices to supply tools, engineers, and technicians to stimulate and guide village work. The president awarded prizes to those provinces, districts, and communities that accomplished the most. Enthusiastic rural Peruvians who adhered to the Indian work ethic truly built much. Yet they became dissatisfied with the blatant pork-barrel politics involved in the program and the highly paid bureaucrats who paid lip-service to the goals of *Indigenismo* in order to obtain foreign loans to pay high salaries.

The rural people who demonstrated that they would work away at their development projects under any national administration had other reasons for disenchantment with Belaunde. Many of them lived in indigenous communities and resented the regime's revocation of their 1963-64 recoveries of lost lands. Many technocratically minded entrepreneurs and white-collar workers who had enthusiastically supported Belaunde when he was inaugurated blamed him for their financial losses when he devalued the currency. Radical urban intellectuals demanded faster and more extreme reforms than Belaunde and parliament achieved, while an exploding university system rapidly trained more new intellectuals to turn radical. The armed forces' own higher education institution, CAEM, successfully introduced the higher-ranking officers to what they would once have dismissed as radical ideas and heightened their intolerance of civilian inefficiency. By 1968, then, the euphoria that greeted Belaunde's regime five years earlier had long since dissipated and been replaced by disillusionment and disgust.

Chapter 11 • A Revolutionary Military Regime, 1968-1975

On October 3, 1968, changes initiated in the armed forces by the French military mission and fostered by the U.S. naval and military missions and by foreign aid matured. Senior armed forces' officers carried out a bloodless coup d'état. Gen. Juan Velasco Alvarado assumed the presidency, and other generals and admirals took ministerial posts. Colonels and captains became chief executive officers of ministerial bureaucracies at the next echelon, with civilians relegated to tertiary roles throughout the government. By October 3, 1974, the regime had held power for the equivalent of a constitutional six-year term. Thus, the Velasco regime took its place as one of Peru's longer administrations by the time it ended on August 29, 1975.

The Velasco high command group labeled itself "The Revolutionary Government of the Armed Forces," and it carried out a series of actions that could only be labeled as socially and economically revolutionary in terms of Peru's past. This regime set out to upgrade the morality of public servants. It launched a radical agrarian reform program. It nationalized numerous petroleum, mining, transport, communication, and fish-processing corporations. It suspended the normal operation of mass-participation political parties and worked to mobilize citizens into occupational groups that might someday replace political parties.

Military leaders carried out the 1968 coup largely from disgust with what they regarded as an immoral sell-out by Fernando Belaunde Terry's civilian administration to the International Petroleum Co. (IPC). A Canadian corporation wholly owned by Standard Oil of New Jersey, IPC exploited north coast Talara oil fields under questionable title. Although politicians of many persuasions had long advocated its expropriation, none in power before Velasco had possessed the courage to do so. No sooner had Velasco completed the coup than he ordered troops to occupy IPC fields at Talara and decreed its expropriation. Within a week the state-owned *Empresa Petrolera Fiscal* was operating IPC's oil field holdings. In July, 1969, Velasco created *Petróleos Peruanos S.A.* (PETROPERU) to conduct Peru's oil businesses directly under the president. A perennial bone of contention in domestic politics became an international issue between Peru and the United States: compensation to the parent corporation.

On its fifth anniversary, the regime purchased Burmah Oil Company's Lobitos Petroleum subsidiary for U.S.$6,000,000. Shortly thereafter it bought Atlantic Richfield's tiny Ganzo Azul for U.S.$185,000. Thus, it rounded out its control of the foreign petroleum concerns operating in Peru when it seized power, having also acquired a Standard Oil of California refinery and stations.

PETROPERU launched an aggressive oil exploration campaign in the Amazon region with foreign corporate participation in the search. Such firms as Union, Occidental, Texas, Tenneco, Pan-Ocean, Getty, Sun, Shell, Superior, Gulf, and Cities Service eagerly loaned cash in exchange for exploration rights and a share of crude production. Occidental brought in three consecutive successful wildcat wells and scheduled commercial production for 1975.

The decisive initial action of the military establishment quickly and crisply altered the tone of national governance and public life. After devaluing Peru's currency, the Belaunde administration had sunk into a miasma of political confusion. The military coup and prompt nationalization of IPC immediately reversed the psychological situation. Members of the armed forces who had been wearing civilian clothing with hangdog looks put on their uniforms with pride. Citizens in all walks of life united behind the generals and gained a new and deeper national pride.

The Velasco regime began calling itself "revolutionary" in a social sense. While it digested IPC properties, it worked on reforms in higher education, rationalization of industry, and similar projects for several months. It did not act rapidly to initiate radical reforms. When the regime did act, it began its social revolutionary program with real agrarian reform.

Early in 1969, a highland estate owner evicted Indian tenants from the property, shooting up the homes of resisting peasants. Officials from the departmental capital city attending a party at the manor house learned of the incident when they saw the bodies of slain peasants stretched out on the porch. One notified Lima officials that despite abundant rhetoric about revolutionary social change peasant repression was still occurring in traditional form. Shortly thereafter, aggrieved peasants picketed the presidential palace on Lima's Plaza de Armas.

Confronted with evidence that the provincial landed elite would continue violent peasant repression, the regime acted. The senior command had already decided never again to allow the landowning elite to place the armed forces in the position of killing one group of citizens to protect vested property interests of another. Velasco's ideologues worked around the clock to prepare a landmark speech for him to deliver on June 24 with a thoroughgoing agrarian reform decree N° 17716. Earlier regimes had made St. John's Day, still widely observed in rural Peru, "Indian Day" as part of the Indian integration showcase effort.

On that day, however, Velasco announced that Peru would abandon colonial racist terminology. Those previously called "Indians" would henceforth be officially termed "peasants" (*campesinos*) as in Bolivia since its 1952 social revolution. With the memorable phrase, "Peasants, the landlord will no longer eat from your poverty," Velasco decreed that rural estates where landlords employed outstandingly repressive measures would be immediately expropriated. Moreover, he decreed a nationwide land expropriation program aimed at converting large estates into workers' cooperatives without production losses. The regime created three types of bonds with which to recompense expropriated landowners which had to be first converted into industrial investments or urban improvements to be eligible for redemption in any near future.

Mobilizing army manpower, Velasco seized key coastal agrarian properties even as he spoke. The army "intervened" in most major sugar-cane growing plantations on the coastal oases. Military technocrats chose to maintain plantation economies of scale, borrowing the cooperative institutional form long advocated by APRA leader Haya de la Torre and similar to the one worked out in the rural peasant context by Cornell's Sierra hacienda experiment for the Peruvian Indian Institute. The regime set out to convert plantation labor forces of from 1,774 to 4,552 workers into producers' cooperatives. Two years later, foreign business observers predicted that military intelligence and agrarian reform agency controls would keep the plantations as state farms until they paid off their bonds. The regime's social action arm, SINAMOS, in April of 1972, however, held elections at the thirteen largest agroindustrial sugar cooperatives. A measure of its devolution of control was that the newly elected president at Tumán was a maintenance mechanic who had been in prison as an agitator until just before the election.

In September of 1969, the agrarian reform bureau began to expropriate those estates with long histories of violent repression of Sierra peasant tenants and all estates with over 500 hectares of agricultural land. Within two years, it had dispossessed owners of three dozen estates in critical regions, shifting permanently the balance of socioeconomic power in the Andes. In the Sierra as on the coast, the regime pursued a policy of establishing production cooperatives and creating integrated rural production organizations. At the same time, it abolished existing landlords' associations.

By the fourth anniversary of the agrarian reform law, the Velasco administration was expropriating land at a 1,300,000 hectare-per-year rate. It celebrated that occasion by handing out to cultivators titles for over half a million hectares, while trying to reassure small and medium commercial farmers that they would not be collectivized.

The revolutionary military regime moved deliberately and with caution in reforming industry. Not until May, 1970, did it publish a draft of a proposed new industrial law, although international companies had already felt its impact. The 1970 Industries Law set up, among other things, a state research-and-development program. The regime's state corporation emerged on January 25, 1972, in Decree N° 19272 which established an *Empresa Estatal Industrias del Peru* (INDU-PERU) to manage nationalized properties and to create associate and mixed ownership companies. Spokesmen warned soon after that foreign companies were no longer welcome and stressed the regime's goal of replacing imported products with domestic ones. In an impressive display of its technocratic orientation and grasp of economic theory far beyond that of nineteenth-century general-presidents, the military regime set about rationalizing motor vehicle production.

In Lima, a baker's dozen of manufacturers assembled in 1968 scores of automobile models, none engineered for local roads or high altitudes. The revolutionary military regime set out to force assemblers to achieve economies of scale and to increase the use of locally made parts. Late in 1969 the regime limited assemblers to one model in each of four passenger car and four truck and bus categories. Early in 1970 it froze prices, called for bids on exclusive assembly concessions, and required 51 percent Peruvian ownership. Chrysler, American Motors, Nissan, Volvo, Toyota, and Volkswagen survived first-round weeding.

By mid-1971, locally manufactured parts were about 23 percent of each assembled vehicle. Five remaining assemblers turned out 16,639 units that year as American Motors dropped out. Early in 1973 the regime cut models back to seven, although a local company specialized in assembling minibuses for urban transport. Negotiations began on exclusive production rights. Sweden's Volvo won the bus and heavy truck contest. In September, 1973, the regime contracted with Volvo to make 160-250 HP engines in a diesel engine plant to be built at Trujillo. The administration chose Trujillo as the site for a new heavy-industry complex to decentralize industrial concentration away from the Lima-Callao metropolitan area. Volvo would own 24 percent, and Peru signed Perkins Engines for a like interest and to manufacture engines up to 150 HP. INDUPERU kept 52 percent ownership. The state company had agreed in July with Massey-Ferguson of Canada to establish a tractor factory, also at Trujillo, with 49 percent Massey-Ferguson participation. At the end of the year, INDUPERU awarded Toyota a tender to build gasoline engines and gear-boxes and to make 1,500 to 2,500 cc. automobiles, signaling the departure of the other assemblers from automobile production. Worldwide inflation then interfered with Peru's drive toward a small, low-cost people's car, but the revolutionary military regime had recast automobile, bus, and truck making in a new mold.

The Velasco government edged state capitalism gradually into mining, although it had acted quickly to recover inactive concessions. Less than a year after seizing power, the military leaders demanded that companies present development schedules for their concessions by the end of 1969. Development work had to begin by April 1, 1970, to win approval. Anaconda, Kaiser, Cerro, and American Smelting and Refining lost major concessions. Southern Peru Copper Co. lost one, but retained its huge Cuajone concession by contracting to raise U.S.$350,000,000 to bring it into production.

Velasco decreed a state monopoly of mineral marketing on April 16, 1970. In June the regime called for bids on a 100,000 ton-per-year copper smelter, a 40,000 TPY zinc refinery and a 70,000 TPY sulphuric acid plant. Then it set up its state mining corporation (MINERO-PERU) in October to manage all state mining. It quickly found foreign engineers to start developing recently reclaimed concessions. Further, the administration extended the principle of "labor communities" sharing in profits and management to the mining industry in mid-1972. The largest labor community consisted of 14,500 Cerro de Pasco workers. A year later, the regime let it be known that it had already been negotiating for a year to purchase Cerro de Pasco. The parent Cerro Corp. broke off talks in September, 1973, accusing Velasco's people of bad faith and double-dealing. The president replied that

Peru could no longer tolerate such conduct. Clearly, the Cerro Corp. left the regime no alternative to nationalization, which it carried out in 1974. The following year the military government nationalized the Marcona Mining Corp., the major iron-ore extractor. Thus the government under the military administration acquired control of the largest foreign corporations that had dominated the national economy and politics for years.

The same nationalistic thrust completely changed the nature of the communications business. Telephone lines had become so scarce relative to the burgeoning Lima population that businessmen advertised in classified newspaper sections offers of S/. 15,000 (U.S.$550 prior to the 1967 devaluation) or more for an existing telephone connection. The Belaunde regime worked out a 1967 agreement to "Peruvianize" ITT's 69 percent share in the *Compañia Peruana de Teléfonos,* to which frustrated clients and employees felt no loyalty. In mid-1969 the military regime denied a rate increase, rescinded the expansion agreement, and obtained ITT concurrence on nationalization. ITT would invest most of its payment in a Sheraton hotel in Lima and an equipment factory. The latter began work at the end of 1970, and the hotel opened early in 1973 on the site of an old penitentiary.

Late in 1969 the military leaders established a state company, ENTEL-PERU, to operate public telecommunications. In mid-1972, it added the *Compañia Nacional de Teléfonos* facilities in northern and central Peru: Piura, Trujillo, Chimbote, Chiclayo, Huancayo, and Ica. In August of the following year, the regime took over the *Sociedad Telefonica del Sur,* which operated telephones in Apurimac, Arequipa, Cuzco, Moquegua, Puno, and Tacna Departments.

Meanwhile, ENTEL-PERU set about creating a truly national telecommunications network. Late in 1971 the regime issued a General Communications Law nationalizing seventeen private television stations. In the middle of 1972 the administration imposed strict controls on television and radio programming. Cigarette and liquor advertisements, violence, and sex were all relegated to hours after 9 P.M. ENTEL-PERU began in 1972 to install a microwave network.

In the transportation industry, the revolutionary military regime solved one foreign investment problem nearly a century after it began. In April, 1971, the Industrial Bank foreclosed its mortgage on the Peruvian Corporation, which had in 1967 defaulted on World Bank and Export-Import Bank lòans to modernize the railroads. The Industrial Bank put the Corporation up at auction, in effect nationalizing its assets. Although British bondholders sent a former ambassador to attempt to obtain some payment, the military leaders finally put an end to that particular foreign capital intervention in Peruvian governance. They set up a state railway company, ENAFER, in late 1972 to operate the railways. By the middle of 1973, ENAFER ordered twenty-five diesel electric locomotives from Canada to renovate the rail transport system.

While problems generated by the Peruvian Corporation had plagued each administration since 1890, the military regime also encountered air-age difficulties. Toward the middle of 1971, the national flag line APSA, controlled by U.S. capital, suspended operations when its aircraft were all repossessed on U.S. and Spanish air fields. The armed forces quickly authorized the military air transport command, SATCO, to expand its commercial flights as an independent entity and to acquire additional jet aircraft. They handicapped Faucett, the highly successful domestic civilian carrier that already flew cargo to the U.S. twice a week, and designated SATCO as the national airline for international flights under the "Aero Peru" label.

A series of problems in the fish-meal industry led the Velasco regime to nationalize fish-meal purchasing and marketing in mid-1970. The following March it issued a law altering property structures in the industry, requiring Peruvian majority ownership, consolidating production groups, and decreeing that workers would share in profits. The state marketing company, *Empresa Pública de Comercialización de Harina y Aceite de Pescado* (EPCHAP), pushed technological improvements. It proved to be unable to market fish meal at its own prices in 1971, forcing producers to carry large stocks while costs mounted. Then EPCHAP overcommitted itself to buyers as the catch plummeted when anchovies disappeared from Peruvian waters. The regime required fish-meal companies to borrow from state banks, so they became mortgaged when production was extremely low in 1972. The Fisheries Minister Javier Tantaleán then announced nationalization of the industry on May 7, 1973.

The regime created another state corporation, PESCA PERU, to operate the industry. U.S., Japanese, Spanish, French, Norwegian, and Scots investors lost properties along with Peruvian entrepreneurs. These and other expropriations caught overseas attention, along with the regime's vigorous defense of Peruvian sovereignty over the nation's fourth zone. During the 1968-74 period, the Peruvian navy alternated with the Ecuadorian navy in arresting the largest number of U.S.-registry tuna clippers within the 200-mile offshore zone.

Far more significant for the average Peruvian, however, has been a drive by the Velasco regime to increase domestic consumption of ocean food-fish. Velasco removed the ocean fisheries component from the Ministry of Agriculture to free it to concentrate on agrarian reform, cooperative formation, research, and extension. He created a Ministry of Fisheries that began operating February 1, 1970, embarking on a strong campaign to augment domestic consumption of food-fish. This meant improving port facilities in numerous small peasant fishing villages. It also meant converting a few such settlements into fully commercial ports, creating cooling and freezing facilities, building a fleet of refrigerated trucks, and enlarging the market distribution system.

The military regime launched this expansion in 1970 by building refrigeration plants in fifteen cities, seven ports, and seven inland reception points. The first locally built trawler began fishing at the end of the year to supply eleven refrigerated trucks. Early in 1971 the regime created an *Empresa Nacional de Puertos*, ENAPUPERU, for uniform port administration and development. It quickly laid out a program to build five fishing complexes on the Pacific, one at Iquitos on the Amazon and one at Puno on Lake Titicaca, plus sixteen new terminals at peasant fishing villages. In a sophisticated diplomatic move, disturbing to U.S. citizens comfortable only when Latin American foreign ministers echo U.S. State Department positions, the regime contracted with the U.S.S.R. to install the largest new food-fishing complex at Paita. At the same time, the United Nations Food and Agriculture Organization installed a hake-filleting plant to produce for export.

Major policy emphasis remained on improving the diet by increasing domestic fish consumption, although the regime also pushed fishing cooperatives. Inland consumption mounted for the first time as refrigerated fish arrived in good condition. Refrigerators opened in Tacna and Arequipa in 1971, and the latter went from forty tons per month to from twenty to thirty tons per week by early 1972. Air Force transports flew refrigerated fish to Ayacucho more cheaply than trucks could haul it. By August the state fish-sales company was operating in Cuzco and Huánuco, and its Arequipa fish restaurant served 2,000 meals a day. The 1972 food-fish catch reached 216,764 tons. Then refrigerated fish depots began operating in 1973 in Cajamarca, Huamachuco, and Huaráz. Thus, the Velasco regime achieved a significant increase in the fish protein consumption of residents of major urban areas where an economical source of protein was sorely needed to augment the diet of most of the populace.

When the Velasco regime discovered that the IPC was able to export funds even after its production facilities had been expropriated, the military launched a bank reformation. This later expanded and extended to other types of financial institutions.

The generals began with the Central Reserve Bank in mid-March, 1969. They decreed governmental appointment for all members of a new six-person board. Just over a year later, the regime restored the bank's authority to issue bank notes and to coin money, while routing half of its annual profit to the treasury. Six months later, Velasco cancelled commercial bank bond-issuing powers, further reinforcing the Central Reserve Bank.

The military regime greatly magnified the role of other state banks in national financing. It encouraged the Central Mortgage Bank founded in 1929 to open branches in Callao, Huancayo, Piura, Trujillo, and Tacna. By 1970 that bank cornered almost 59 percent of internal savings in 32,524 new family accounts. Its S/. 1,000 certificates accounted for 39 percent of all securities transactions on the Lima stock market. Tax exonerations for up to thirty years on low-cost houses upped construction from 17,000 units in 1970 to over 80,000 in 1971, creating a booming demand for mortgages. U.S. AID helped with two loans; the second early in 1972 enabled savings and loan associations to cut their interest rates to five percent.

The Velasco regime's greatest banking venture expanded the role of the National Bank. In mid-1970, the government used the *Banco de la Nación* to take over Peru's second largest commercial bank, the *Banco Popular*. This gave the National Bank 149 branches in many cities. It also acquired the Continental and International banks.

At the same time, the regime regulated commercial banks so as to force significant increases in size. A 1968 decree raised capital requirements for Lima banks from S/. 10,000,000 to S/. 60,000,000 with an early 1971 deadline. In May, 1970, a new decree upped the requirement to S/. 150,000,000, at a time when only Peru's largest bank met the standard. Smaller private banks were forced to merge with larger commercial banks or the *Banco de la Nación*. Only a few pre-1969 banks survived. By late 1971, the revolutionary military regime's policies created a four-bloc banking system in Lima. The government dominated credit with the *Banco de la Nación,* the Continental, International, and *Banco Popular,* besides specialized banks for agriculture, industry, mining, and housing. Conducting 34 percent of the city's banking operations, the *Banco de Crédito* constituted a bloc in itself. The remaining private banks, Wiese, *Banco de Lima,* and Commercial, made up the third bloc. Branches of the foreign First National City, Bank of America, Bank of Tokyo, and Bank of London and South America comprised the fourth bloc.

Toward the end of 1971 the regime acted to preserve provincial banks against predation by capital city banks struggling to meet capitalization requirements. It protected Trujillo, Huancayo, Ica, Cuzco, Arequipa, and Iquitos banks, setting their minimum capital at S/. 20,000,000. Two years later the *Banco Nor-Peru* of Trujillo indicated that it did not need protection when it invaded Lima, opening a branch on the Plaza San Martín. Later in 1973, West Germany's

Commerzbank also opened a Lima office. Thus competition continued to be lively in Peruvian banking.

The revolutionary regime established an entirely new financial institution in 1971. COFIDE followed the Chilean Production Development Corporation and Mexican *Nacional Financiera* model of an autonomous public corporation to administer state shares in companies and to form new ones. The government subscribed 80 percent of its shares, leaving 20 percent to private investors. The private sector shares achieved immediate success. They yielded an 8 percent dividend, tax-free; purchasers could also deduct share cost from taxable income. The U.S. AID program promptly transferred seven projects to COFIDE.

The Velasco regime employed COFIDE to carry out what might be termed "gentle" nationalization of foreign-owned enterprises. By April, 1971, COFIDE held 20 percent of the shares of *Empresas Eléctricas Asosciadas* (EEA) and 31 percent by year's end, making EEA virtually a state company. A year after EEA finished expensive expansion work, the Ministry of Energy and Mines revalued its assets, forcing it to increase equity capital under the electrical industry law. COFIDE supplied the new capital, thereby gaining greater ownership. In 1972 the regime established ELECTROPERU, a state company to acquire all private electric companies. The regime also assigned capital value to "public domain property" utilities used and assigned that value to COFIDE. Thus it acquired 35 percent of *Servicios Eléctricos* serving Chiclayo, Supe, Chincha, Ica, and Pisco, and named four directors to its board. In this manner COFIDE acquired participation in numerous other companies. In 1973 the state employed this device to take over EEA. Swiss stockholders were left to wonder just what future benefits they might receive from their shares in EEA.

Some observers of the military regime who are less cosmopolitan than its leaders confuse Peru's foreign-policy opening toward Soviet nations with a leaning toward Communism. They would do well to remember the regime's continued campaign against domestic Communism, on the one hand, and its real encouragement of a capitalistic stock exchange on the other. The Velasco regime, however radical its social goals for agrarian reform, and no matter how garrison-statist some of its governing techniques, consistently pursued a kind of populist small-scale capitalism-encouragement policy.

Physically centered in Lima commercial banks, the stock exchange did relatively little to generate public participation in corporate financing or to raise venture capital prior to 1968. The military leadership established a National Securities Commission along the lines of the U.S. Securities and Exchange Commission. Beginning operation in January, 1971, the reformed exchange registered only three new securities in six months. Then activity increased, although trading continued to be concentrated in a few standard issues, especially bank bonds. By early 1973 the exchange listed seventy-four companies and was setting records for daily sales volume.

In other moves aimed at strengthening Peru's economy, the military regime in May, 1970, required all foreign-currency accounts to be converted into soles and forced citizens to convert cash holdings abroad into soles in Peru. In mid-1971, it monopolized the marketing of pearls, precious metals, and gems in the *Banco Minero del Peru*. It also channeled insurance company profits within the country, via the *Banco de la Nación,* outlawing re-insurance outside Peru. Likewise, it reduced foreign ownership of insurance companies below 20 percent.

Not all aspects of national governance proved as amenable to military solutions as those already discussed. Creole and Mestizo emulation of Spanish food preferences and denigration of central Andean domesticated plants as "Indian" food continued to contribute to poor domestic nutrition and costly food imports. In mid-1971 the Velasco regime extended its state corporatism drive to food importation. Decree N° 18871 monopolized all food imports in the *Empresa Pública de Servicios Agropecuarios* (EPSA), established in December, 1970. Early in 1971 the regime prohibited importing some 207 food items so as to improve Peru's balance-of-payments position. Such prohibitions left untouched the major food drain on foreign exchange. Since colonial times, Peru's culturally Hispanic population has consumed more wheat bread and pasta than the country was able to grow itself. Even the revolutionary military regime appeared unable to modify the food habits involved.

Consequently, Peru purchased 200,000 tons of Canadian wheat in 1969, besides other imports. EPSA ordered 110,000 tons of Australian wheat early in 1971, and by May was authorized to buy 225,000 tons from Canada. In 1972, Peru had to import U.S.$60,800,000 worth of wheat, representing a 22% increase since 1968. In 1973 wheat imports more than offset the value of cotton exports.

Like other leaders of developing nations attempting to control an economy, Peru's ruling officers found themselves running out of beef early in 1972. They imposed rationing, but EPSA had to import beef. Colombian and Bolivian beeves came to Lima by air, swiftly raising air cargo tonnages. At this time when air space was needed, however, strangely enough the regime did nothing to dampen enthusiasm for such luxury items as the excellent beers brewed in Peru. All hops and half the barley used are imports from Czechoslovakia, Germany, and the U.S. Thus, Peru spends heavily for overseas food purchases in spite of such military successes as its food-fish expansion program.

A major earthquake on May 31, 1970, added a huge natural catastrophe to the burdens of a regime trying to achieve a more equitable distribution of income. The military leaders rebudgeted great sums for immediate disaster relief and long-term regional rehabilitation. The quake epicenter was not far from the industrial city of Chimbote. The earthquake leveled nearly every building there; damage extended from Talara with 600 houses demolished south to Huacho on the Pacific coast, affecting Ancash Department most of all. Scores of farming and ranching settlements suffered severe losses in the Sierra. Falling walls and collapsing roofs killed an estimated 50,000 persons and left over 500,000 homeless. Earth tremors set off secondary deglaciation disasters. One avalanche buried 3,500 people in the city of Yungay. Devastated settlements may not be rebuilt for a generation, so great was the capital loss.

The regime soon established an interministerial committee for reconstruction and rehabilitation, CRYRZA, later called ORDEZA. At times it seemed seriously unaware of the actual human problems of survivors and seldom familiar with peasant views of priorities and values. Disaster relief flowed in volume from the U.S., U.S.S.R., Sweden, Germany, the United Kingdom, and other nations. CRYRZA settled on a long-range development strategy, but bogged down in bureaucratic regulations and studies. Finally, four years after the earthquake, the new ORDEZA organization began the major tasks of reconstruction. As a result of the disaster, the social structure of many places has been radically altered, with peasants assuming more important roles than before.

Benign compared to many military regimes, the Velasco administration displayed its authoritarian character most overtly in legislating by decree and in its intolerance of media criticism. Many revolutionary military leaders apparently could not brook printed criticism.

One of Peru's most able investigative journalists, Enrique Zileri Gibson, repeatedly "got the goat" of members of the military establishment. Early on, the Minister of Justice deported Zileri to Spain because he felt insulted by an article in the foremost biweekly news magazine, *Caretas*, which Zileri coedited. In December, 1970, Zileri was fined S/. 100,000 and given a suspended six-month jail sentence for his reply to letters to the editor on censorship. He lost an inspired court suit in 1972 and accumulated another suspended six-month sentence. That still failed to halt Zileri. Two years later, *Caretas* was closed. Zileri's early deportation put the press on notice how the military leaders would interpret a freedom of the press law on the books.

Early in 1970, the regime decreed a new press law that allowed heavy fines for injuring the prestige or dignity of public institutions or individuals. Another provision allowed newspaper employees to publish opinions on the editorial page. Thus, the regime could whipsaw owners between the two decrees, taking them to court for publishing criticism or for refusing to publish it. The regime required all editors to be citizens. In 1972 it used a continuous-residence requirement to oust the elitist long-time editor of the major Lima daily *La Prensa*. Then it fined his nephew who took over the editorship for publishing a story that had already appeared in Mexico City.

In mid-1973 employees struck *El Comercio*, Lima's oldest and most right-wing daily. The Minister of Labor settled the strike after twenty-nine days, forcing management to hire an outside management study, pay for an independent audit, and make several changes.

The culmination of the Velasco regime's feud with the newspaper press came at the end of July, 1974, when the administration seized eight independent metropolitan papers and appointed state officials to manage each one. Velasco reportedly had shown increasing anger over press charges that his administration was coming under growing Marxist influence. Whatever his motives, Velasco demonstrated to the world that the institutional training of Peruvian officers failed to equip them to bear the press criticism every elected politician lives with all the time.

The radical changes being decreed and carried out by the armed forces appear to forecast a dramatic new course for Peru during the last of the twentieth century. If political continuity is maintained, then 1968 will probably become the most significant year since 1821, or even since Viceroy Toledo. By 1972, for the first time, coastal and urban populations gained national numerical dominance, constituting a major demographic shift from pre-Columbian, colonial, and republican patterns. What this portends for the tenacious Andean traditions and culture when considered alongside the post-1968 social, economic, and political reforms gives one much room for speculation.

Perhaps the most crucial question concerning the military regime is the extent to which it can impose its distinctive brand of political mobilization on people in nonmilitary occupations. The longer a military regime remains in power, the more necessary some effective form of alternative decision-making becomes if the rule of the armed forces is not to become permanent. Peru's military social revolution appears to have ended the political and economic power of the "oligarchy" that dominated life until 1968. However badly their decisions may have served the majority, the interrelated members of the "oligarchy" did provide a civilian social organization to make key national decisions. The military regime has also prevented the mass-participation political parties from functioning, particularly in the area of posing serious alternatives to specific measures of the social revolution. The longer political parties are inhibited, the less likely they will be able to govern well if and when the military establishment should decide to relinquish its control.

The military leadership may be content to continue in power indefinitely. Such a course means that it must devise a mechanism for the transfer of power within the military institutions. President Francisco Morales Bermúdez's most bloodless of coups as prime minister may indicate that such a mechanism has been perfected.

If the military leaders intend to turn power over to, or even to share it with, civilians through channels other than historic parties, they must create decision-making organizations. They have indicated that they intend to structure decision-making through occupational groups by creating industrial communities, rural cooperatives, and allowing them to use major metropolitan newspapers as a forum for expressing their particular problems. The military administrators may well find that creating viable policy-making organization in other occupational sectors is far more difficult than in the armed forces. There are powerful dynamics inherent in many sectors that militate against armed-forces-style unity of values and institutional loyalty.

In agriculture, each family's interests tend to make it competitive with every other farm family, rather than cooperative. The centuries-old ability of rural peasants to thwart national plans drawn up on the desks of idealistic Lima bureaucrats could well frustrate the regime's effort to mobilize farmers as an occupational category.

In mining and plantation farming, workers belonged by 1968 to unions that trained workers to use strikes and other tactics to improve their lot. Although mine owners, in compliance with the revolutionary policy that would in time make workers the owners of the companies, have transferred shares into the industrial community, the workers continue to demand shorter hours, higher wages, and fringe benefits, rather than management responsibility. Workers continue, in other words, to support their unions and to regard government bureaucrats as another kind of management.

These two examples illustrate that the dynamics of present Peruvian society is the result of many interacting forces operating over a very long time. Peru is really an ancient society even though it is often classified as a developing nation. Long-standing environmental, biological, and cultural patterns limited the rapidity and extent of change achieved by the conquering Incas and Spaniards. Once Peru settled into its historic mold, these same patterns likewise reduced the impact of new influences brought in by Spanish royal or republican reformers. The military regime that seized power in 1968 gained during its first seven years in power greater leverage in dealing with socioeconomic and political problems than any other political group since independence. It could conceivably break the historic mold and define quite a different future—yet the environmental, the biological, and many of the cultural constraints are still very strong. We shall see.

Political Chronology

5500 B.C.	Indians domesticate llama, guinea pig, gourds, squash, quinoa, amaranth, and lay foundations for sedentary life.
3800 B.C.	Maize cultivation in Sierra allows villages to develop.
1400 B.C.	Pan-Andean Kotosh-Chavín culture spreads.
1200 B.C.	Regional cultures develop large irrigation works.
A.D. 500	Pan-Andean Huari and Tiahuanaco empires spread.
A.D. 1000	Regional states hold sway.
1438-71	Inca conquest state begins rapid expansion under Pachacuti Inca Yupanki.
1471-83	Topa Inca expands *Tawantinsuyu* to northern Chile and Argentina.
1477	Incas conquer Chimú kingdom.
1483-1524	Huayna Capac reigns expanded frontiers; alternative capital established at Quito.
1492	Spain completes reconquest of Peninsula; expels Jews; Columbus initiates biological and cultural exchanges between Old World and New.
1503	Spain establishes *Casa de Contratación* in Seville to control trade with New World; Queen Isabella authorizes *encomienda*.
1509	Spaniards colonize Isthmus of Panamá.
1512	Spanish monarchs issue Laws of Burgos to protect Native Americans.
1513	Vasco Núñez de Balboa discovers the Pacific Ocean.

1516   Hapsburg Charles I succeeds to crowns of Castille and Aragon.

1519   Charles I elected Emperor Charles V of Holy Roman Empire;
        Panamá city founded.

1524   Sapa Inca Huayna Capac and heir apparent Ninan Cuyuchi
        and millions of subjects die of smallpox; Inca War of Succession
        begins; Pizarro-Almagro expedition explores west coast of South
        America south from Panamá.

1529   Pizarro contracts with Spanish crown to conquer Indians along
        200 leagues of west coast.

1532   Pizarro lands in *Tawantinsuyu;* captures Atahuallpa and seizes
        control; founds municipalities; grants *encomiendas.*

1533   Pizarro occupies Inca capital city, Cuzco.

1535   Pizarro founds colonial capital city, Lima.

1536   Manco Inca leads Inca forces in unsuccessful attempt to dis-
        lodge Spaniards.

1537   Diego de Almagro seizes Cuzco, begins private army civil wars.

1538   Hernando Pizarro executes defeated Diego de Almagro.

1541   Almagro partisans kill Francisco Pizarro.

1542   Charles V promulgates "New Laws" that prohibit enslaving In-
        dians, limit *encomiendas;* first viceroy's enforcement generates
        renewed civil war; loyalists defeat and execute Diego de Almagro
        the younger.

1544   Gonzalo Pizarro's coup d'état kills Viceroy Blasco Núñez de
        Vela.

1548   Lima *audiencia* President Pedro de la Gasca defeats Gonzalo
        Pizarro, restores royal authority.

1551   Antonio de Mendoza arrives as second viceroy; sugar cane intro-
        duced; First Ecclesiastical Council of Lima.

1555   Charles V abdicates; Philip II succeeds; patio process of silver re-
        covery perfected in New Spain.

1556   Third viceroy, Andrés Hurtado de Mendoza, Marqués de
        Cañete, arrives to heighten respect for royal authority.

1559   *Audiencia* of Charcas established; royal mercury monopoly ex-
        tended to colonies.

1561-64 Fourth Viceroy Conde de Nieva.

1565   *Audiencia* of Lima President Lope García de Castro (acting vice-
        roy, 1564-69) introduces *corregidores de indios;* Philip II be-
        gins to sell notary office in Peru.

1569-81 Fifth Viceroy Francisco de Toledo recasts conquest culture into
        colonial pattern.

1571   Toledo orders Indians to congregate in villages.

1572   Toledo defeats Neo-Inca state; executes Tupac Amaru.

1574   Toledo decrees *mita de minas*.

1575   Toledo creates Spanish-style municipal offices among Indians.

1581-83   Sixth Viceroy Martín Enriquez de Almansa; Archbishop Toribio de Mogrovejo arrives, begins reforms.

1589-96   Viceroy García Hurtado de Mendoza, Marqués de Cañete; imposes transaction tax (*alcabala*).

1598   Philip II dies; Philip III succeeds.

1700   Hapsburg Charles II dies; Bourbon Duke of Anjou, grandson of Louis XIV of France, succeeds as Philip V.

1701   War of Spanish Succession begins.

1702   Philip V invades Italy; Anglo-Dutch fleet assaults Cádiz.

1704   British seize Gibraltar; Catalonia declares for Austrian Archduke Charles.

1705   British capture Barcelona, land Archduke Charles.

1706   British take Majorca.

1707   Manuel de Oms de Santa Pau, Marqués de Castell dos Rius, arrives as Peruvian viceroy.

1711   Austrian Emperor Joseph dies of smallpox; Archduke Charles succeeds to Austrian throne.

1713   Peace of Utrecht.

1734   Spanish Prince Charles conquers Naples; is crowned King of Sicily.

1737   Ignacio Torote rebels on Peru's jungle frontier.

1739   Philip V creates Viceroyalty of New Granada.

1741   War of Austrian Succession begins.

1742   Juan Santos Atahuallpa rebels on central Sierra jungle frontier of Peru.

1746   Philip V dies; Ferdinand VI succeeds; major Lima earthquake.

1748   Treaty of Aix-la-Chapelle ends War of Austrian Succession.

1759   Ferdinand VI dies; his half-brother Charles II, King of Sicily, succeeds, enters Madrid in 1760, and loses wife.

1761   Viceroy Manuel de Amat y Junient refurbishes Lima.

1762   Spain enters the Seven Years' War.

1767   Charles III expels Jesuits from Spanish territories.

1776   Charles III creates Viceroyalty of Río de la Plata; violent Peruvian protests against *repartimiento;* Manuel de Guirior viceroy.

1780   José Gabriel Condorcanque rebels as Tupac Amaru II; Agustín de Juárequi viceroy.

1781   Spain invades Minorca, occupies Florida, executes Tupac Amaru II and his family.

1783	Treaty of Versailles ends War of American Independence; Spain retains Florida, Minorca.
1784-90	Viceroy Teodoro de Croix divides Peru into seven Intendencies.
1787	Charles III creates *audiencia* of Cuzco; has census taken of Spain's population.
1788	Charles III dies; his son Charles IV succeeds.
1789	The French States-General convenes, initiates modern period of world affairs.
1790-96	Viceroy Francisco Gil de Taboada y Lemos conducts censuses of Peruvian population.
1793	Revolutionary France declares war on Spain.
1795	Spain cedes half Santo Domingo to France; peace restored.
1796	Treaty of San Ildefonso allies Spain with France.
1801	Spanish-French armies invade Portugal; Gabriel de Aviles viceroy of Peru.
1802	Peace of Amiens.
1808	Napoleon Bonaparte occupies Madrid; Charles IV abdicates, his son Ferdinand VII succeeds; Napoleon makes his brother Joseph king of Spain.
1809	Royal officials quash independence movements in Quito, La Paz, and Chuquisaca.
1810	Caracas council assumes executive powers; Buenos Aires claims self-government; Hidalgo raises cry of popular revolution in New Spain.
1812	Free Spanish government proclaims constitution; Wellington retakes Madrid from French.
1814	Ferdinand VII reinstalled on throne in Madrid, repudiates constitution; Napoleon abdicates; Cuzco rebels.
1815	Royalists defeat Cuzco rebellion; Napoleon returns to France, loses decisive battle at Waterloo.
1816-21	Lt. Gen. Joaquín de la Pezuela viceroy; Confederated States of the Río de la Plata forms in 1816.
1818	José San Martín decisively defeats royalists in Chile; rebels create Pacific fleet.
1819	Rebel Admiral Lord Cochrane lands San Martín's forces in Peru; Free New Granada and Venezuela unite.
1820	José Bernardo Tagle declares independence at Trujillo, followed by "solid North."
1821	San Martín declares Peru independent; abolishes Indian tribute, personal services; frees children of slaves; José de la Serna replaces Pezuela in coup d'état.

1823	San Martín departs; generals conduct first republican coup d'état making José Riva Aguero president; Simón Bolívar arrives; Riva Aguero exiled.
1824	Viceroy Serna capitulates after losing Battle of Ayacucho; Bolivarian secularization.
1825	Peru creates court system; abolishes titles of nobility; Bolivia becomes independent.
1826	Bolívar departs; Andrés Santa Cruz acting president; Callao forts capitulate; Indian tribute reestablished.
1827	Congress elects José de la Mar president.
1828	Peru declares war on Gran Colombia and is defeated.
1829	Gamarra-Gutierrez coup d'état deposes José de la Mar.
1829-33	Agustín Gamarra's first term as president.
1833-36	Luís José Orbegoso's presidential term.
1836-39	Confederation of Bolivia with North Peru and South Peru under Andrés Santa Cruz.
1838-39	Peruvian exiles obtain Chile's intervention to destroy Confederation.
1839-41	Marshal Agustín Gamarra's second term; Minister Ramón Castilla signs first guano contract.
1841-45	Political chaos after Gamarra dies in battle while invading Bolivia.
1845-51	Gen. Ramón Castilla's first regime; first period of tranquil government since independence.
1851-55	Gen. José Rufino Echenique regime.
1854	Echenique and Castilla both decree freedom of slaves during fighting over presidency.
1855-62	Marshal Ramón Castilla's second regime.
1862-63	Marshal Miguel San Román's regime; dies in office.
1863	Second Vice-President Pedro Diez Canseco's brief government; Congress makes *sol* basic monetary unit.
1863-65	Gen. Juan Antonio Pezet, First Vice-President, negotiates with Spain over treatment of immigrants.
1865	Gen. Pedro Diez Canseco provides transitional government.
1865-68	Col. Mariano I. Prado's first regime goes to war with Spain.
1866	Spanish fleet bombards Callao but is repulsed.
1868	Pedro Diez Canseco's third term after revolt against Prado; signs Arequipa railroad contract; holds elections.
1868-72	Col. José Balta's administration begins feverish railroad construction.
1872-76	Manuel Pardo, first civilian president, faces financial reckoning

	with guano concessionaires; creates Civil Guard, municipal police.
1876-79	Mariano I. Prado's second regime; foreign debt service halts in 1879.
1879-83	War of the Pacific with Chile.
1879	Nicolás de Piérola's coup deposes absent Prado.
1881	Chile occupies Lima; Francisco García Calderon occupation president.
1883-85	Gen. Miguel Iglesias makes peace with Chile.
1886-90	Col. Andrés A. Cáceres regime after he deposes Iglesias by coup d'état.
1890-94	Col. Remigio Morales Bermúdez administration.
1894-95	Gen. A. A. Cáceres's second term; deposed by Piérola's coup d'état.
1895-99	Nicolás de Piérola's regime greatly changes Peru.
1899-1903	Eduardo López de Romaña's civilian regime.
1903-04	Manuel Candamo administration; dies in office.
1904-08	José Pardo, Manuel's son, elected to first term.
1908-12	Augusto B. Leguía elected to first term.
1911	Commandant Oscar R. Benavides captures Colombian fortified post on jungle frontier.
1912-14	Guillermo Billinghurst elected on populist platform.
1914-15	Oscar R. Benavides leads coup d'état and regime.
1915-19	José Pardo elected to second term.
1919-30	Augusto B. Leguía leads preemptive coup d'état, serves additional terms after amending constitution.
1920	Constitution legalizes indigenous communities.
1930-31	Series of juntas.
1931-33	Commandant Luís M. Sánchez Cerro who deposed Leguía by coup d'état elected, then assassinated.
1933	Constitutional Congress writes new constitution.
1933-39	Gen. Oscar R. Benavides's second regime.
1939-45	Manuel Prado y Ugarteche, Mariano's son, elected to first term.
1941	Border war with Ecuador; U.S. arbitration.
1945-48	José Luís Bustamante y Rivero elected president with APRA support.
1948-56	Gen. Manuel A. Odría leads coup d'état; holds election; enfranchises women.
1956-62	Manuel Prado y Ugarteche elected; deposed by army high command coup d'état.

1962-63   Generals Ricardo Pérez Godoy and Nicolás Lindley overthrow
          Prado and successively head military government.
1963-68   Fernando Belaunde Terry elected under military supervision,
          deposed by coup d'état.
1968-75   Gen. Juan Velasco Alvarado heads revolutionary military regime.
1975   Gen. Francisco Morales Bermúdez, Velasco's prime minister,
          ousts Velasco to assume the presidency, continuing the revolu-
          tionary program.

A Selective Guide
to the Literature on Peru

SELECTED STUDIES IN ENGLISH

Highly recommended as a conceptually fundamental introduction to all New World history is Alfred W. Crosby's *The Columbian Exchange: Biological and Cultural Consequences of 1492* (Westport, 1972). George M. Foster's *Culture and Conquest* can help on this subject, especially on Iberian antecedents of colonial patterns.

To understand the important dynamics of Peruvian society, Thomas R. Ford's *Man and Land in Peru* (Gainesville, 1955) is quite instructive although its statistics are dated.

Stories, essays, and notes by American engineer Hans Otto Storm, collected by David Greenhood in *Of Good Family* (New York, 1948) afford an unusually sensitive technician's view of social structure.

A series of writers has attempted to capture the essence of prehistoric Peru and the nation of their time, going beyond incidents of travel to compiling statistics and analyzing natural and human resources. English antiquarian Clements R. Markham pioneered with *Peru* (Philadelphia, 1891) and *A History of Peru* (London, 1892). Charles R. Enock's *Peru* (New York, 1908) is an early twentieth-century example. R. J. Owens'

Peru (London, 1963) provides a good introduction to the country and its socioeconomic conditions with very brief historical background. Perhaps the best such volume is *Peru in Four Dimensions* (Lima, 1964) by David A. Robinson, a long-time resident who knew what matters, so stressed demography, geography, and technification, yet with scant temporal perspective. Sometime British ambassador Robert Marett wrote another *Peru* (London, 1969) summarizing selected sources of historical and social information.

GEOGRAPHY

The best geographic description is J. A. Tosi's *Zonas de Vida Natural en el Perú* (Lima, 1960), unfortunately rare even in libraries. Emilio Romero's *Geografía Económica del Perú* (Lima, 1961, 3d ed.) long influenced thought about national geography in earlier editions.

Justino M. Tarazona S. compiled legislation concerning internal political geography in *Demarcación Política del Perú* (Lima, 1946, rev. ed. 1967) and *Prontuario de la demarcación política de Perú* (Lima, 1970).

César García R., *Diccionario de la Demarcación Política del Peru 1821-1971* (Lima, 1941) was an outstanding analysis of international frontiers. Washington Cano in *Historia de los límites del Perú* (Lima, 1962), Gustavo Pons Muzzo in *Las fronteras del Perú, historia de los límites* (Lima, 1962), and Alberto Wagner de Reyna in *Los límites del Perú* (Lima, 1961) discuss international boundaries and their historic definition.

A classic work on the great Marañon River region translated into English by Harriet de Onís is Ciro Alegría's *The Golden Serpent* (New York, 1963).

The Andes. One of the oldest but still best analyses of Peruvian geography is *The Andes of Southern Peru* (New York, 1916) by Isaiah Bowman. A smaller-scale regional study by Hans Kinzl and Erwin Schneider, *The Cordillera Blanca* (Innsbruck, 1950), includes superlative photographs and basic map.

The altitude factor is summarized in an encyclopedic review of research on human and animal life in the heights, *Aclimatación en los Andes* (Lima, 1960) by Carlos Monge M., the physician who first scientifically described hypoxia. *High Altitude Diseases, Mechanism and Management* (Springfield, 1966) by Carlos Monge M. and his physician-son Carlos Monge C., sums up, in technical English, decades of basic research. Jean McClung takes up a crucial high-altitude population trend factor in *Effects of High Altitude on Human Birth* (Cambridge, 1969).

PRE-HISPANIC SOCIETIES

Many armchair and some field archeologists have tried their hands at synthesizing available research reports into readable form. Discoveries occur so rapidly that every summary seems outdated by the time it appears. Informative general summations include J. Alden Mason, *The Ancient Civilizations of Peru* (Harmondsworth, 1957), G. H. S. Bushnell, *Peru* (New York, 1957, rev. ed. 1963), Edward P. Lanning, *Peru before the Incas* (Englewood Cliffs, 1967). Still useful summaries appear in the *Handbook of South American Indians* (Washington, 1946-50) edited by Julian H. Steward. Later works build on Philip A. Means, *The Ancient Civilizations of the Andes* (New York, 1931; New York, 1964).

Reconstructions of pre-Incaic cultures include Elizabeth P. Benson's *The Mochica* (New York, 1972), Victor W. von Hagen's *The Desert Kingdoms of Peru* (New York, 1964) on both Mochica and later Chimú kingdoms on the north coast, and Hermann Buse's *Introducción al Perú* (Lima, 1965). Julio P. Tello's *Chavín* (Lima, 1960) presents this pioneer excavator's early interpretation, since sustained. *The Upper Amazon* (New York, 1970) by Donald Lathrap gives the most knowledgeable review of early archeology and ethnohistory of that area.

Inca. A fine, readable, unromanticized account is Alfred Métraux's *The Incas* (London, 1965). Useful is Burr C. Brundage's *Empire of the Inca* (Norman, 1963). Specialized but informative are *El Imperio Incaico* (Buenos Aires, 1946) and *Los Incas* (Seville, 1956) by Roberto Levillier. Louis Baudin wrote a stimulating polemic based on modern political dialectic, *L'Empire Socialiste des Inka* (Paris, 1928) translated by K. Woods as *A Socialist Empire: The Incas of Peru* (Princeton, 1961). Baudin's mistitled *La Vie Quotidienne du Temps des derniers Incas* (Paris, 1955) achieves a less doctrinaire description of Inca culture, translated by Winifred Bradford as *Daily Life in Peru under the Last Incas* (New York, 1962). Older but interesting are *The Incas of Peru* (London, 1910) by Clements R. Markham, and *Del Ayllu al Imperio* by Luís E. Valcárcel (Lima, 1925).

Specialized but indispensable for understanding Inca taxation is Sally F. Moore's *Power and Property in Inca Peru* (New York, 1958) and for understanding the conquest state Joseph Bram's *An Analysis of Inca Militarism* (New York, 1941). Charles Gibson, *The Inca Concept of Sovereignty and the Spanish Administration in Peru* (Austin, 1948) is instructive about the postconquest colonial as well as Inca regime. Burr C. Brundage's *Lords of Cuzco: A History and Description of the Inca People in their Final Days* (Norman, 1967) deals with the same transition. Catering to the nontechnical reader are *Daily Life in Ancient Peru* by Hans D. Disselhoff (New York, 1967) and *Highway of the Sun* by Victor W. von Hagen (London, 1956). Hiram Bingham, later a U.S. Senator, explored *Machu Picchu, A Citadel of the Incas* (New Haven, 1930).

THE COLONIAL PERIOD

Most prolific historian of the viceroyalty is the Jesuit Rubén Vargas Ugarte. His multivolume *Historia General del Perú* (Lima, 1966) is well-written, illustrated, and printed, a viceroy-by-viceroy elitist account with scattered hints of social history. An older polemical author of historiographic interest, Ricardo Cappa "wounded" Incas, harbingers of independence and republican leaders with *Historia compendiada del Perú con algunas apreciaciones sobre los viajes de Colon y sus hechos* (Lima, 1886), motivating Ricardo Palma and Eugenio Larrabure y Unánue to rebuttals. Cappa later wrote the massive *Estudios críticos acerca de la dominación española en América* (Madrid, 1889-97).

The Spanish conquest fascinates historians. Gen. Felipe de la Barra's *El indio peruano en las etapas de la conquista y frente a la república* (Lima, 1948) gives a technical interpretation of Inca military operations followed by a history of Indian affairs. Fullest modern analysis is John Hemming's *The Conquest of the Incas* (New York, 1970). Eloquent if dated is William H. Prescott's *History of the Conquest of Peru* (New York, 1847). Edward Hyams and George Ordish in *The Last of the Incas* (New York, 1963) and Lieselotte and Theo Engl in *Twilight of Ancient Peru: The Glory and Decline of the Inca Empire* (New York, 1969) treat the same theme. James Lockhart wrote the outstanding sociobiographical analysis of the first 168 conquerors in *The Men of Cajamarca* (Austin, 1972) and the best social history of conquest culture in *Spanish Peru 1532-1560* (Madison, 1968). Philip A. Means' *Fall of the Inca Empire and the Spanish Rule in Peru 1530-1780* (1931; New York, 1964) influences later writers. Chronicles of conquest and colonial travel provide indispensable information, but Native American writings are extremely rare. Thus, *Comentarios Reales y Historia General del Perú* by the half-Inca Garcilaso de la Vega (Madrid, 1963) and *El primer nueva crónica i buen govierno* by provincial noble Phelipe Guamán Poma de Ayala (Lima, 1956) are the most important sources, even though one spoke from a preconquest elite viewpoint and the other composed a unique cry for social justice in the colonial provinces.

Monographic studies of special aspects of colonial life include *Vida intelectual del virreinato del Perú* by Felipe Barreda L. (Lima, 1906, 1964), *Historia del tribunal de la inquisición de Lima, 1569-1820* (Santiago, 1956), and *La imprenta en Lima, 1584-1824* (Santiago, 1966) by José Toribio Medina; on intellectual trends, the Inquisition, and printing, respectively. Rubén Vargas U. treats colonial religion in *Historia del culto de María en Iberoamerica y de sus imágenes y santuarios mas celebrados* (Buenos Aires, 1947) and *Historia del Santo Cristo de los milagros* (Lima, 1966) as does Luís Martín in *The Intellectual Conquest of Peru: The Jesuit College of San Pablo 1568-1767* (New York, 1968). Robert D. Wood on *La educación de los indios andinos durante la época colonial* (Lima, 1967) on Indian education; Daniel Valcárcel in *San Marcos: Universidad Decana de América* (Lima, 1968) on the institution of higher learning that likes to define itself as the oldest in the Americas; and *Reforma de San Marcos en la época de Amat* (Lima, 1955) on university reform under a Bourbon viceroy, describe the church influence on education.

The stubborn persistence of Native American beliefs shows through the colonial facade in *La extirpación de la idolotria en el Perú* (1601, Lima, 1920) by Pablo J. de Arriaga, translated by Clark L. Keating as *The Extirpation of Idolatry in Peru* (Lexington, 1968), and *Dioses y Hombres de Huarochirí* (Lima, 1966) by Francisco de Avila.

W. F. D. Purser surveyed in *Metal-Mining in Peru, Past and Present* (New York, 1971) the activity basic to the colonial economy. Arthur P. Whitaker concisely presents the social and economic impact of the Santa Barbara mine in *The Huancavelica Mercury Mine* (Cambridge, 1941). José Toribio Polo's *Reseña histórica de la minería en el Perú* (Lima, 1911) was ambitious yet sketchy. Alejandro Garland essayed a basic analysis of payments to the crown in *Remesas del Perú a la corona de España en la época del coloniaje* (Lima, 1904).

Analyses of other aspects of colonial labor include Fernando Silva Santisteban on *Los obrajes en el virreinato del Perú* (Lima, 1964), the best work on cottage textile industry; Enrique Torres Saldamando with *Apuntes historicos sobre las encomiendas en el Perú* (Lima, 1967), brief but valuable; and Frederick P. Bowser on *The African Slave in Colonial Peru 1524-1650* (Stanford, 1974), which is helpful yet incomplete.

Colonial governance has been sketched in by John P. Moore with *The Cabildo in Peru under the Hapsburgs: A Study in the Origins and Powers of the Town Council in the Viceroyalty of Peru, 1530-1700* (Durham,

1954), and *The Cabildo in Peru under the Bourbons: A Study in the Decline and Resurgence of Local Government in the Audiencia of Lima 1700-1824* (Durham, 1966). Carlos Deustua P. gives essentials but few details of late Bourbon administrative change in *Las intendencias en el Peru (1700-1796)* (Seville, 1965) while J. R. Fisher's *Government and Society in Colonial Peru: The Intendent System 1784-1814* (London, 1970) benefits from archival discoveries.

A lighter side of colonial life appears in *Historia Taurina del Perú 1535-1935* (Lima, 1936) by José Emilio L Calmell L., on bull-fighting.

Inca rulers confronted by Europeans have attracted biographers, such as Juan José Vega with *Manco Inca: El gran rebelde* (Lima, n.d.), and outstandingly María Rostworowski de Diez Canseco whose *Curacas y sucesiones costa norte* (Lima, 1961) analyzed cultural differences by examining the lives of Native American leaders.

Viceroys have also attracted a few biographers. Jorge Basadre contributed *El Conde de Lemos y su tiempo* (Lima, 1948), Roberto Levillier *Don Francisco de Toledo, supremo organizador del Peru: su vida, su obra (1515-1582)* (Buenos Aires, 1935), and Arthur F. Zimmerman *Francisco de Toledo, Fifth Viceroy of Perú* (Caldwell, 1938) on the most influential viceroy. Monseñor Carlos García I. composed a four-volume biography of *Santo Toribio* (Lima, 1906-08) on the third centenary of his death. Elías del Carmen P. eulogized the *Vida admirable de San Francisco Solano* (Lima, 1904), and Domingo Angulo wrote well of *Santa Rosa de Lima* (Lima, 1917).

Schoolteachers and newsmen have published a huge number of provincial monographs which include sections on local history. They tend to be derivative and questionably accurate. In the hands of a master, however, local history is unsurpassed. The *Historia de Huánuco de la era prehispánica a nuestros días* (Buenos Aires, 1959) demonstrates that José Varallanos is a master.

Freed from Spanish colonial rule by Argentina and Venezuelan-Colombian leaders and troops, Peruvians have since sought national heroes. One result is a special kind of nationalistic interpretation of the revolt of José Gabriel Condorcanqui. The fullest English account, *The Last Inca Revolt 1780-1783* by Lillian E. Fisher (Norman, 1966) makes dull reading. Emilio Del Solar's *Insurección de Tupac Amaru, sus antecedentes y efectos* (Lima, 1962) betrays its thesis origins. Broader in scope is *Tupac Amaru el rebelde, su epoca, sus luchas y su influencia en el continente* by Boleslao Lewin (Buenos Aires, 1943), while *La rebelión de Tupac Amaru* by Daniel Valcárcel (México, 1947) is intensely nationalistic. Francisco A. Loayza edited *Mártires y heroines* (Lima, 1945) in a frank search for heroes. Daniel Valcárcel also summarized eighteenth-century Native American revolts in *Rebeliones indígenas* (Lima, 1946).

WARS OF INDEPENDENCE

The government has undertaken to publish a mass of analysis and documentation of the struggle for independence. Planned are seven volumes on *Ideólogos*, four on *La rebelión de Tupac Amaru*, seven on *Conspiraciones y rebeliones en el siglo XIX*, one about *El Perú en las Cortes de Cadiz*, four concerning *La acción patriótica del pueblo en la emancipación*, five reporting *Asuntos militares* and three *La marina*, three about *La expedición libertadora*, one on *Cabildos*, one analyzing *Símbolos de la patria*, two describing *Misiones peruanas 1820-1822*, and two *Misiones y documentación de Cancillerías extranjeras*, two on the *Obra gubernativa de San Martín* with one of *Epistolario peruano de San Martín*, two describing *El primer congreso constituyente*, two from the *Archivo Riva Agüero*, three from *Archivo Torre Tagle*, one from *Archivo Reyes*, a disproportionate five about *La universidad*, two on *La Iglesia*, three analyzing *Asuntos económicos*, two of *Documentación oficial española*, three on the press, *Periódicos*, one of *Poesía de la emancipación*, two on *El teatro y la independencia*, eight of *Memorias, Diarios y crónicas*, three of *Relaciones de viajeros*, with one map volume, *Cartografía histórica*, one of *Iconografía* and one of *Bibliografía*. This set should prove invaluable and lead to a revision of some current interpretations.

The sixth volume of Vargas U.'s *Historia General del Perú* deals with *Emancipación* (1816-1825). Other interpretations include José M. Valega, *La gesta emancipadora del Perú* (Lima, 1940), the defensive José A. de Izcue analysis *Los peruanos y su independencia* (Lima, 1905) and the specialized *La emancipación frente al indio peruano* by Juan José Vega (Lima, 1958) on republican legislation on Indian Affairs from 1821 to 1830.

Biographies of freedom fighters abound. David Bushnell's collection of primary sources about *The Liberator, Simon Bolivar* (New York, 1970) makes fascinating reading. Luís Alayza y Paz Soldán studied *El gran mariscal José de La Mar* (Lima, 1942) from a Peruvian viewpoint. Pío Jaramillo A. in *Vida del gran mariscal José de La Mar* (Quinto, 1950) and Alberto Muñoz V. in *El gran mariscal José de La Mar* (Cuenca, 1939) from an Ecuadorian point of view. Alfredo Guinassi Morán wrote of the Venezuelan *General Trinidad Morán, 1796-1854: Estudios Históricos y biográficos* (Arequipa, 1918, 1940; Caracas, 1954). Julio Días A. deals with the Bolivian *El mariscal Santa Cruz y sus generales* (La Paz, 1965). Rubén Vargas U. describes the Peruvian leader *Ramón Castilla* (Buenos Aires, 1962), republican strongman-innovator written about more than any other president. The best of the other biographies are by Gen. Felipe de la Barra, *Castilla, Conductor Militar* (Lima, 1942), Félix Denegri Luna, *En torno a Ramón Castilla* (Lima, 1969), and Alberto Regal, *Castilla Constructor* (Lima, 1967) on public works, and *Castilla, Educador* (Lima, 1968) on educational policies. Néstor Puertas Castro celebrates *El general Vidal, procer de la independencia Americana y jefe supremo de la República a traves de sus memorias* (Lima, 1950) as does Geraldo Arosemena G. in *El general Francisco de Vidal* (Lima, 1971).

Miguel A. Martinez deals with *El mariscal de Piquiza don Agustín Gamarra* (Lima, 1946), Luís Alayza y Paz Soldán with the great civilian *Hipólito Unánue* (Lima, 1952), Evaristo San Cristoval with *Manuel Ignacio de Vivanco* (Lima, 1959), and *El gran mariscal Luís José de Orbegoso, su vida y su obra* (Lima, 1941), as did César García. R. in *Orbegoso, Una vida heroica* (Lima, 1940).

THE NINETEENTH CENTURY

Far and away the outstanding historian of independent Peru is Jorge Basadre. The 1968 edition of his *Historia de la República del Perú* contains in 16 volumes the fullest available chronicle from independence to the end of Leguía's regime. Firmly focused on elite institutions and individuals, Basadre's work nonetheless incorporates more social history than Vargas U.'s final four volumes of *Historia General del Perú* (Lima, 1971) going to the end of the War with Chile, Pedro Dávalos y Lisson's older *Historia republicana del Perú* (Lima, 1931-39), and especially Manuel Nemesio Vargas' even older *Historia del Perú independiente* (Lima, 1902-40) or Mariano Felipe Paz Soldán's *Historia del Perú Independiente* (Buenos Aires and Lima, 1870-1929, 4 vols.). Basadre's early *Perú: Problema y posibilidad* (Lima, 1931) holds historiographic interest, like earlier, smaller editions of his *Historia*. . . . Frederick Pike's *The Modern History of Peru* (New York, 1967) characterizes Peruvian historical writing as civil war (following Basadre) and constitutes one prochurch battle in that struggle. National histories such as Pedro Dávalos y Lisson's *La primera centuria* (Lima, 1919-26), Luís H. Delgado's *Historia Republicana del Perú* (Lima, 1933), Raúl Rivera S.'s *Historia del Perú* (Lima, 1968), and Leonidas Castro B.'s *Geohistoria del Perú* (Lima, 1962) tend to be so polemical as to make consultation of even more polemical primary sources highly advisable.

Useful specialized histories include: José Pareja Paz Soldán, *Historia de las constituciones nacionales* (Lima, 1943) and Javier Vargas, *La Constitución de 1860* (Lima, 1961) on the fundamental document which lasted longer than any other; Ernest Yepes, *Perú 1820-1920. Un siglo de desarrollo capitalista* (Lima, 1972); Luís H. Delgado, *Historia del Senado del Perú (1829-1929)* (Lima, 1929); Alejandro Freundt Rosell's compilation on supreme court justices, *La corte suprema de la república desde su fundación: cuadro cronológico de sus miembros* (Lima, 1923); Román Alzamora, *Historia del Derecho Peruano* (Lima, 1875), the first history of national law, and Manuel Belaunde Guinassi's more up-to-date *Programa razonado de historia del derecho peruano* (Lima, 1961); and Alejandro Revoredo's *La obra nacionalista y democrática del partido civil* (Lima, 1931) on the civil party movement.

The first volume of Carlos Dellepiane's *Historia militar del Perú* (Lima, 1931-36) deals with the independence battles, the second with international conflicts. Although not superseded, it is superficial battlefield history.

Mariano Felipe Paz Soldán began analysis of the Peru-Bolivia union in his partisan *Historia del Perú Independiente 1835-1839* (Buenos Aires, 1888). José de la Riva Agüero y Osma began a confederation laudatory trend with *La Historia en el Perú* (Lima, 1910). The second volume of Jorge Basadre's *La iniciación de la república* (Lima, 1930) deals with the confederation, based on materials in the National Library since burned. Later, Jorge Cornejo Bouroncle, *La confederación Perú-Boliviana* (Cuzco, 1935) and Carlos Neuhaus Rizo Patrón, *El estado Sud-Peruano* (Lima, 1946) reconsidered the period. Ernesto Barros Jarpa, *La segunda independencia* (Santiago, 1956) extols Chilean policy toward the confederation. Gonzalo Bulnes, *Historia de la campaña de Perú en 1838* (Santiago, 1878), Ramón Sotomayor Valdes, *Campaña del ejercito chileno contra la Confederación Perú-Boliviana en 1837* (Santiago, 1896), and Fabio Galdamez Lastra, *Historia militar de Chile. Estudio crítico de la campana de 1838-39* (Santiago, 1910) nationalistically analyze Chilean intervention.

The pivotal conflict with Spain is clearly described by William C. Davis in *The Last Conquistadores* (Athens, 1950), but best analyzed by Pedro de Novo y Colson in *Historia de la guerra de España en el Pacífico* (Madrid, 1882), nationalistically summarized by newspaperman Enrique Chirinos Soto in *La guerra del Perú y España* (Lima, 1966). Carlos E. Grez Pérez, *Los intentos de unión Hispano-americana y la guerra de España en el Pacífico* (Santiago, 1928) reported a significant aspect of Hispanic union attempts. Adolfo Calderón Cousiño's *Breve historia diplomática de las relaciones chilenos-peruanos* (Santiago, 1919) dealt with this conflict as well as the later Perú-Chile war.

Primary sources are indispensable for domestic events. Juan Bustamante's *Los indios del Perú* (Lima, 1867) was a report from a battlefield in the long race war.

The traumatic War of the Pacific generated a plethora of chronicles of specific campaigns, but a surprisingly scant analytical military and diplomatic literature and no social or economic history. The Venezuelan Jacinto Lopez, *Historia de la guerra del guano y del salitre* (New York, 1931) takes Perú's side. Víctor M. Maurtua's *La cuestión del Pacífico* (Lima, 1901) gives the classic Peruvian position. Alberto Gutierrez attempts to absolve Bolivia of blame in *La guerra de 1879* (Paris, 1912) and *La guerra de 1879, nuevos esclarecimientos* (Paris, 1920). Chilean sources include Diego Barros Arana, *Historia de la guerra del Pacífico (1879-1880)* (Santiago, 1880-81), which scoffs at a 48% officer Peruvian army; Gonzalo Bulnes's authoritative *Las causas de la guerra entre Chile y el Perú* (Santiago, 1910), and *La guerra del Pacífico* (Valparaíso, 1912-19; Santiago, 1955-56, 3 vols.) with two volumes on campaigns and one on the occupation; Manuel Jordan Lopez's *Historia diplomática de la guerra del Pacífico* (Santiago, 1957), Hernán Ramirez Necochea's Marxist *Historia del Imperialismo Chileno* (Santiago, 1960); Luís Langlois's *Influencia del Poder naval en la historia de Chile desde 1810 hasta 1910* (Valparaíso, 1911) following Mahan's thesis of the decisiveness of naval power; and the Swedish officer Wilhelm Ekdahl's technical *Historia militar de la guerra del Pacífic entre Chile, Perú y Bolivia 1879-1883* (Santiago, 1917-19, 3 vols.). The war yielded a large harvest of martyr-heroes. *El contralmirante Miguel Grau* by Geraldo Arosemena G. (Lima, 1946) stands out among biographies of that naval leader. *Francisco Bolognesi* by Eudoxio H. Ortega (Lima, 1963) represents eulogies of the most admired martyr of land war. Among the victors, the merciless raider *El Príncipe rojo Patricio Lynch* by Manuel G. Balbontin (Santiago, 1963) tells of the slashing general who won most attention.

The Treaty of Ancón left conflicting territorial claims to generate many studies, exemplified by Víctor Andrés Belaunde's *Nuestra cuestión con Chile* (Lima, 1919) and Anselmo Banlot Holley's *Tacna y Arica después del tratado de Ancón* (Santiago, 1917).

Biographies of public figures tend to be as polemical as the subjects. In *Biografías de generales republicanos* (Lima, 1963) Manuel de Mendiburu brought personal participation and writing ability as well as prejudices to bear on 19 early republican caudillos. He put together the largest biographical collection, *Diccionario histórico-biográfico del Perú* (Lima, 1931-34) for the independence movement and early republic. Son Oscar de Santa Cruz's *El gran mariscal Andrés de Santa Cruz* (La Paz, 1913) and document collection called *El general Andrés de Santa Cruz* (La Paz, 1924) illuminate that Bolivian participant in early Peruvian governance. Manuel Bilbao lauded his subject, *Historia del general Salaverry* (Lima, 1853). A descendant chronicled *Los generales Diez Canseco* (Lima, 1950) by Ernesto Diez Canseco. Similarly, Jorge Arías Schreiber Pezet recalled *El general Juan Antonio Pezet* (Lima, 1963), last early republican leader. Both Evaristo San Cristoval, *General Mariano Ignacio Prado, su vida y su obra* (Lima, 1966) and Luís H. Delgado, *Historia del general Mariano Ignacio Prado* (Lima, 1957) examined the leader of the Restoration and war against Spain. Jacinto Lopez's *Manuel Pardo* (Lima, 1947) on Prado's Minister of Exchequer and later president and civil party founder reprinted seminal Pardo essays. Evaristo San Cristobal in *Manuel Pardo y La Valle: su vida y su obra* (Lima, 1945) also reprinted documents and lauded his subject. An assassinated president received the attention of Geraldo Arosemena G. in *El coronel José Balta* (Lima, 1945) and Mario Bazan, *El coronel José Balta* (Lima, 1962). Luís H. Delgado's *La obra de Francisco García Calderón* (Lima, 1934) chronicles the Chilean occupation-president. Jorge Dulantro Pinillos' *Nicolás de Piérola* (Lima, 1947) is partisan and long yet stops at 1899. Alberto Ulloa's *Don Nicolás de Piérola: una época de la historia del Perú* (Lima, 1949), maturer, captures more of the pivotal nature of Piérola. Pedro Dávalos y Lisson's *Leguía 1875-1899* (Barcelona, 1928) on the nineteenth-century career of the twentieth-century dictator is ultraconservative.

Some foreign citizens profoundly affected Peru. J. Peter Grace in *W. R. Grace* (New York, 1953) lauded his robber-baron ancestor. Probably as influential, *Henry Meiggs, Yankee Pizarro* (Durham, 1946) was ably portrayed by Watt Stewart. F. A. Eustis praised *Augustus Hemenway: Builder of the United States Trade with the West Coast of South America* (Salem, 1955).

Among economic leaders, José M. Velez Picasso's *Ricardo Bentin* (Lima, 1953) treats a mining entrepreneur who led recovery after the War of the Pacific. Carlos Camprubi A.'s *José Payan y de Reyna* (Lima, 1967) deals with a Cuban banker leading the same effort.

Dr. Juan B. Lastres's *Daniel A. Carrión* (Lima, 1957) describes the pioneer researcher-martyr on the Andean *verruga* disease.

Two women attracted biographers because of flamboyant actions, not because they were typical. Charles N. Gattey's *Gauguin's Astonishing Grandmother* (London, 1970) describes a natural daughter of a powerful

Arequipa family which drew her eloquent literary venom after she traveled to Peru to seek recognition. Jorge Cornejo Bouroncle's *Doña Francisca Zubiaga de Gamarra, la mariscala* (Cuzco, 1948) chronicles the militant wife of a two-term president who took matters into her own hands on occasion.

An Italian immigrant professor, Antonio Raimondi, pioneered scientific study of natural and human resources with *El Perú* (Lima, 1874, 5 vols., 1965 facsimile ed.), a classic source for generations of armchair scholars.

Several institutional analysts have delved into nineteenth-century origins of important twentieth-century phenomena. For banking, Gianfranco Bardella's *Setenta y cinco años de vida económica del Perú 1889-1964* (Milan, 1964) traces the Bank of Italy-Banco de Crédito. Carlos Camprubi A.'s *Historia de los bancos en el Perú 1860-1879* (Lima, 1957) chronicles banking to the War of the Pacific, and his *Un siglo al servicio del ahorro 1868-1968* (Lima, 1968) the savings bank of the Lima Beneficent Society. Another contribution to economic history is F. Mario Bazan's *El proceso económico del Perú* (Buenos Aires, 1954) dealing with the gold standard, loans, balance of payments, and foreign exchange from 1860 to 1950. Broader in scope is Emilio Romero's *Historia económica del Perú* (Lima, 1939; Buenos Aires, 1949; Lima, 1968).

Peter Klaren places the origins of the major political party in sugar plantation formation in *La formación de las haciendas azucareras y los orígenes del APRA* (Lima, 1970). Carlos Jimenez Correa's *Evolución histórica de la industria minera en el Perú* (Lima, 1924) is less technical than José Toribio Polo's *Reseña histórica de la minería en el Perú* (Lima, 1911).

Brian Fawcett in *Railways in the Andes* (London, 1963) summarizes a significant influence. Only Rubén Vargas U. has produced general church history: *Historia de la Iglesia en el Perú. Tomo V: 1800-1900* (Burgos, 1962). Other studies deal with religious orders or local diocesan history. Gen. Felipe de la Barra's *La abolición del tributo por Castilla y su repercusión en el problema del indio peruano* (Lima, 1956) deals with a mid-century attempt to abolish Indian head-taxes. Otherwise, often obscure provincial authors have paid attention to events fundamentally important in shaping twentieth-century Peru. Juan José del Pino described provincial Native American uprisings in *Las sublevaciones indígenas de Huanta 1827-1896* (Ayacucho, 1956). Ernest Reyna in *El amauta Atusparia* (Lima, 1932) reconstructed an 1885 Indian rebellion in the Callejón de Huaylas. Cuzqueña Clorinda Matto de Turner's novel *Aves sin nido* (Lima, 1889) made a turning point in elite attitudes toward Native Americans.

Héctor Centurión Vallejo's *Esclavitud y Manumisión de negros de Trujillo* (Trujillo, 1954) treats manumission by a law professor-landlord on the north coast six years prior to legal emancipation.

THE TWENTIETH CENTURY

Basadre's history of the republic provides the best framework for understanding the first third of this century. Yet national policies have been set since the time when his monumental work stops, in an intellectual climate generated since 1928. That year José Carlos Mariátegui published *Siete Ensayos de Interpretación de la realidad peruana* (Lima, 1928), the first and profoundly influential Marxist analysis which became Peru's largest best-seller. It is translated by Marjory Urquidi as *Seven Interpretive Essays on Peruvian Reality* (Austin, 1971). *La realidad nacional* (Paris, 1931) by Arequipa's elitist professor-diplomat Víctor Andrés Belaunde collects articles from *Mercurio Peruano* of 1929 and 1930 posing a constructive alternative to Mariátegui. While sounder, Basadre's *La multitud, la ciudad y el campo en la historia del Perú* (Lima, 1929) achieved only two editions and his *Perú: problema y posibilidad* (Lima, 1932) one. Belaunde followed up with *Meditaciones peruanas* (Lima, 1932) and *Peruanidad* (Lima, 1942). Alfonso Benavides Correa's *Reflexiones sobre el sentido de la historia peruana* (Lima, 1949) contributed a different view. Luís A. Sanchez's best single book, *El Perú, retrato de un pais adolescente* (Lima, 1963), berates his countrymen for their immaturity.

Ricardo Martinez de la Torre's *Apuntes para una interpretación marxista de historia social del Perú* (Lima, 1947, 4 vols.) is powerful though little controlled Marxist analysis that is valuable for its documentation.

Peruvian historians hesitate to begin the task of summarizing the period since Leguía's fall, although partisan source materials abound. José Pareja Paz Soldán rounded up 26 of them to initiate the work in *Visión del Perú en el siglo XX* (Lima, 1962-63, 2 vols.) with chapters on special topics. Many foreign students have contributed valuable specialized analyses. Robert J. Alexander's selection of material to translate in *Aprismo: The Ideas and Doctrines of Victor Raul Haya de la Torre* (Kent, 1973) is somewhat biased, but discussions of APRA usually are. William J. Dennis, *Tacna and Arica, an Account of the Chile-Peru Boundary Dispute* (New Haven, 1931) carries the story of the territory legacy of the War of the Pacific into this century. Some of the best available guidelines for U.S. policy toward Peru appear in Daniel A. Sharp's collection *U.S. Foreign Policy and Peru* (Austin, 1972). James Carey's *Peru and the United States*

1900-62 (Notre Dame, 1964) is less policy-science oriented. Alberto Wagner de Reyna's *Historia diplomático del Perú 1900-1945* (Lima, 1964, 2 vols.) is nationalistic.

A number of young political scientists have made analyses of various aspects of Peruvian governance and political mobilization. The indifferent quality of most of these specialized studies may be summed up by pointing out that none of the lot, however sophisticated the author's use of quantitative methods or grandoise political theory, appears to have taken into account the extension of suffrage to women at the end of the Odría regime. Most informative, perhaps because it focuses on local political mobilization with ethnographic detail, is *Politics in the Altiplano* by Edward Dew, good in describing Mestizo mobilization of rural peasants (Austin, 1969). Useful in relating the rise of APRA as a regional movement is *Modernization, Dislocation, and Aprismo: Origins of the Peruvian Aprista Party, 1870-1932* by Peter F. Klaren (Austin, 1973). Quantitative depiction of APRA's regional voting strength constitutes the principal contribution of *The Politics of Reform in Peru* by Grant Hilliker (Baltimore, 1971) although it fails to place that phenomenon accurately in sociocultural context. *Pressure Groups and Power Elites in Peruvian Politics* by Carlos A. Astiz (Ithaca, 1969) imposes foreign class categories on Peruvian reality and presents gossip as evidence in attempting to come to grips with militarism.

John M. Baines treats *Revolution in Peru: Mariategui and the Myth* (Alabama, 1972). More specialized and sounder are *Labor and Politics in Peru: The System of Political Bargaining* (New Haven, 1965) by James L. Payne; *Health Manpower in Peru* (Baltimore, 1969) by Thomas L. Hall; *The Government of the Executive of Modern Peru* (Gainesville, 1967) by Jack W. Hopkins; *The Peruvian Industrial Labor Force* (Princeton, 1967) and *Industrialization and the Distribution of Wealth in Peru* (St. Louis, 1967) by David Chaplin; and *The Economic Development of the Western Montaña of Central Peru as Related to Transportation* (Lima, 1958) by Wolfram U. Drewes. Thomas M. Davis, Jr. correctly chronicles *Indian Integration in Peru* (Lincoln, 1970) from 1900 to 1948 as an elitist effort that largely failed. Howard Handelman's *Struggle in the Andes* (Austin, 1975) sketches peasant mobilization in Peru in 1963.

Participant records of events remain as important now as in earlier times as do monographs prepared close in time to events they analyze. Francisco Chirinos Soto, *84 horas de lucha por la constitución* (Arequipa, 1962) accuses Fernando Belaunde T. of playing human chess with his partisans while the author tried to negotiate an APRA-Acción Popular accord to avoid a military coup. Arnold Payne analyzes the result in *The*

Peruvian Coup D'Etat of 1962 (Washington, 1968). Hugo Blanco records
his turn to peasant revolt in *Land or Death* (New York, 1972).

Liisa North included Peru in a comparative analysis of military intervention in governance in *Civil-Military Relations in Argentina, Chile and
Peru* (Berkeley, 1966). Benito Lazo long ago posed the question of power
in *El poder de la fuerza y el poder de la ley* (Lima, 1947). In this century, Edwin Elmore raised the issue in *En torno al militarismo* (Lima,
1920), Luís H. Delgado in *El militarismo en el Perú 1821-1930* (Lima,
1930) and *La espada en el Perú 1821-1931* (Lima, 1931). Víctor Villanueva's *El militarismo en el Perú* (Lima, 1962) signaled military concern
over social issues. His *Un Año bajo el sable* (Lima, 1963) records military
governance following a 1962 coup. Leonidas Castro B.'s *¡Golpismo!* (Lima,
1964) studies that coup and its antecedents. Gen. Felipe de la Barra's *Ob-
jetivo: Palacio de Gobierno* (Lima, 1967) places forceful changes of administration in perspective from independence to 1962.

Several social scientists have analyzed the crucial distribution of power.
Emilio Romero's *El decentralismo* (Lima, 1930) raised the question of
overwhelming concentration of power in Lima, since turned even more
acute and reconsidered in Emilio Romero and César Levano, *Regionalismo
y centralismo* (Lima, 1969). Richard H. Stephens seems quite perceptive
of reality in *Wealth and Power in Peru* (Mutuchen, 1971). Giorgio Alberti and Rodrigo Sánchez's *Poder y conflicto social en el valle del Mantaro 1900-1974* (Lima, 1974) examines changes in Lima's central Andean
hinterland. In *Los dueños del Perú* (Lima, 1964, 1968 3d ed.), Carlos
Malpica makes a fundamental contribution to publicizing elite concentration of land ownership. His more historical *Crónica del hambre en el Perú*
(Lima, 1966) is less dramatic. French sociologist François Bourricaud describes differential access to power in *Power and Society in Contemporary
Peru* (New York, 1970) and *La oligarquía en el Perú* (Lima, 1969) with
Jorge Bravo Bresani, Henri Favre, and Juan Piel. Julio Cotler's functional
analysis *La mecánica de la dominación interna y del cambio social en el
Perú* (Lima, 1967) is perceptive. Wilfredo Kapsoli E.'s *Luchas obreras por
la conquista de las ocho horas de trabajo* (Lima, 1969) chronicles the struggle for an 8-hour workday.

Earlier, in *La tierra* (Lima, 1921) Víctor G. Maita called attention to
the increasing severity of land-tenure inequality already signaled in *Tierras
indígenas y cuestiones sociales* (Lima, 1920) by Abel Gutierrez Ocampo,
and Philip A. Means in *Indian Legislation in Peru* (Baltimore, 1920).
Luís E. Valcárcel's *Tempestad en los Andes* (Lima, 1927) stands out
among pro-Indian works, in part for his influence on Mariátequi. Erasmo
Roca's *Por la clase indígena* (Lima, 1935) includes a report of the first

governmental investigation of contemporary Native American conditions in 1920-21.

Petroleum and its politics generated a large polemical literature. An early contribution is *La industria petrolera en el Perú* (Lima, 1912) by Ricardo Deustua. In *La cuestión Brea y Pariñas* (Lima, 1916) Manuel Quimper became an energetic defender of national rights. In *El Imperialismo Petrolero y la agresión económica en el Perú* (Lima, 1930), Carlos A. Butron kept the issue alive. Deputy Alfonso Benavides C. led the campaign to nullify the Leguía regime's arrangements in parliament and with *El Petoleo peruano* (Lima, 1961) and *Oro negro del Perú* (Lima, 1963).

The Lequía regime generated numerous personal panegyrics such as José E. Bonilla's *El siglo de Leguía* (Lima, 1928) comparing Leguía to Ceasar, Alexander, Napoleon, and Washington, among others. After his death, Lequía continued to be attacked by Dora Mayer de Zulen in *El Oncenio de Leguia* (Callao, 1932, 2 vols.) and Abelardo Solís in *Once Años* (Lima, 1934), and defended by Abel Ulloa Cisneros, *Escombros 1919-1930* (Lima, 1934), Clemente Palma, *Había una vez un hombre* (Lima, 1935), and Manuel A. Capuñay, *Leguía* (Lima, 1951). Carlos Miró Quesada Laos praised the officer who overthrew Leguía in *Sanchez Cerro u su tiempo* (Buenos Aires, 1947).

Biographers even honor civilians who never became president. José Pareja Paz Soldán evokes *El Maestro Belaunde* (Lima, 1968) the diplomat-educator. Lima's enterprising publisher Juan Mejía Baca brought out in *Perú Vivo* (Lima, 1966) autobiographies of 8 eminent civilians, authors, and educators ranging from an engineer and economist to two *indigenistas*. Luís H. Delgado's *Cincuenta años del periodismo* (Lima, 1953) applauds the impact of a newspaper owner-editor.

Volumes like *Who's Who* record achievements of a wide selection of important Peruvians. José D. Cortés pioneered with *Diccionario Biográfico* (Paris, 1875) with 5 Peruvian collaborators. Juan Pedro Paz-Soldán later produced the national *Diccionario Biográfico de peruanos contemporáneos* (Lima, 1917) containing data available nowhere else. William B. Parker's *Peruvians of To-Day* (Lima, 1919) followed quickly for English speakers. Raúl D. Garbín, Raúl D. Garbín, Jr., and Julio Cardenas Ramirez prepared *Diccionario Biográfico del Perú* (Lima, 1944). Ronald Hilton's *Who's Who in Latin America* (Stanford, 1946-51) includes Peruvians in one of its seven volumes. Manuel Beltroy assembled *Peruanos Notables de Hoy* (Lima, 1957). Several profit-motivated volumes of this style describe bankers and other professionals.

While a few individuals have played outstanding roles in this century, mass decisions add up to fundamental change. Thus, quantitative history increases in importance. In 1919, Alberto Alexander R. published an *Estudio sobre la crisis de la habitación en Lima* (Lima), a study of short housing. Carlos Jimenez Correa's *Estadística industrial del Perú* (Lima, 1922) encouraged the compiling of industrial statistics. Oscar F. Arrus in *El costo de vida en Lima y causas de su carestia* (Lima, 1925) began cost-of-living analysis. César A. Ugarte's *Bosquejo de historia económico del Perú* (Lima, 1926) stimulated economic history. Alberto Arca Parro *Censo Nacional de Población y Ocupación de 1940* (Lima, 1944) led the first modern enumeration of Peruvian population. Enumeration recurred in 1961 and 1972. Dario Saint Marie S. in *Perú en Cifras 1944-1945* (Lima, 1945) brought together not only statistics on many aspects of life, but also historical sketches. The Bureau of Statistics and Census has for many years issued a very instructive *Anuario estadístico del Perú*. Rómulo Ferrero contributed *Tierra y Población en el Perú* (Lima, 1938) on man-land ratios and *La historia monetaria del Perú en el presente siglo* (Lima, 1953) on money. The Economic Commission for Latin America's *Analyses and Projections of Economic Development: VI: The Industrial Development of Peru* (New York, 1959) provides data on industrial development. With *Migración e Integración en el Perú* (Lima, 1963) H. F. Dobyns and Mario C. Vázquez focused attention on the basic demographic process of internal migration. Oscar Valdivia Ponce's *Migración Interna a la Metrópoli: Contraste cultural, conflicto y desadaptación* (Lima, 1970) constitutes but one follow-up among many.

Quantitative regional studies have proliferated. An early example was *La Demografía y los Recursos humanos* (Lima, 1959) of southern Peru by Richard P. Schaedel with José A. Tejada and Leonardo Pérez Saco—one of many studies of the region carried out then. The Instituto de Planeamiento de Lima prepared an *Estudio para el desarrollo económico y social del departamento de Lambayeque* (Lima, 1968).

Useful institutional histories include Jorge Basadre and Rómulo Ferrero's *Historio de la cámara de comercio de Lima* (Lima, 1963); Hermann Buse, *Huinco: 240,000 KW* (Lima, 1965) on Lima's electric company; Alberto Fernández Prada Effio, *La aviación en el Perú, 1751-1942* (Lima, 1969, 2d ed.) on aviation; Jorge Castro Harrison, *Proceso histórico de la educación en el Perú* (Pueblo Libre, 1959) on education; Hermilio Valdizán, *Diccionario de Medicina peruana* (Lima, 1923-60, 6 vols.) and Juan B. Lastres, *La medicina en la república* (Lima, 1951) on medicine Carlos Miró Quesada Laos, *Historia del periodismo peruano* (Lima, 1957) on newspapers although biased by family and metropolitan orientation; Neptalí Benvenutto *Historia de las carreteras del Perú* (Lima, 1952) on highway construction; Julio César Nieri, *El correo en el Perú* (Lima, 1935) on postal service; Rómulo Merino Arana, *Historia policial del Perú durante la república* (Lima, 1965) on the police; Manuel D. Velasco Núñez's *Compilación de la legislación indigenista concordada* (Lima, n.d.) pulls together laws on Indian affairs. A stellar example of a provincial monograph is *Ensayo monográfico de la provincia de La Mar* by Antonio Vilchez A. (Lima, 1961) which led guerillas to rebel in 1965 in La Mar Province.

THE REVOLUTIONARY MILITARY REGIME

The authors rely on their personal acquaintance with people and events in characterizing this regime. Some useful attempts at analysis have begun to appear in doctoral dissertation form, yet evaluation lies in the future.

Antimilitarist Víctor Villanueva quickly reacted to the 1968 coup d'état with *Golpe en el Perú* (Montevideo, 1969) and *¿Nueva mentalidad militar en el Perú?* (Buenos Aires, 1969). President Juan Velasco Alvarado speaks for himself in *Velasco: la voz de la revolución: discursos* (Lima, 1970).

SOCIETY AND CULTURE

Social scientists have studied a fair sample of the thousands of rural settlements in Peru. They have begun to analyze important aspects of urban life. Their findings describe modern Peru better than they account for its historic development. One of the best statements of this historic importance of the Columbian exchange new race is José Varellanos' *El cholo y el Perú* (Buenos Aires, 1962). The Interamerican Committee on Agricultural Development presents massive evidence of unequal access to land in *Tenencia de la Tierra y desarrollo socio-económico del sector agrícola: Perú* (Washington, 1966). Mainly urban and most instructive is Humberto Rotondo's *Estudios sobre la familia en su relación con la salud* (Lima, 1970). Specialized but significant is Daniel Goldrich, Raymond B. Pratt, and C. R. Schuller, *The Political Integration of Lower-Class Urban Settlements in Chile and Peru* (St. Louis, 1968).

Indian Affairs. Indigenista literature abounds. Good examples include Dora Mayer de Zulen's *El indígena a los cien años de república libre e independiente* (Lima, 1921); Luís F. Aguilar's *Cuestiones indígenas* (Cuzco, 1922); and J. Antonio Almanza's *También el indio ruge* (Cuzco, 1933). Such writing is increasingly outmoded by social scientific studies. Hildebrando Castro Pozo's *Nuestra comunidad indígena* (Lima, 1924),

Mariátegui's seven essays, and Moisés Saenz's *Sobre el indio peruano y su incorporación al medio nacional* (Mexico, 1933) achieved a major conceptual transition. Thirty years later Peruvian social scientists make mature policy-science statements regularly. José Matos Mar's *Idea y diagnóstico del Perú* (Lima, 1966) analyzes sociocultural pluralism. José R. Sabogal Wiese edited *La comunidad andina* objectively if sympathetically toward Native Americans. Fernando Fuenzalida, Enrique Mayer, Gabriel Escobar, François Bourricaud, and José Matos Mar collaborated on *El indio y el poder en el Perú* (Lima, 1970), a politically leftist general statement. Robert G. Keith, Fernando Fuenzalida, José Matos Mar, Julio Cotler, and Giorgio Alberti's *La hacienda, la comunidad y el campesino en el Perú* (Lima, 1970) of the same orientation does not supersede Mario C. Vázquez's *Hacienda, peonaje y servidumbre en los Andes peruanos* (Lima, 1961), a succinct technical characterization based on personal studies in several areas. Henry F. Dobyns summarized selected characteristics of 1,600 peasant communities that complement haciendas in *The Social Matrix of Peruvian Indigenous Communities* (Ithaca, 1964) and *Comunidades Campesinas del Perú* (Lima, 1970). Ulrich Peter Ritter analyzed cooperative behavior in greater detail in a smaller sample in *Comunidades indígenas y cooperativismo en el Perú* (Bilbao, 1965). Studying representative settlements, Alfred A. Buck, Tom T. Sasaki, and Robert I. Anderson contribute to health policy with *Health and Disease in Four Peruvian Villages* (Baltimore, 1968).

An outstanding analysis of a local area in historic perspective, *Huaylas* by Paul L. and Mary French Doughty (Ithaca, 1968) describes a highly self-reliant Mestizo administrative district in the Callejón de Huaylas in rich detail. François Bourricaud's *Changements a Puno: etude de sociologie andine* offers sophisticated synchronic comparison of city and hinterland. Richard N. Adams' *A Community in the Andes* (Seattle, 1959) places Muquiyauyo in Mantaro Valley developmental context. Julio Cotler's *Los Cambios en la propiedad, la comunidad y la familia en San Lorenzo de Quinti* (Lima, 1959) summarizes agroeconomic changes in cheese-making peasant communities in an administrative district on the Andean western slope. Fernando Fuenzalida, José L. Villarán, Jurgen Golte, and Teresa Valiente, *Estructuras tradicionales, y economía de mercado: la comunidad de indígenas de Huayopampa* (Lima, 1968) details how another such community shifted into commercial fruit-growing. Julian H. Steward's *Contemporary Change in Traditional Societies. Vol. 3. Mexican and Peruvian Communities* (Urbana, 1967) incorporates Louis Faron's analysis of evolution of Chancay Valley haciendas and communities and Solomon Miller's on a northern Sierra hacienda-plantation transformation. Henri

Favre, Claude Collin-Delavaud, and José Matos Mar compare three haciendas in the central Sierra, central and north coast in *La hacienda en el
Perú* (Lima, 1967) with analysis of historic evolution of large properties
and their influence on rural society. José Matos Mar, José Portugal Mendoza, and others outline local history of the oasis next south from Lima in
El valle de Lurín y el pueblo de Pachacamac: cambios sociales y culturales
(Lima, 1964). E. A. Hammel's *Power in Ica* (Boston, 1969) deals with
another near south coast oasis.

Many fine studies of single settlements illuminate specific aspects of
rural society. W. W. Stein's *Hualcán* (Ithaca, 1961) describes a half-free-
holder, half-serf hamlet in the Callejón de Huaylas. Mario C. Vázquez's
Educación rural en el Callejon de Huaylas: Vicos (Lima, 1965) sums up
cultural patterns inhibiting rapid education of Native American enclaves.
H. F. Dobyns, P. L. Doughty, and H. D. Lasswell in *Peasants, Power and
Applied Social Change* (Beverly Hills, 1971) report consequences of gov-
ernment-university intervention to move a hacienda population toward
economic and social autonomy at Vicis, Ancash.

Oscar Núñez del Prado's *Kuyo Chico* (Chicago, 1973) recounts a similar anthropology professor's government-contracted intervention near
Cuzco. Rural sociologist Manuel Alers-Montalvo's *Pucará* (Lima, 1968)
augments understanding of the Mantaro Valley analyzing government-
encouraged innovations in tuber production. Hernán Castillo, Teresa Ego-
ávil de Castillo, and Arcenio Revilla C. in *Carcas: The Forgotten Community* (Ithaca, 1964) paint a sad portrait of a village disintegrating by
emigration and mortgaging land to finance religious festivals. In the south,
Jorge A. Flores Ochoa's *Los Pastores de Paratia* (Mexico, 1968) describes
high plateau pastoral specialists. Harry Tschopik's *The Aymara of Chucuito, Peru: Magic* (New York, 1951) is still useful although overreliant
on Mestizo information. For the edge of the Amazon rain forest, David A.
Andrews and colleagues' *Paucartambo, Pasco, Peru: Whence . . .
Whither* (Ithaca, 1965) describes a colonization zone stimulated by government agricultural extension efforts.

On the dry western slope, George M. Korb's *Ticaco* (Ithaca, 1966)
quantitatively describes an Aymara-speaking colony in Tacna Department.
Earl W. Morris, L. A. Brownrigg, S. C. Bourque, and H. F. Dobyns in
Coming Down the Mountain (Ithaca, 1968) look at a mixed farming
peasant community and its urban Huacho and Lima colonies in terms of
national-local institutional links. P. L. Doughty and Luís Negrón in
Pararín (Ithaca, 1964) examine specialists in high-altitude cattle grazing
who turned to mechanized farming after reclaiming low-altitude oasis
fields. John Gillin in *Moche* (Washington, D.C., 1947) describes a Na-

tive American dairy and truck farming enclave on the outskirts of Trujillo.

Amazon Basin Native Americans, once largely ignored, now receive increasing study and integrative effort. Outstanding authority is Stefano Varese, with *La sal de los cerros* (Lima, 1968) on the rain forest Campa tribesmen, and *The Forest Indians in the Present Political Situation of Peru* (Copenhagen, 1972). John H. Bodley, *Tribal Survival in the Amazon: The Campa Case* (Copenhagen, 1972) offers another view. Hallucinogenic healing is the subject of *Visionary Vine* by Marlene Dobkin de Ríos (San Francisco, 1972).

International Migration. Political preoccupation with encouraging European immigration and discouraging other forms of population growth appear in such works as *La imigración en el Perú* (Lima, 1891) by Pedro Paz Soldán y Unánue writing under the pseudonym Juan de Arona, and *Colonización de la costa peruana por medio de la inmigración europea* (Lima, 1900) by Carlos Larrabure y Correa; *El Perú actual y las colonias extranjeras 1821-1921* (Bergamo, 1924) by Enrique Centurión y Herrera; *La inmigración y su desarrollo en el Perú* by Mario del Río (Lima, 1929), and *La vita Italiana nella republica del Perú* by Emilio Sequi and Enrique Calcagnoli (Lima, 1911). Intellectuals like policy-makers viewed coastal Chinese and Japanese colonies gained during the last half of the nineteenth century as problems. Thus, dispassionate analyses tend to come from outsiders such as Watt Stewart in *Chinese Bondage in Peru* (Durham, 1951) dealing with the 1849-74 period.

Folklore. Oral tradition often illuminates consequences of colonial or republican policies. A most significant compendium is *La medicina popular peruana* of Hermilio Valdizán and Angel Maldonado (Lima, 1922), on folk medicine. Interesting are Carlos Camino Calderon's *Diccionario folklórico del Perú* (Lima, 1944) drawing on Lima and the north coast, and Lauro Pino's *Jerga criolla y peruanismos* (Lima, 1968), a short dictionary of modern slang. Robert J. Smith's *The Art of the Festival* is an outstanding treatment of popular religion (Lawrence, 1976).

BIBLIOGRAPHY

The two contemporary giants among Peruvian historians also dominate the field of historical bibliography. Jorge Basadre followed his history of the republic with a two-volume critical *Introducción a las bases documentales para la historia de la república del Perú con algunas reflexiones* (Lima, 1971), the best available. Rubén Vargas Ugarte's *Manual de estudios peruanistas* (Lima, 1959) reached its fourth edition then, slighting the postindependence period and Basadre. Vargas U. also compiled *Biblioteca peruana: manuscritos peruanos* (Lima, 1935) and *Manuscritos peruanos en las bibliotecas y archivos de Europa y América* (Buenos Aires, 1947). Their efforts are amplified by military historian Gen. Felipe de la Barra in *Fichero bibliográfico historico militar peruano* (Lima, 1970) and earlier works, and the *Catálogo del Archivo Histórico Militar del Perú* (Lima, 1962-70) issued by the Centro de Estudios Histórico-Militares; Alberto Tauro in *Guía de estudios históricos* (Lima, 1955) and as editor of *Anuario bibliográfico peruano* published by the Biblioteca Nacional; and Carlos Moreyra y Paz Soldán's *Bibliografía regional peruana* (Lima, 1967). A fine pioneer work on historiography was José de la Riva Agüero y Osma's *La historia en el Perú* (Lima, 1910).

Bibliographies have begun to appear for specialized fields. Carl Herbold, Jr. and Steven Stein annotated only 102 volumes in *Guía bibliográfica para la historia social y política del Perú en el siglo XX 1895-1960* (Lima, 1971). Politician-professor Luís A. Sánchez contributed the fullest guide to national literature, *Contribución a la bibliografía de la literature peruana* (Lima, 1969). The sociologist José Mejía Valera annotated *Fuentes para la historia de la filosofía en el Perú*. Pedro Ugarteche and José Pareja Paz Soldán's *Al servicio de una bibliografía de historia internacional diplomática del Perú* (Lima, 1942) explored resources of the Ministry of Foreign Affairs.

Bibliography of interethnic affairs appears best of all. Héctor Martínez A., Miguel Cameo C., and Jesús Ramirez S. compiled a 1,703-item *Bibliografía Andina peruana 1900-1968* (Lima, 1969). Mario C. Vázquez annotated English-language publications for local social scientists in *Bibliografía peruana de ciencias sociales publicada en inglés 1945-1965* (Lima, 1967). César Augusto Angeles Caballero and Mildred Merino de Zela compiled *Bibliografía del Folklore peruana* (México, 1960). Paul Rivet and George G. Crequi-Montfort compiled a massive *Bibliographie des langages Aymara et Kicua* (Paris, 1951-56).

Tables

TABLE I. THE HISTORIC DEMOGRAPHY OF PERU AND THE GROWTH OF LIMA.

Date	Peru			Lima			
	Population	Number Annual Change	% Annual Change	Population	Number Annual Change	% Annual Change	% Total Change
1523*	32,000,000						
1530*	16,000,000	−2,285,714	−7.1				
1548	8,285,000	−428,611	−2.6				
1570	2,738,500	−252,114	−3.0				
1614				26,441			
1650	3,030,000	+3,644	+0.1				
1700				37,259	+126	+0.47	
1796	1,076,122	−13,382	−0.5	52,627	+160	+0.43	5.0
1825	2,488,000	+48,685	+4.5				
1836	1,373,736	−97,660	−3.9	55,627	+75	+0.14	4.0
1850	2,001,203	+44,819	+3.2				
1857				94,195	+1,837	+3.3	
1862	2,487,916	+40,559	+2.0	89,434	−952	−1.0	3.5
1876	2,651,840	+11,709	+0.5	100,156	+766	+0.8	3.8
1891				103,956	+253	+0.2	
1898				113,409	+1,350	+1.3	
1903				130,089	+3,336	+2.9	
1908				140,884	+2,159	+1.7	
1908†				172,927			
1920†				223,807	+4,240	+2.5	
1931†				373,875	+13,642	+6.1	
1940	6,207,967	+55,564	+2.0	562,885	+13,188	+9.4	9.0
1961	9,906,746	+176,132	+2.8	1,632,370	+50,928	+9.0	16.4
1972	13,572,052	+333,209	+3.3	3,002,043	+124,516	+7.6	22.1

* Estimates based upon H. F. Dobyns, "Estimating Aboriginal American Population," *Current Anthropology* (Vol. 7, No. 4), 1966.
† Province of Lima. After 1908, population growth and settlement size made the province the meaningful unit for measurement.

Sources: Perú, *Censo Nacional de Poblacion y Ocupación, 1940*; M. F. Paz Soldán, *Diccionario Geográfico Estadístico del Perú* (1862 and 1876); Perú, *Censo Nacional de Población, 1961 and 1972, Resultados Preliminares.*

TABLE 2. BIRTH AND DEATH RATES FOR PERU PER 1,000 IN 1940 AND 1972.

Date	Birth Rate	Death Rate
1940	50.0	32.6
1972	43.4	12.3

Source: *America en Cifras, 1972.*

TABLE 3. POPULATION OF PERU BY DEPARTMENT, REGION, RATE OF GROWTH, AND PERCENT URBAN FOR 1940, 1961, AND 1972.

Area	Total 1972	% of Total	Coast	Sierra	Jungle	Urban	% 1961-72 Increase	Total 1961	% Urban	% 1940-61 Increase	Total 1940	% Urban
Peru 1940			25	62	13	35	—	—			6,207,967	
Peru 1961			39	52	9	47		9,906,746		59.6		
Peru 1972	13,572,052	100	45	44	11	60	36.9	—				
Amazonas Dept.	196,469	1.4	—	33	67	34	65.9	118,439	39	81.8	65,137	41
Ancash	726,668	5.4	34	66	—	47	24.7	582,598	33	37.1	424,975	23
Apurimac	307,805	2.3	—	100	—	23	34.9	228,223	20	—11.6	258,094	14
Arequipa	530,528	3.9	15	85	—	82	56.5	338,881	64	28.8	263,077	59
Ayacucho	459,747	3.4	—	91	9	33	11.9	410,772	25	14.4	358,991	24
Cajamarca	916,331	6.8	—	82	18	18	22.7	746,938	15	51.1	494,412	14
Callao Prov.	315,605	2.3	100	—	—	99	47.8	213,540	96	159.5	82,287	99
Cuzco Dept.	712,918	5.2	—	85	15	36	16.5	611,972	32	25.8	486,592	25
Huancavelica	331,155	2.4	—	96	4	21	9.3	302,817	19	23.8	244,595	15
Huánuco	420,764	3.1	—	79	21	27	27.9	328,919	21	40.5	234,024	19
Ica	357,973	2.6	100	—	—	72	39.9	255,930	54	81.6	140,898	44
Junín	691,130	5.1	—	82	18	60	32.6	521,210	49	21.5	428,855	39*
La Libertad	806,368	5.9	61	39	—	59	38.5	582,243	42	51.9	383,252	31
Lambayeque	515,363	3.8	100	—	—	73	50.5	342,446	62	72.1	198,890	51
Lima	3,485,411	25.7	93	7	—	94	71.6	2,031,151	86	145.2	828,298	76
Loreto	494,935	3.6	—	—	100	50	46.8	337,094	39	99.9	168,611	32
Madre de Díos	21,968	0.2	—	—	100	43	47.5	14,890	25	200.8	4,950	26
Moquegua	74,573	0.6	59	41	—	71	44.5	51,614	48	51.1	34,152	24
Pasco*	176,750	1.3	—	78	22	60	27.7	138,369	35	53.1	90,353	—*
Piura	854,668	6.3	77	23	—	52	27.8	668,941	45	63.7	408,605	36

Puno	779,594	5.7	—	96	4	24	13.6	686,260	18	25.1	548,371	13
San Martín	224,310	1.7	—	—	100	59	38.7	161,763	59	70.1	94,843	56
Tacna	95,623	0.7	73	27	—	80	44.8	66,024	70	81.6	36,349	53
Tumbes	75,399	0.6	100	—	—	74	35.1	55,812	61	117.1	25,709	42

* The Department of Pasco was created in 1944 from portions of Junín. The figures for both departments are adjusted here to show what they would have been in 1940.

Sources: Peru, *Censo Nacional de Población y Ocupación, 1940; Censo Nacional de Población* (VI) *1961; Censo Nacional de Población* (VII) *1972.*

TABLE 4. CITIES WITH MORE THAN 20,000 INHABITANTS, 1940-72.

City	Zone	1961 Population	% Increase 1940-1961 Total	Year	1972 Population	% Increase 1961-1972 Total	Year
Lima	C*	1,436,231	175	8.3	2,973,845	107	9.7
Callao	C*	204,990	124	5.9	312,332	52	4.7
Greater Lima		1,641,221	167	7.9	3,286,177	100	9.0
Arequipa	H*	158,685	122	5.8	304,653	91	8.2
Trujillo	C*	103,020	170	8.0	241,882	134	12.1
Chiclayo	C*	95,667	203	9.6	189,685	98	8.9
Chimbote	C	59,990	1313	62.5	159,045	165	15.0
Piura	C*	72,096	158	7.5	126,702	75	6.8
Cuzco	H*	79,857	96	4.5	120,881	52	4.7
Huancayo	H*	64,153	140	6.6	115,693	80	7.2
Iquitos	J*	57,777	81	3.8	111,327	92	8.3
Ica	C*	49,097	134	6.3	73,883	50	4.5
Sullana	C*	34,501	63	3.0	60,112	74	6.7
Pucallpa	J	26,391	1014	48.2	57,525	117	10.6
Tacna	C	27,449	149	7.0	55,752	103	9.3
Cerro de Pasco	H	21,363	19	0.9	47,178	120	10.9
Pisco	C	22,112	55	2.6	41,429	87	7.9
Puno	H	24,459	77	3.6	41,166	68	6.1
Huánuco	H	24,646	105	5.0	41,123	66	6.0
Juliaca	H	20,351	237	11.2	38,475	89	8.0
Cajamarca	H	22,705	58	2.7	37,608	65	5.9
Huacho	C	22,806	75	3.5	36,697	60	5.4
Ayacucho	H	23,768	42	2.0	34,593	38	3.4
Tumbes	C	20,885	238	11.3	32,972	57	5.1
Talara	C	27,957	115	5.4	29,884	6	0.5
Huaraz	H	20,345	84	4.0	29,719	46	4.1
Chincha Alta	C	20,817	67	3.1	28,785	38	3.4
Pativilca	C††	(15,327)	198	9.4	28,369	85	7.7
Tarma	H††	(15,452)	110	5.2	28,100	81	7.3
Other Cities		24,724†	—	—	224,866**	54	4.9
TOTALS		2,766,842	196	9.3	5,624,281	103	9.3
Percent of the National Population		28%				41%	

* Cities over 20,000 in 1940.
† The only city was La Oroya, H.
** Includes Chulucanas C, La Oroya H, Barranca C, Chepén C, Ilo C, Tarapoto J, Chocope C, Huaral C, Tingo María J, in order of size.
†† Not added to 1961 total. Pativilca includes Paramonga.
C = Coast, H = Highland, J = Jungle-Amazon basin

Sources: Perú, *Censo Nacional de Población y Ocupación*, 1940: *Censo Nacional de Población* (VI) 1961 and *Censo Nacional de Población* (VII) 1972.

TABLE 5. NATIONAL BUDGETS BY PRESIDENTIAL ADMINISTRATION, 1900-1970.

Administration	Years	Average Annual Budget*	Average Yearly Percent of Budget						
			Congress	Govt. Admin.†	Development	Education	Military	Foreign Relations	Non Budget Costs
Lopez de Romaña	1900-03	13.9	2.9	57.3	3.6	—	24.1	5.2	6.9
Candamo	1904	18.9	2.4	57.5	6.3	—	23.0	5.2	5.6
Pardo	1905-08	25.6	3.2	57.9	8.7	—	20.9	2.8	6.5
Leguía	1909-12	30.0	3.0	63.6	6.2	—	21.5	3.2	2.5
Billinghurst	1913	45.4	2.6	50.4	5.6	—	20.0	3.3	18.1
Pardo	1916-19	49.6	2.9	58.1	6.8	—	16.1	1.8	14.3
Leguía	1920-30	123.6	2.4	49.0	9.3	—	14.7	2.5	22.1
Samanez	1931	131.4	1.0	54.3	6.7	—	16.1	1.7	20.2
Sánchez Cerro	1932	97.0	2.8	64.6	8.4	—	20.5	2.6	1.1
Benavides	1933-39	187.4	1.1	45.2	9.0	9.3	17.5	2.5	15.4
Prado	1940-45	402.6	1.7	41.9	5.3	8.7	19.3	2.6	21.1
Bustamente	1946-48	921.6	1.0	44.0	12.1	14.3	20.7	2.1	5.8
Odria	1949-56	2,267.6	1.6	46.4	10.4	16.7	23.9	2.2	—
Prado	1957-62	5,660.1	2.7	41.8	7.4	25.4	21.1	1.6	—
Pérez	1963	15,026.4	2.2	42.4	18.5	19.3	16.8	0.8	—
Belaunde	1964-68	19,962.9	2.2	35.9	17.7	27.5	15.8	0.8	—
Velasco	1969-70	38,650.0	—			22.5	18.9	0.8	—

* Expressed in millions of soles.
† Category includes smaller ministries such as Justice, Labor, and Exchequer.

Sources: Perú, *Anuario Estadístico*, 1955, 1966; United Nations, *Statistical Yearbook*, 1972.

TABLE 6. PERUVIAN INTERNATIONAL TRADE, COST OF LIVING, AND MONEY, 1900-1970.

		1900	1920	1925	1930	1940	1945	1950	1960	1965	1970
Exports in dollars		9.3	76.9	—	66.8	65.7	—	186.5	433.1	667.3	1,004.0
Imports in dollars		4.8	39.9	—	39.7	51.6	—	185.2	374.7	729.4	619.0
% Exports (a) / Imports (b)											
The Americas	a	39.1		61.9			82.1			54.2	40.0
	b	18.1		44.4			88.9			59.0	54.3
United States	a	21.2		34.8			33.9			33.7	32.9
	b	8.9		38.7			56.4			39.8	32.1
Chile	a	13.5		8.4			19.2			2.6	0.6
	b	3.9		3.0			5.8			0.9	1.8
Argentina	a	—		7.7			3.2			2.9	1.3
	b	—		.9			13.7			6.8	6.5
Canada	a	—		6.9			—			0.8	0.4
	b	—		0.5			4.8			4.3	4.5
Mexico	a	0.1		—			5.1			0.7	1.3
	b			—			1.5			0.5	2.0
Europe and Asia	a	60.9		38.1			11.8			54.3	59.7
	b	80.1		51.1			9.8			40.1	42.0
United Kingdom	a	46.4		34.1			6.2			5.8	2.5
	b	46.7		18.9			3.4			5.2	4.3
West Germany	a	21.2		1.7			—			12.5	15.0
	b	15.6		11.0			—			11.7	12.2
France	a	2.7		0.6			0.6			2.2	1.8
	b	6.7		3.6			—			1.9	1.9
Holland	a	—		0.3			—			9.1	9.6
	b	—		2.3			—			2.4	2.1
Japan	a	—		0.3			—			9.2	13.5
	b	—		1.0			—			7.1	7.9

Cost of Living Index in Lima (1934–36=100)	—	136.4	109.7	118.7	—	481.5	1,021.8	1,565.3	1,771.6
Exchange rate, Sol to U.S. dollar	4.82	4.59	3.53	6.17	—	15.48	27.3	26.8	43.8

Sources: Peru, *Anuario Estadístico*, 1925, 1946, 1950, 1955, 1969; Peru, *Boletín de Estadística Peruana*, 1961; Pan American Union, *América en Cifras*, 1972.

TABLE 7. FIRST LANGUAGE AND EDUCATION CHARACTERISTICS OF THE POPULATION OVER 5 YEARS OF AGE, 1961-72 (HUNDREDS).

First Language Spoken*

	Total Number (100%)	Quechua No.	%	Aymara No.	%	Other Native† No.	%	Spanish No.	%	Other Language** No.	%
1972 Total	11337.1	3015.2	27	332.5	3.0	119.3	1.0	7740.9	68	50.6	0.4
Men	5676.7	1481.2	26	167.3	3.0	59.0	1.0	3900.2	69	28.6	0.5
Women	5660.4	1533.9	27	165.2	3.0	60.2	1.0	3840.7	68	21.9	0.4
Urban pop.	6839.3	1094.3	16	83.4	1.0	31.2	5.5	5528.2	81	45.8	0.7
Men	3414.8	546.7	16	46.4	1.0	14.9	4.4	2752.5	81	28.3	0.8
Women	3424.4	547.5	16	37.0	1.0	16.2	.5	2775.6	81	20.0	0.6
No school	1145.7	346.9	30	19.5	1.7	11.0	1.0	753.6	66	19.1	1.7
Men	415.4	92.1	22	5.1	1.2	3.7	.9	308.9	74	9.1	2.2
Women	730.0	254.7	35	14.3	2.0	7.3	1.0	444.7	61	1.0	0.1
University	319.3	18.3	6	1.5	.5	0.5	.2	287.3	90	9.9	3.1
Men	202.7	13.2	7	1.2	.6	0.3	.1	179.3	88	6.7	3.3
Women	117.5	5.1	4	0.3	.3	0.2	.2	108.0	92	3.1	2.6
Rural pop.	4497.8	1920.8	43	249.1	5.5	88.1	2.0	2212.6	49	4.8	10.1
Men	2261.9	934.4	41	120.9	5.3	44.1	1.9	1147.6	51	2.8	10.1
Women	2235.9	986.3	44	128.1	5.7	43.9	2.0	1065.0	48	1.9	0.1
No school	2279.7	1169.8	51	120.8	5.3	56.8	2.5	919.3	40	1.2	0.1
Men	854.7	422.1	49	39.6	4.6	24.9	2.9	362.4	42	.6	
Women	1424.9	747.7	52	81.2	5.7	31.9	2.2	556.8	39	.6	0.1
University	12.5	1.7	14	0.3	2.4	0.1	0.8	9.7	78	.5	4.0
Men	8.7	1.3	15	0.2	2.3	0.1	1.1	6.4	74	.3	3.4
Women	3.8	0.4	11	0.03	0.8	0.03	0.8	3.2	84	.1	2.6

1961 Total	8235.2	2685.8	33	290.1	3.5	213.2	2.6	4945.2	60	57.1	0.7
Men	4085.3	1305.9	32	142.3	3.5	102.2	2.5	2479.8	61	35.0	0.9
Women	4149.9	1379.8	33	147.7	3.6	110.9	2.7	2465.4	59	24.1	0.6
Urban Pop.	3361.2	786.8	23	49.3	1.5	62.8	1.9	3001.5	89	48.8	1.5
Men	1968.5	392.0	20	27.3	1.4	29.6	1.5	1484.4	75	28.5	1.4
Women	1992.6	394.8	20	20.0	1.0	33.1	1.7	1517.1	76	20.4	1.0
Rural Pop.	4263.9	1898.9	45	24.7	5.8	150.4	3.5	1943.6	46	8.1	0.2
Men	2116.7	913.9	43	115.0	5.4	72.6	3.4	995.3	47	4.4	0.2
Women	2157.2	985.0	46	127.7	5.9	77.8	3.6	948.3	44	3.7	0.1

* The bilingual population is included but cannot be accurately distinguished in census reports; thus, it is not separately reported here.

† Includes aboriginal languages spoken by some 54 ethnolinguistic groups living in the Amazon basin area of the country.

** Includes all foreign languages. The largest group were those speaking Japanese, followed by English, German, Chinese, and Italian.

Sources: Perú, VI Censo Nacional de Población, Vol. I, Tomo III (1966); Perú, Censos Nacionales: VII de Población, II de Vivienda: Nivel Nacional, Tomo II (1974).

TABLE 8. LAND AREA, ARABLE LAND, AND POPULATION DENSITY
ACCORDING TO NATURAL AREAS IN 1972.

	Total	Coast	Highlands	Jungle
Territory				
Km²	1,285,120	160,502	388,176	736,442
Percent	100	13	30	57
Arable land and Pasture*				
Km²	28,043	6,901	17,460	3,682
Percent	100	24	63	13
Population Density				
(Total Area/Km²)	10.5	37.9	15.4	2
Population Density				
on Arable Land				
and Pasture	483	883	343	401

* Based upon the amount of land reported as actually used.

Sources: Perú, *Anuario Estadístico, 1966;* Comité Interamericano de Desarrollo Agricola (CIDA), *Tenencia de la Tierra y Desarrollo Socio-económico del Secto Agricola: Perú.*

TABLE 9. LAND TENURE AND INCOME IN PERU IN 1961.

Type of Holding	Number of Holdings	Percent	Average Size Hectares	Percent of Area	Average Operator Income (Dollars)
National Total	851,192	100.0			
Large Estates	10,462	1.2	1,338.1	75.2	20,374
Small Estates	23,250	2.7	43.3	5.4	3,184
Family Farms	98,370	11.6	8.9	4.7	940
Minifundia	719,110	84.4	1.9	6.0	413
Communities	(808)	0.1	1,985.1	8.6	166 to 915
Serfs & Peons	—	—	—	—	240
Coast	54,320	100.0			
Large Estates	920	1.7	1,126.0	80.0	33,862
Small Estates	2,000	3.7	39.0	6.0	2,592
Family Farms	6,200	11.4	8.4	4.0	832
Minifundia	45,200	83.2	2.9	10.0	506
Communities	—	—	—	—	—
Serfs & Peons	—	—	—	—	318
Highlands	708,050	100.0			
Large Estates	8,912	1.3	1,284.8	75.0	17,132
Small Estates	19,100	2.7	39.8	5.0	3,233
Family Farms	88,500	12.5	8.2	4.8	736
Minifundia	590,730	83.5	1.2	4.7	269
Communities	(808)	0.1	1,985.1	10.5	166 to 915
Serfs & Peons	—	—	—	—	116 to 170
Jungle	89,630	100.0			
Large Estates	627	0.07	2,406.4	73.6	10,127
Small Estates	2,151	2.4	78.1	8.2	3,612
Family Farms	3,675	4.1	27.3	4.9	1,214
Minifundia	83,177	92.8	3.3	13.3	442
Communities	—	—	—	—	—
Serfs & Peons	—	—	—	—	240

Note: These are the best data available on land tenure prior to 1969 and all figures approximate reality. All data on Communities comes, for example, from the highlands, yet there were in 1961 1,650 government-registered Communities, a number which has materially increased since then. There were no reliable data in 1961 of virtually any sort for Community lands or populations. From the colonial period to the present, it has been impossible to obtain nationwide land tenure data other than estimates.

Source: Comité Interamericano de Desarrollo Agricola (CIDA), *Tenencia de la Tierra y Desarrollo Socio-económico del Sector Agricola: Perú.*

Index